I Am a Pencil

A Teacher, His Kids, and Their World of Stories

✺   ✺   ✺   ✺   ✺   ✺

SAM SWOPE

AN OWL BOOK

Henry Holt and Company   New York

KH

Owl Books
Henry Holt and Company, LLC
Publishers since 1866
175 Fifth Avenue
New York, New York 10010
www.henryholt.com

Henry Holt® and 🏰® are registered trademarks of
Henry Holt and Company, LLC.

Library of Congress Cataloging-in-Publication Data
Swope, Sam.
 I am a pencil : a teacher, his kids, and their world of stories / Sam Swope.—1st ed.
 p. cm.
 ISBN-13: 978-0-8050-7851-0
 ISBN-10: 0-8050-7851-7
 1. English language—Composition and exercises—Study and
teaching (Elementary)—United States—Anecdotes.   2. Children of
immigrants—Education (Elementary)—United States—Anecdotes.   3. Swope, Sam.
I. Title.
LB1576.S96 2004
372.62'3—dc22   2004042475

Henry Holt books are available for special promotions and
premiums. For details contact: Director, Special Markets.

Originally published in hardcover in 2004 by Henry Holt

First Owl Books Edition 2005

Excerpts from "The Juniper Tree" from *The Juniper Tree and Other Tales* translated by
Lore Segal and Randall Jarrell, and pictures by Maurice Sendak. Translation copyright
1973 by Lore Segal. Pictures copyright 1973 by Maurice Sendak. Reprinted by permission of Farrar, Straus and Giroux, LLC.

Designed by Kelly S. Too

Printed in the United States of America

1 3 5 7 9 10 8 6 4 2

1/04/06

For all the Mrs. Duncans

I am a pencil
ready to write
my life

JESSICA
(fourth grade)

CONTENTS

GRADE FOUR: THE ISLAND PROJECT

GRADE FIVE: THE TREE PROJECT

AUTHOR'S NOTE

This book is a distillation of thousands of pages of material, including journal entries, transcriptions of tape-recorded student conferences and classes, and the students' writing. Permission to publish the children's writing and details about their lives was granted by their parents. To protect my students' privacy, I've changed the names of children, parents, teachers, and school. Unless otherwise stated, the students' writing has been corrected for grammar and spelling.

"The Blackbird Is Flying" and "The Little Liar" originally appeared, in slightly different form, in *Teachers & Writers*; portions of this book also appeared, in very different form, in *Teacher Magazine* and *The Threepenny Review*.

For financial support, the author wishes to thank the Overbrook Foundation, the Spencer Foundation, Teachers & Writers Collaborative, Teaching Tolerance, and the Thomas Phillips and Jane Moore Johnson Foundation.

I Am a Pencil

Preface

✤   ✤   ✤

The Blackbird Is Flying

I

Among twenty snowy mountains,
The only moving thing
Was the eye of the blackbird.

First we went over some hard words—*pantomime, indecipherable, Haddam, lucid, euphony,* and *equipage.* Then, as I handed out copies of "Thirteen Ways of Looking at a Blackbird," I told the fifth graders, "This is a famous poem written by an American businessman named Wallace Stevens. I'm telling you that so you know you can be a writer and still have another career." I said, "Before we discuss it, I want you to read it silently."

My students put their elbows on their desks and leaned over the poem. I'd been teaching writing to this class for three years, since they were in third grade. I knew them well. They were a smart group, immigrants or the children of immigrants to Queens, New York. They came from twenty-one countries and spoke eleven languages. A majority were from Latin America, and most of those were from Ecuador, but Colombia, Cuba, the Dominican Republic, Guyana, and Uruguay were also represented. Two had Puerto Rican fathers. Ten were listed on the roster as Asian, but that covered a lot of ground, including Bangladesh, Cambodia, China, Hong Kong, India, Korea, Pakistan, Taiwan, Thailand, and Vietnam. One student was Turkish. The class had also had an Egyptian boy and a half-Croatian, half-Bosnia-Herzegovinian girl, but they'd since moved.

The kids knew English, more or less, but some still thought in their native tongues, and I could see them translate what I said inside their heads. Most were poor, their sights set on doctoring as the clearest way up the American ladder, and although they enjoyed reading and writing, they thought math and science were the only subjects that really mattered.

Their fifth-grade classroom was crowded, not much space for anything but students, tables, and chairs. But it was a bright, tall room, at the top of a fat old brick schoolhouse. Its ceilings were high; the windows started eight feet up the wall, so that even when standing you had to look up to look out. All you ever saw was sky. It was like being in a deep box with the lid ajar.

Stevens writes of twenty snowy mountains. It was late January, nearly seventy degrees and sunny. We were hot. "El Niño!" cried my students. "Global warming!" What could they know of mountains and blackbirds? The school had no recess, and when the kids were not in class, most were stuck in tiny apartments, forbidden to play in the city streets.

The room was silent as the children read.

II

> I was of three minds,
> Like a tree
> In which there are three blackbirds.

The first stanza's moving blackbird "eye" becomes the "I" that is the poet in the second stanza, where the blackbirds are an unsettling metaphor for the poet's thoughts. Throughout this poem, Stevens juxtaposes the actual blackbird with the blackbird of his mind. At least I think that's what he's doing, but it's hard to know for sure. It's a fair question: Is "Thirteen Ways of Looking at a Blackbird" too difficult for fifth graders?

Kenneth Koch, a poet whose book *Wishes, Lies and Dreams* became my bible for teaching poetry, shows in *Rose, Where Did You Get That Red?* that adult verse can be used to inspire children to write poems. He recommends poems by Blake, Donne, Whitman, Lorca, Ashbery, and others, each providing an example of what he calls a "poetry idea." Koch makes a special pitch, however, for "Thirteen Ways of Looking at a

Blackbird," finding in it both a "gamelike quality" that is appealing to children and an obvious poetry idea: write about an ordinary object in as many different ways as you can. This assignment was well-suited for my yearlong unit on trees, and I hoped it would help my students approach our subject from new and interesting directions.

I waited for the children to finish reading the poem. One by one they looked up, faces blank. *Uh-oh,* I thought. The less confident cast sidelong glances round the room, checking to see if others were as lost as they. I told them, "This is a difficult poem. Don't worry if you didn't understand it. But before we discuss it, I'd like to hear your first reactions."

Not a hand went up. Everywhere I looked, eyes avoided mine.

I called on Simon, a bright-eyed kid with ears that stuck out. Simon was the baby of a Dominican family, so lovable and so well loved he never was afraid to say he didn't know. "This is like a college poem, Mr. Swope," he said. "Why'd you give us a college poem for?"

"Yeah," said Rafael. "I didn't understand a word of it!"

"Yeah," said Aaron. "I thought I was falling asleep!"

Smelling blood, everyone perked up, eager to join an uprising: "Yeah!" "Yeah!" "Yeah!"

"It's not a poem!"

"It's like a set of instructions!"

"Directions to see a blackbird!"

"It's a how-to thing!"

"It's got numbers!"

"Yeah, it's, like, so weird!"

I was of three minds: I am a rotten teacher; this is a rotten class; Stevens is a rotten poet.

III

> The blackbird whirled in the autumn winds.
> It was a small part of the pantomime.

Stevens's economy of language is impressive. In just two lines he moves us from a single bird to the whole sky. If this were a scene in a movie, the soundtrack would be silent as the camera tracked the bird then gradually pulled back to reveal an autumn panorama in which the ever-smaller blackbird soared.

"Now I'll read the poem out loud," I said. "Just make yourselves comfortable and listen." I turned out the lights; the room went gray and dusky. Several students put their heads down. It's a marvelous thing, reading to children. My voice, Stevens's poem, blackbirds in the room. No one fidgeted, no one whispered, and when I finished, the poem hung in the air.

"Reactions?"

Students lifted their heads, rubbed their eyes. I called on Mateo, a polite boy whose mother had wanted to be a schoolteacher back in Ecuador. He smiled apologetically, sorry to disappoint.

"Come on, Mateo," I said. "What did you think of the poem when you heard it read out loud?"

"When you read it, it made more sense."

"Okay," I said. "In what way did it make more sense?"

He smiled and squirmed, nothing to say.

Rosie, a thoughtful Indian girl with long beaded braids, put it this way: "When you read something, you can't explain the feeling—it's the feeling you have, whatever you do."

"What do you mean, 'whatever you do'?"

"When you read this, it's a feeling. It gives you a feeling."

"What feeling?"

"I can't explain it."

Is this enough? To read a poem out loud, cast the spell, give your students a feeling, then move on? Not talk about what can't be talked about? Perhaps, but even if we say that sometimes the reading of a poem is enough, is "Thirteen Ways of Looking at a Blackbird" that sort of poem? I doubt it. If I had let it go, Stevens's words would have whirled around the room and vanished.

It's a tough poem to hold on to. It has no characters, no plot, no humor, no rhyme, no clear-cut beat, no uplifting sentiments, and its pleasures are subtle, quiet, abstract. Koch is right. "Thirteen Ways of Looking at a Blackbird" is a puzzle, a Cubist collage—precisely the kind of poem you get to know better by talking about it. But how to do that with a room of ten-year-olds?

Following Koch's advice, I focused on the poem's more accessible sections, then asked the children to write about a tree in as many ways as they could. Most came up with four or five separate thoughts, of which these, each from a different student, are typical:

It looks like eyes on the trunk.
A stick with a bee hive on the end.
I wish it was spring so my tree could grow leaves.
A tree is a place that keeps people trapped inside.
You are the wall I hate that covers the sun when I'm cold.

I was both heartened and disappointed. They'd gotten the poetry idea, as Koch promised, but they hadn't written poems. To help them do so, I decided we'd discuss the poem line by line but in small groups and then, using Stevens's poem as a model, write "Thirteen Ways of Looking at a Tree."

Later, after I explained the task, Rosie, a deep-thinking, no-nonsense girl, looked at me and said, "Let me get this straight: You want us to use all thirteen techniques but with different words, and about a tree?"

"Yes, that's the idea, but if a section seems too hard," I hurried to add, "skip it. Make up something all your own."

"No, no, it's not too hard," she assured me. "No problem."

The world around the tree
Was hectic and moving
Yet it stood still
With a brave heart.

ROSIE

IV

A man and a woman
Are one.
A man and a woman and a blackbird
Are one.

Here the style of the poem changes. In plain, declarative sentences, Stevens announces a spiritual idea of unity. We are all one. There's nothing more to say.

I met with students in groups of five or six. What a difference intimacy makes! One group was all boys, and by the time we got to this part of the poem, each of them was fighting to be heard. Simon, the boy who'd scolded me for giving them a college poem, was so eager to talk he couldn't sit still.

"Simon, please don't stand on your chair."

"But I want to say what section four means!"

"Okay, what's section four mean?"

"It means a man and a woman get married and become one because they love each other so they're not two separate people."

Cesar disagreed. "No, it means, like, the man and woman do, like, a matrimony and then they look at blackbirds and see the blackbirds do the same."

"But a man and a woman and blackbird are not going to get married!" said Gary.

"No, not like get married exactly," explained Cesar, "but birds, people, they do basically the same—"

"No!" said Simon. "He said that a woman and a man and a blackbird are one. He's not comparing them."

"Then what is Stevens doing with the blackbird here?" I asked Simon.

Simon went quiet for a moment; then he said, "It might be that that bird's their pet."

Everyone liked this idea. "Maybe they are bird lovers," suggested Rafael. "The man and the woman, they get married, so then they treat the blackbird like a child."

Cesar smiled, happy at that thought. "Part of the family," he sighed.

> *You are one.*
> *So am I.*
> *But trees are part of us*
> *Also.*
>
> NOELIA

V

> I do not know which to prefer,
> The beauty of inflections
> Or the beauty of innuendoes,
> The blackbird whistling
> Or just after.

I begged him, "Miguel, write! Write something! Try!"

He hadn't written a thing for months, he rarely had his homework, and in class he couldn't sit still. Miguel was immensely confident, capable of unusual, interesting thought, yet lazy and disorganized, angry and socially awkward. He often drew while other children wrote, but he wasn't very good at it, and what he drew upset me.

"May I see?"

Miguel had scrunched his drawing in a corner of the page. It was typically sloppy and mostly indecipherable. There were scratchy men with limbs that didn't bend, and there were guns and bombs. At least he had a bird, an eagle decently drawn, but even it was bleeding from the heart. There were blotches of explosion and lots of smudgy death, not the joyful ruin happy children draw, no flashing zigzag lines and gaudy color.

"Oh, Miguel," I sighed. "Why are your pictures always so violent?"

He smiled, happy to be noticed, and continued drawing. We had had this conversation many times before.

"It worries me, Miguel. It makes me feel like you're not happy."

"Oh, I'm happy, Mr. Swope. I just like drawing violence, that's all."

I knew him well enough to say, "This picture makes me think you're going to grow up and be a mass murderer, Miguel, and I think you can do a little better than that."

Miguel giggled as he kept on drawing.

"Do me a favor. Stop drawing and try to write. Write at least one way of looking at a tree, okay? You can do this."

"Okay," he said, and cheerfully pulled out his writing folder.

> It grows big
> but he
> is small
> although
> big things
> are happening inside.
>
> MIGUEL

There are no euphonies here, and even though his poem isn't perfectly clear, it has some interesting innuendo going on, a lot of promise. I gave it a *Good!!!*

But it's hard to know what I responded to—the poem itself, or the boy behind it; my student as he was, or as I wanted him to be.

VI

Icicles filled the long window
With barbaric glass.
The shadow of the blackbird
Crossed it, to and fro.
The mood
Traced in the shadow
An indecipherable cause.

This section was a class favorite, with its prison made of ice, its menacing shadow, and its goose bumps sort of evil. Yet when I asked Su Jung how she'd do something similar but with a tree, she shook her head and told me that was hard.

Her classmates disagreed.

"I know!"

"Through the icy window—"

"The tree—"

"Or its shadow—"

"It looks like a monster or something—"

"Suddenly the wind blows and you see this branch—"

"And it looks like a hand—"

"Yeah, and you get scared—"

"And you see a UFO!"

As other children huddled around and spun this silly horror, Su Jung sat in silence. She was often quiet, not always by choice. Sometimes she'd join in a discussion, then startle us by going mute, eyes looking out at me as from a cell. She couldn't speak, not even when she wanted to. No one could explain these strange and sudden silences, least of all Su Jung. It was as if she were under a curse, and in a way, tragic girl, she was. When you suffer as a child and have the blackbird's shadow in your heart, do you lose the fun of fear, the happiness of horror? Throughout the years I had her as a student, Su Jung didn't write of happy-ever-afters. No prince rode into her stories.

We want to know our students, and knowing, try to help. I searched her writing, certain that I understood, but is her life, as I have described it, her deciphered cause? Am I so wise? Can I say I know this child so well I see into the window of her soul? What arrogance is that?

Su Jung's only comment on this section was "I don't like looking out an icy window 'cause I feel like it's destroying my eyesight."

"Because you can't focus?"

"Exactly."

> *The tree is an angel*
> *That god sent down*
> *To watch over the earth.*
> *But in the winter*
> *The snow covers its eyes*
> *So it can't see.*
>
> SU JUNG

VII

> O thin men of Haddam,
> Why do you imagine golden birds?
> Do you not see how the blackbird
> Walks around the feet
> Of the women about you?

It's hard to look at the world and really see it.

One day we went to Central Park and drew trees. I was watching Rafael, a skinny Cuban kid with shiny blackbird hair.

"Rafael, why are you coloring the tree trunks brown?"

"'Cause that's what color they are."

"Take a look around you. What color is the bark?"

He squinted at some nearby trees and said, "It's brown."

"No, it's not. It's gray."

"No, it's not. It's brown."

"Look!" I told him. "Use your eyes!"

Rafael looked again, and when he saw that I was right, he said, "I don't care what color real trees are. In comics, trees are brown."

Rafael's parents were divorced. To support her son and daughters, his mother worked six days a week as a receptionist. She was a kind, decent woman with a sad smile, and she always looked tired. She came to school several times, worried about Rafael. He didn't read books, was bored by school, didn't do his homework, hadn't tested well. All he cared about was comics and cartoons. What should she do?

"Buy him paper and paints and markers," I said. "Send him to art class."

"I don't want to encourage him."

"His comics are really good. Maybe he'll be an artist."

"That's what I'm scared of," she said. "An artist's life is very hard."

"It's scary, yes. But if he is an artist, there's nothing you can do. You won't change that. It'll be better for Rafael, and better for you, if you encourage him."

This made her sad.

"Don't worry, he'll be fine. I think he's got a gift. Besides, there's money in cartoons."

It was easy to see Rafael as an artist type. He was a loner, quiet, quick to cry, but with a rattlesnake temper when roused. He loved to dance. Although happy when I let him make a comic instead of writing, when I didn't, Rafael would make a comic anyway, drawing one in words. It didn't matter what sort of writing I got him to do—essay or story or poem—it was always a comic strip struggling to get out.

When Rafael handed in his "Thirteen Ways of Looking at a Tree," I asked him, "While you were writing this, did you glance at a real tree even once?"

"No."

I threw up my hands and said, "Rafael!"

"Heh, heh, heh," he answered, mimicking Beavis.

But Rafael was right, just following the master. I don't imagine Wallace Stevens sat on some old rock while writing of the blackbirds at his feet.

> *O crazy mimes of Staten Island*
> *Stop giving free performances*
> *To the tree, can't you see the*
> *Tree is one of you, you mimes,*
> *The Tree is a very still mime!*
>
> RAFAEL

VIII

I know noble accents
And lucid, inescapable rhythms;

But I know, too,
That the blackbird is involved
In what I know.

In the beginning was the thump, screech, and grunt. Then came words, or was the whistle first? Long before our noble accents, back when speech was being made, what models did our early wordsmiths use? Where did the sounds of language come from—the whoosh of wind, a gurgling stream, the songbird warble? Somewhere lost in time, did Nature help to shape our tongue, and so inform our thought? Is that what Stevens meant: "the blackbird is involved in what I know"?

I asked Fatma, a gloomy Pakistani child and the school's top speller, what she had made of "Thirteen Ways." She didn't like it, telling me, "The thing is, it doesn't say very much, but then you don't understand it."

Good point. Even when his words are simple, reading Stevens is like trying to understand a language you don't know very well. You have to do a lot of guessing.

But Noelia, a carefree Caribbean child, showed her gap-toothed smile and said, "That's why I like this poem."

"Explain."

"Because I didn't understand it!"

"But why do you like that?"

"Because I learn new things," she said. "And it's kind of weird."

"Weird is good?"

"Oh, yeah! Weird is def-i-nite-ly good."

Noelia loved the funniness of words, their boing-a-doing and tickle: "In-you-EN-doe!" "YOU-fun-knees!" But with Stevens I suspect she loved the word *equipage* best of all, and when I said, "That word is kind of fun to say. Let's say it all together," Noelia pogoed up and down and shouted out of sync, "Equipage! Equipage! Equipage!"

Later, I told this story to a friend of mine, a fan of Wallace Stevens's and a poet. When I was done, she asked, "That's how you pronounce it? Are you sure that it's eh-kip´-ij?"

"No, I'm not sure," I said. "How would you pronounce it?"

"It's French. I think it's eh´-kee-pahj."

"My God, how stupid. Yes, of course you're right." What was I thinking?

But then I looked *equipage* up and found we both were wrong. A French word, yes, but come to us by way of England, its Gallic murmur filtered through a Henry Higgins nose. It's eh´-kweh-pij.

> *The hands of*
> *the tree*
> *reach for the*
> *sunlight*
>
> GARY

IX

> When the blackbird flew out of sight,
> It marked the edge
> Of one of many circles.

If Stevens were my student, I'd have written in the margin: "Interesting image, Wallace, but I'm not quite sure what you're referring to here. What circles do you mean exactly?"

If I think about my students, though, I can see them in my mind—or sort of can—the whole class in a circle, holding hands.

> *When the*
> *tree shakes*
> *its arms*
> *I still see the*
> *mark*
> *left behind.*
>
> ELLA

X

> At the sight of blackbirds
> Flying in a green light,
> Even the bawds of euphony
> Would cry out sharply.

I told each group, "I have no idea what this section means. Don't bother imitating it. Just make up something of your own. Now, let's move on."

I didn't understand the section, true enough, but that's not why I hurried to get past it. I wanted to move on because of the word *bawd*. I had looked it up, expecting it to mean libertine, but *bawd* instead means prostitute.

It wasn't that I didn't think the kids could handle that. They watched TV, they flipped the bird, they spat out words both coarse and sexual. Some of them knew a lot more than they should have. My worry was their parents, who didn't know how much their children knew (or half-knew, even worse) about the whores who nightly worked the nearby strip with all the garish lights. My worry was the school board and the armies of the right.

> *I looked out my window*
> *And there the tree stood,*
> *Gazing into my eyes*
> *Like it knew something.*
>
>   ROSIE

XI

> He rode over Connecticut
> In a glass coach.
> Once, a fear pierced him,
> In that he mistook
> The shadow of his equipage
> For blackbirds.

This one's fun. The glass coach crossing Connecticut is a nice touch, kind of surreal, with the rider—I see someone noble—vulnerable, exposed, as though inside a bubble. Then the sudden fear, a gasp!

"How would you do that, but with a tree?" I asked one of the groups, and had them write.

Whip-smart Ella needed time to think, but not too much. That girl could get her words down quick.

> *As I ride the bus*
> *along the road*
> *I see the tree*
> *moving but not*
> *me, am I crazy?*
>
>   ELLA

Yes! She'd even got the startle right, the shock we feel when things aren't what we think.

Ella came from Hong Kong, skinny as a stick, and everything with her was fast, fast, fast. On Field Day, when the whistle blew, off she'd fly and leave the rest behind. In class, no sooner did I give a task than snap! she had it done—and neatly, too. And when it came to math, her hand shot up, the numbers figured out inside her calculator head. There's more: eager to grow up, she was the first to place a hand on her hip, roll her eyes, and say to me, "Oh, please!" And long before the other girls, Ella played the teen and wore short shorts, her shirttails knotted up above her little belly button.

> *Two birds on a*
> *tree. Two minds*
> *in one. As two*
> *minds in one*
> *thought.*
>
> ELLA

Brava! Not only had she understood the birds as metaphors for thought but she'd extended that and made them metaphors for love. I told her, "Ella, this is really good. Profound, in fact, and beautifully expressed."

She said, "I got this idea from a commercial."

"What idea?"

"The two always stick together," she said and slyly smiled.

I said I didn't understand, but Ella swatted at the air and gave a huff and told me, "Never mind!"

Then Noelia turned to me and said, "It's from a toothpaste commercial, and part of it is tartar control and part is whitening, and together they are one."

XII

> The river is moving.
> The blackbird must be flying.

Jessica thought too much, which made her stories so complex and so confused that the only way for her to end them was to write, "To Be

Continued!" And when she made her first attempts to mimic Stevens, her words were typically perplexing:

> *The land was*
> *of five minds*
> *like my tree.*

I said, "Don't think, Jessica. Just write whatever comes into your head." Later, when our work that day was done, among the other bits she handed in was this:

> *My tree is so big*
> *that no one*
> *really notices.*

The next day I read her poem to the class but Jessica cried out, "Hey! That's not mine!"

"It has your name. It's in your handwriting."

"I'd remember if I wrote it."

I handed her her paper, which she studied, disbelieving.

"You wrote it, that's for sure, and good for you," I said. "That is a good poem."

Jessica looked surprised. "It is?"

"Yes."

"Oh!" she said, and beamed with pride.

Then she got to thinking, and later said to me, as if confessing, "That poem that I wrote you liked? I don't know what it means."

XIII

> It was evening all afternoon.
> It was snowing
> And it was going to snow.
> The blackbird sat
> In the cedar-limbs.

There's a lot of quiet in this poem.

Earlier, while discussing the blackbird whirling in the silent autumn winds, Miguel said, "I think what Wallace was trying to say is, like, the blackbird would make no noise when he was going through the wind and so he was like part of the stillness of what was around him."

"But if he was part of the stillness," said Maya, "he shouldn't be moving, right?"

"Stillness can also mean quiet," I said. "It doesn't only mean motionless."

"Oh," said Maya, dreamy-eyed, her straight black hair so long that it was like a cape.

I asked Jorge, "What is Stevens doing in this final section?"

Speaking softly, Jorge said, "It's the end of his poem, so it's gonna be, like, it's gonna be darkness, and it's snowing a little, but it was gonna snow more, so he has to go home."

"Why does the poet end with this simple image?"

"Because he probably doesn't want to write no more and so he wants to end it in a way that people can understand."

"Mmm-hmmmm. How do we know that it's ending?"

"He's saying it's evening and he has to go to sleep or something."

Sleep, perhaps, or maybe there is a deeper stillness here, the blackbird on the snowy limb a metaphor for death. Many children heard the poem's darker echoes, but Maya, who loved horror, reveled in them. "Isn't thirteen a dreaded number?" she had asked me with a hopeful smile. "Isn't black an evil color?"

"Yes," I said. "That's in the poem, too."

Maya was a model student with a peaceful, pleasant manner. When we studied Stevens, I didn't sense that anything was wrong, and didn't know her favorite uncle had just died, or that her best friend had betrayed her. It wasn't until later that her mother called to tell me that Maya was often overwhelmed with tears and cried out to her parents, "I want to die! I want to die!"

> As still as night
> as night is
> still
> the wind blows
> the bird chirps
> the dog barks
> but still
> the tree is still.

The bark falls off
but there is no sign
of pain, or suffering.
How can this be?
No pain,
no nothing that a
human has.
So giving
and strong,
nothing really
in its way.

MAYA

We worked with Stevens for two weeks. And then, at the darkening end of a February day, several children read their poems to the class, and we said good-bye to blackbirds. Everyone was tired, yet everyone seemed happy. It was time to go home.

"All right," I said. "That was good. Thank you. That was very interesting."

When I asked Simon if he liked the poem now, his face lit up. "Oh, yeah, a lot!" he said, and others quickly cried out they did, too—Oh, yeah! yeah! yeah!

The Box Project

✿ ✿ ✿

Becoming Mr. Swope

I was a writer, children's books mostly, funny stories in which anything could happen. Every morning I got up at six, fed Mike, my cat, and got to work. I spent a lot of time inside my head with giants and ogres, fairies and talking animals, and when I went out into the city, I was a danger, sometimes so lost in thought I'd cross the street against the light, only snapping to at the blare of a horn. To free my life for writing, I'd pared it down to the essentials: a small Manhattan rental, no kids, no car, not even a TV.

I'm not a famous writer now and wasn't then, nor had I published much—nothing in some time. Still, I kept going through the motions, throwing words at the computer, screen after screen of promising beginnings, bits of characters, half thoughts, every day more words; but they never added up to anything, no book had taken shape in much too long, and I had grown discouraged.

When Teachers & Writers Collaborative asked me to run a ten-day writing workshop with a third-grade class, I was grateful for the change. And so it was one bright October morning I set out for Queens. The rush-hour subway was crowded, nine-to-fivers cheek by jowl, waiting to be delivered to their particular station of hell. I closed my eyes, blacked out the world, unable to relax until we reached Grand Central, the last stop before Queens, at which point every passenger but me got off. Delighted to be alone, I took a seat, crossed my legs, and opened my copy of the *New York Times*. The train lurched and slowly rumbled into the tunnel under the East River, where it gradually picked up speed, climbed upward, and flashed into the light of day (a blinding change but welcome), then rattled down the elevated tracks that run through Queens.

Though visible behind me, just across the river, the towers of Manhattan seemed a world away. Queens is different, its buildings only a few stories high, and from the train I had a view both intimate and vast, with fleeting glimpses into windows just across the way, and beyond, a panorama of tarred and shingled rooftops, chimneys, antennae, trees, satellite dishes, phone poles, car washes, small factories, and billboards. Planes flew low not far off, on their way into La Guardia.

I reached my stop, got off the train, and clanked down the metal staircase to the street. As soon as I was in the noisy chaos underneath the El, I felt like a tourist. I'd never seen a place like this, so foreign yet without a single ethnic identity, not a Chinatown or a Little Italy but an Immigrant World, a place where everything was all tossed in together: Colombian hairdressers, Indian spice shops, Korean wedding stores, Italian bakeries, storefront mosques, Dominican lawyers, Pakistani candy shops, Chinese green markets, Irish pubs, Mexican groceries, Hindu temples, English-language schools, and restaurants of every description. It was exotic, with a Third World flavor, but nothing felt permanent, as if this were a way station, like the intergalactic bar in *Star Wars,* a place where travelers stop en route to somewhere else.

The blocks surrounding the school were residential, frame houses from the 1920s and brick apartment buildings from the 1950s—no hint from their exteriors what nationalities might live inside. It was a quiet, peaceful neighborhood, here and there a little front-yard garden, several good-sized trees. I didn't see a lot of litter. The school itself was the old-fashioned kind, a looming pile of brick and stone from 1910, back when schools were built to look impressive.

I was early, in time to see the grown-ups bring their little ones to school. What a sight! Hand in hand they came from every direction: boys and girls with Cuban dads in baseball caps, bearded Sikhs in turbans, high-heeled Latinas with painted nails, Indonesian women covered in veils, Chinese grandmas in Mao jackets and sneakers, Hindus with red dots on their foreheads. It felt epic, all these immigrants, these hopeful parents who had somehow made their way to Queens and then sought out the school, the purpose of their journey, so that their kids could have a better life.

In children's stories, wanderers find safe haven—for Snow White, a cottage in the woods; for Dorothy, the Emerald City—and when I poked my head in Mrs. Duncan's classroom, I found mine. It seemed a world unto itself, bright with sun, a maple tree outside the window, a place both orderly and purposeful, with eight-year-olds of every color and each one so attentive to their teacher, a woman of nearly fifty and with eyes the color of the sea. She noticed me and smiled, gestured warmly, welcomed me inside.

"You must be Mr. Swope," she said.

That wasn't true. I wasn't Mr. Swope and never had been. I'd always been just Sam. Yet I made no objection, and so it was I was renamed. At a stroke, rechristened. In a way, reborn—although I didn't know that yet.

"Class," said Mrs. Duncan, "this is the special guest I was telling you about. Mr. Swope is a real writer, but not just any kind of writer: he writes stories for children. And he's here to help you write stories, too."

The class let out a cheer so loud I was a bit embarrassed, a bit ashamed, and a bit delighted.

"Hi, guys," I said.

We gathered at the back of the room, the reading corner. The children sat at my feet while I sat on a chair, like Mother Goose. I read a picture book I'd written, *The Araboolies of Liberty Street,* about a fantastical family with skin of every color—orange, pink, green, and blue. This fun-loving clan travels from a faraway island to a place where difference and laughter are forbidden. I'd written the book never thinking one day I'd be reading it to real-life Araboolies, but here I was and there they were.

When I finished, the children clapped, I blushed, and a boy at my knee said, "I have a question."

"Shoot."

"Do you think I'm a boy or a girl?"

I was taken aback, didn't know what to say. Wondering what trick he was up to, I stalled, took my time, studied him carefully. "Hmmmmm," I said. He was tall and wore jeans and a T-shirt. His glasses, tied around his neck with a shoelace, were so big they covered half his face. He had a wisp of a mustache, and his black hair was cut short, fuzzy as a baby bird's. I almost called his bluff and said he was a girl, but instead I played it safe and said, "I think you're a . . . boy."

"No, I'm a girl."

I looked in disbelief, but other kids assured me it was true, Fatma was a girl.

"Everyone thinks I'm a boy," said Fatma with a shrug.

I felt awful. Trying to repair the damage, I said, "That's just because your hair's so short and because you're so wonderfully tall . . ." But my blather didn't fool Fatma. She had my number and turned away, her shoulder like a door shut in my face.

When Mrs. Duncan told me later that Fatma was the most advanced writer in the class, it didn't surprise me. Lots of writers begin life as confused, manipulative, or self-destructive children, don't they? I hoped Fatma would forgive me and that we'd be friends. I wanted to welcome her, a fellow writer, to the club. I wanted to let her know that one day everything would be okay.

Mrs. Duncan

Mrs. Duncan lived in the Queens home she'd grown up in, sharing it with her husband, who was also a teacher, and their golden retriever. They had no children. She'd been teaching in the same school for twenty-six years and arrived each morning long before her students to get ready for the day. Like Mary Poppins, Mrs. Duncan ran a tight ship and liked things done spit-spot. Her students hung their coats in an orderly fashion, lined up for lunch according to height, and knew when it was their turn to wash the board or sweep the floor. She gave homework every night and expected the children to be in school every day, on time, prepared to give their very best: "Do I make myself clear? Everybody got that?" Complaining, talking out of turn, and cruelty were not allowed, end of story. "Excuses? I don't even want to *hear* about it."

When her students behaved well, she smiled and gave them stickers, and when they were out of line, she'd summon them to the hallway and lecture them on the importance of doing their duty, living up to their responsibilities, and treating their classmates decently. "Sometimes I feel like such a nag," she said, but she got results, and parents begged her to transfer to the next grade and teach their children again. As far as the kids were concerned, though, the most important thing about Mrs. Duncan was that she was so much fun.

"This is a special class," she told me. "Every one of them is smart, well-adjusted, and sweet. Every single one. That doesn't happen anymore."

Write a Story, Any Story

For my first assignment I said, "Write a story, any story you want. Just make it be your own, not one copied from TV or a book. Make it something unexpected. Surprise me. Have fun!"

The kids were eager to please their writer. As they rushed to get out paper and pencils, Miguel raised his hand. He was tall, a bit overweight. There were darkish rings around his eyes, like a raccoon's.

"Um, Mr. Swope? Where do you get your ideas?"

"Oh, gosh. That's a hard question. Mostly they just pop into my head from out of the blue."

Miguel nodded thoughtfully, but he looked perplexed, so I tried a different tack and said, "Ideas are everywhere. You just have to look for them. Why, I bet you'd even find an idea on the floor if you looked carefully enough."

Miguel glanced under his desk, then looked at me: *Yeah, right.*

To prove my point, I showed a sudden interest in the area near his feet. "Hey, what's that?" I said, and made my way through the classroom as the other kids craned their necks, trying to see. When I reached Miguel's desk, I got on my hands and knees and peered into the crack between the floorboards. "Well, what do you know?" I said. "There's a teeny tiny family down there, and they're sitting on a teeny tiny sofa, watching a teeny tiny TV."

Noelia joined me. She stuck her eyeball up against the crack and cried, "I see them, Mr. Swope! There's the teeny tiny family!"

"See?" I said to Miguel. "Ideas are everywhere."

"You can't see ideas."

"Oh, yeah? Then I guess you wouldn't mind if I looked in your ear."

Miguel's eyes popped wide. With a giggle, he shrugged okay, and I peered into his ear like a doctor. "Aha," I said. "Just as I thought. There *is* an idea inside that head of yours, and it's a doozie." I handed him his pencil and said, "You can do this. Everyone can do this. Just start writing. An idea will come. I promise." I stood beside him, waiting patiently. He squirmed for a moment, then said, "Can I write something, like, autobiographical?"

I was impressed he knew this word and said, "That would be great."

Miguel got to work. The room was quiet. Everyone was writing.

I was amazed at myself. Where had this character called Mr. Swope come from? I hadn't planned him; he'd arrived full-blown, a jack-in-the-box surprise who was part Mister Rogers, part David Letterman, part me. I joined Mrs. Duncan at the back of the room. We stood together and watched the children write their stories, both of us moved by this simple, everyday miracle.

"How did you do that?" she said.

I hadn't done anything.

She said, "I was always taught to have them map their stories out before they begin."

"I've never been able to outline," I told her. "I've tried, but it's never worked for me. Most of my ideas come while I'm writing."

"I was worried when you set them free like that, to write whatever they want. I was sure most of them would freeze up, not know where to begin." She studied her class for a moment, trying to figure this out, then decided it must be me and said, "You're a Pied Piper."

I liked her calling me the piper, but if there was any magic going on, it was a magic that had more to do with books than me, the magic any published writer would bring into a classroom. Still, it was appealing to think there might be truth in what she said. Was it possible I had an undiscovered talent, a gift for inspiring kids to write?

Miguel raced up to me, clutching his paper. "Mr. Swope, look at my autobiography!" He was so proud of himself.

"Let me see," I said.

In the year 1987 a child was born. His birthday was December 25 and this child grew smart, strong and respectful. When he grew bigger he knew how to multiply. This kid was Miguel. He was born in Ecuador and had a lot of interest in writing, coloring, multiplying. Then one day he wanted to try something new. His cousins asked him Hey Junior. Want to play basketball? I said Sure but please try to call me Miguel. I'm not pushing you, but just try. We went to play basketball until Splash! One cousin fell in quicksand! He was drowning. Then the other fell in. I was the only one left. I couldn't just stand there and look at them drown. So I grabbed them and we washed our selfs. Then we headed to go play basketball. We played basketball for 7 days without coming home but we did buy drinks and food. Then we slept in the basketball stadium for 7 days.

"That's just the first chapter," Miguel explained.

I told him he'd done a good job. I said I looked forward to reading more about Miguel. Then I asked him if he was really born on Christmas Day.

He looked at me, confused, wondering why I'd ask such a thing.

"You wrote here you were born on December twenty-fifth."

Miguel read what he'd written. "Oh, that's a mistake," he said, and quickly got out his eraser.

I wondered if I'd just learned something about Miguel. Had he made a Freudian slip? Did he subconsciously think of himself as Christ? No sooner did I have these thoughts than they were chased away when Aaron waved his story in my face.

"Mr. Swope, is this right?"

"What do you mean: Right? There is no right or wrong in stories."

"Just read it, Mr. Swope!"

Aaron was a tiny kid, the shortest in the class, with soft brown hair and laughing eyes. I liked his handwriting immediately. It was sloppy but passionate and expressive, and even though his punctuation was poor, his grammar bad, and his spelling worse, it wasn't hard to translate what he'd written:

THE SUMMER SANTA

Once upon a time not so long ago, one winter there was a mighty heat. And it was so hot there was not a drop of snow. All the kids shouted, "Santa isn't going to come!" But suddenly a light came. Somebody was skateboarding with incredible skill. It was Santa! Go, Santa! Go, Santa! He gave a present to each kid. So the elves were spreading rainbows everywhere. All the people were happy that Santa came. Then he made some snow fall down from the air. I ran and pulled his beard down. "I'll get you, kid!" he said. And he wasn't Santa! Hah! It isn't Santa?! So now nobody else believes in Santa, but I still do. I wish Santa was here.

"This is a riot," I said. "Hey, class, listen to the great story Aaron wrote!" I read "The Summer Santa" out loud and then suggested we act it out, right then and there. "Quick, let's push the desks aside to make a stage," I said.

I was as eager to try this as they were. I'd gotten the idea from a terrific book by Vivian Paley called *Wally's Stories*. Wally's a naughty kindergartner whose stories are acted out in class, and the experience transforms him, the class, and the teacher. It's the sort of book that makes you feel you've learned the secret of teaching and if only every classroom was this way, we'd have a perfect world.

I said, "Since Aaron wrote the story, he gets to choose the actors. Aaron, who's going to play your narrator?"

"Me."

"And who's going to play Santa?"

There were many volunteers, but no one waved his hand more ardently than Miguel, yet Aaron picked Kwan-Yin, and Miguel slumped, his face dark.

I told Miguel, "Don't be upset if you're not chosen. When we act one of your stories you can cast yourself in every single part."

"Yes!" said Miguel, temporarily mollified, but when Aaron didn't choose him to play any other part, either, Miguel got desperate. "What about the reindeer?" he said. "Who's gonna play the reindeer?"

"Aaron's Santa doesn't have any reindeer."

"But Santa always has reindeer."

"In stories, anything can happen," I said. "The writer is the boss. Since this is Aaron's story, we have to act it out the way he wrote it."

The world premier of "The Summer Santa" lasted three minutes, tops, but it was memorable. Skinny Kwan-Yin made a crowd-pleasing Santa, wiggling onto the stage to simulate a skateboard. Maya and MeiKai, as elves, hurled rainbows in the air like confetti, and Gary and Ibrahim, as the kids, shivered mightily when it began to snow. All the while Aaron stood off to the side watching and nodding his head as if to say, "Perfect, this is perfect."

My favorite part was the ending, which I found pretty subtle. After the narrator unmasks Santa, no one else believes in Santa anymore. Except, ironically, the narrator, his imagination defiant but a little lonely: "I wish Santa was here."

I think I knew where Aaron was coming from. At his age, I was a passionate believer in Santa. When my brothers tried to prove he didn't exist, I always ran to Dad, who told me not to listen: of course Santa Claus was real. But then one day at church the minister made a call for gifts so poor kids in our town would get some presents Christmas morning.

What?

Didn't Santa visit the poor?

When I asked Dad to explain, he gave me a look that said how sad he was to see me growing up. I took the loss of Santa hard, my first death, my first betrayal, and with Dad out of the game, that meant I was on my own, like Aaron: I wish Santa was here.

Once the curtain came down on "The Summer Santa," lots of kids were eager for their stories to be acted out next, but Mrs. Duncan said, "We can't today. It's almost time for dismissal. We have to clean up." Then she took me by surprise by asking, "What homework would you like to give, Mr. Swope?"

I hadn't realized I was expected to give homework, so I furiously dug through my mind and remembered the best assignment I was ever given, one that changed my life. "On your way to school tomorrow," I told my students, "notice something new, something you've never seen before, some little thing you'll be glad you saw."

I remember doing that homework. I remember walking to school as a little boy, amazed at all the things I'd never noticed. Better still, everywhere I looked, there was so much more to see! A crack in the sidewalk, a cat in a window, an anthill by a tree. For some reason, the discovery of this hidden world, a world that was mine for the looking, made me enormously happy.

Today, years later, even when on a familiar route traveled a thousand times—to the market, say, or the Laundromat—if I have my wits about me and remember to look, I still see something new, some little thing I've never seen before.

Which One Is Su Jung?

I wished I had a story of my own from third grade. I must have written some, but I don't remember any, and none has survived. Were they early versions of the stories I write now? Or something different? Would I remember writing them? At any rate, at home that night with their first stories, I made a ceremony of the moment—put on some quiet music, poured a glass of wine, sat in my favorite chair, and with my cat curled in my lap, started reading.

Two kids were absent that day, leaving me with twenty-six stories representing various genres. Nine kids made up Halloween stories. Six wrote adventures. Four turned in fairy tales. Two were inspired by *The Araboolies*. There was also a mystery and a tall tale, and one kid, Okan, had written instructions on how to fly an airplane. Elena and Nicole, I was disappointed to find, had written only a sentence fragment each. As Mrs. Duncan had feared, they must have frozen, not known what to write, and somehow managed to look busy and escape our notice.

There was a wide range in technical skills, from Allegra's barely readable scrawl to Fatma's complex sentences. I could often hear the grammar of their native languages inside their English, but in terms of content I saw little evidence of foreign cultures. Most stories were short, just several paragraphs, but some went on for pages. The writing often took wild leaps in logic and could be bewildering, like this story Gary wrote, which I excerpt here uncorrected:

Once upon a time George Corbet wanted to discover a diffrent planet. He found a world were he found a door. He opened it people that were 50 feet. Then were pets 30 feet. He named it Bigfoot planet. People played boxing gloves were 10 feet. Soon they buyd balls like basketball but they had mouths!!! Sharks were very eatless. Soon sharks were gettin bigger and bigger! When everybody was sleeping it was 11:00 AM! It was 3:00 AM when I told everyone to vote for me as president.

If you get the opportunity to read a third-grade class's stories in a single go, don't. Read a few at a time. Otherwise, they start to mush together, sound the same, and it's hard to find the virtues in a single one; your brain gets tired figuring out what word they've tried to spell, what's being said, what's going on; you become frustrated, bored, cranky, depressed, and finally you want to scream, the task of teaching seems so hopeless. But then, if you are lucky, you happen on a story like this one:

LIVING IN THE JUNGLE

Once upon a time, a family took a vacation in the jungle. There were lions roaring and monkeys singing as soon as I got out of the car. I was not too sure I liked this place. . . .

The house was very messy and dirty. There was dust all over the place. I couldn't believe I would have to live there for two months. . . . There was only one room in this house. I really didn't want to have a vacation there. It was terrible.

I was sooooooo mad. I was really furious. I wanted to cool off my head, so I went for a walk in the jungle. While I was walking, I found a cottage that looked puzzled. So I went inside and I saw a man in there. . . . I asked the man, "What is it like living in a jungle?" The man said, "Living in a jungle can be scary. But sometimes it can be the best thing."

I came out of the house and cleaned the dust from our house. When one month passed, I went again to the strange cottage and stepped inside. When I found nobody there, I went very slowly back home. I was very worried. I had to do something to find that man. I called out, "Dad, take me for a drive!" He shouted back, "Later, I'm busy right now!" I went upstairs to my room. I was talking to myself. "Why do I have to have a vacation in the jungle? It's a terrible place." I told my mom. She cried, "You have to learn to like this place." As soon as I heard that, I fell to the ground. I was terrified!

All of a sudden, my mom woke me up and said, "Wake up, you have to go to school." I said, "How come we are here?" My mom said, "What do you mean?" I was puzzled. I got ready to go to school. I was thinking, "Well, at least it was a dream."

Here was an authentic and original voice, a cry from the heart, a story full of image and mystery, with its singing monkeys, messy house, the stranger in the cottage, and what anger—yes! This is the way a writer writes—bravely and with passion, charging into story like a child who stomps into the jungle, come what may.

Who was this Su Jung? What sort of name was that? Korean? Was Su Jung a girl or boy? The next day, first thing, I asked Mrs. Duncan, "Which one is Su Jung?"

"She's the tall girl in the middle of the room with the blue ribbon in her hair."

Su Jung was sitting quietly, copying an assignment off the blackboard, unaware that I was watching her.

I asked Mrs. Duncan, "What's she like?"

"I don't have a handle on her yet. She's very quiet, very sharp, and very serious."

I gave Mrs. Duncan Su Jung's story. "Look what she wrote."

She read it quickly. "Hmmmmm. You could read a lot into that. That the jungle is the city, a dirty, scary place that Su Jung has to learn to like . . ."

"Or maybe the jungle stands for her whole life."

"And the cleaning! You hear that a lot from these kids. I read it all the time in their journals. They have a lot of chores and do a lot of cleaning."

When I handed the stories back to the class, I saved Su Jung's for last. I crouched beside her chair and placed her story on her desk. (Ella, seated next door, pretended not to eavesdrop.) I told Su Jung, "I liked your story a lot. It's really good."

Su Jung's eyes were fixed on a spot on her desk. Her heart was pounding through her T-shirt.

"You're from Korea?" I asked.

She gave a single nod.

"Did you live in a city there?"

She shook her head.

"A village?"

Another nod.

"How old were you when you came to America?"

She answered so softly I couldn't hear.

"I'm sorry. What did you say?"

"Four."

"Was that 'four'?"

A nod.

"I see. Do you remember Korea?"

No response.

"When you lived there, did you ever visit a jungle?"

She shook her head.

"In your story, that man inside the cottage, who was he and where'd he go?"

Another shake. She didn't know.

"It doesn't matter," I said. Then I talked about the story's ending. I told her children often end their stories by waking from a dream, and I thought she understood me when I said, "But happy endings shouldn't come so easily in stories since they don't come easily in life. Anyway, congratulations. Very nicely done."

She didn't look at me or say a thing, but her hands gripped the sides of her desk, making her knuckles white.

I Do! I Do Believe in Fairies!

Mrs. Duncan had selected *Peter Pan* for the class play. It was an abridged version, just twenty minutes long, but there was a lot to be done, so my workshops had to be suspended while the class rehearsed, painted the sets, made the costumes, and learned the songs and dances. Having known my students for only a few weeks, already I had to say good-bye, but I promised to return to see the show.

The famous play about the boy who won't grow up was written by James Barrie, and his biography is worth the telling. Born in Scotland in 1860 to a large family of modest means, Barrie was six years old when his older brother, David (tall, handsome, athletic, charming), died in a skating accident, a death that destroyed Barrie's mother. She retired to her bedroom, shades drawn, for over a year. The playwright later wrote he'd longed to make things right for her, to become so like his brother that his mother wouldn't see the difference. It was a hopeless dream. Inevitably, James got older while his brother, like all children who die, remained forever young: a boy who never grew up.

Strangely, Barrie himself didn't grow much, as if his body were trying not to. He was quite short, barely five feet, and had a high, thin, boyish voice. Some suggest Barrie had a glandular condition that arrests puberty and in extreme cases leaves one psychologically a child of twelve, but at any rate the grown-up Barrie was unquestionably young in spirit, with a passion for games and make-believe.

Before writing *Peter Pan,* Barrie was an established author of adult novels. He didn't think of writing for children until he was in his forties and befriended a married woman named Sylvia Llewelyn Davies and her five young sons, one of whom was named Peter. The boys adored Mr. Barrie, and he, who had no children of his own, loved them. Much to the discomfort of Mr. Llewelyn Davies, Barrie played with the boys for hours in Kensington Gardens, acting out elaborate adventures involving pirates, Indians, shipwrecks, desert islands, and a character called Peter Pan.

Those stories formed the basis of Barrie's play, which, first performed in 1904, was an immediate and enduring success, the most famous play for children ever written. It made Barrie fabulously rich. Then tragedy struck. Mr. Llewelyn Davies died, followed not long after by his wife. Barrie's playmates were now orphans, and he adopted them. One by one, though, the boys grew up. One by one, they lost interest in their writer, their Peter Pan, and came to look on him as an embarrassment.

While the class got ready for their play and I stayed home, I not only found I missed the kids, but realized I'd stumbled into a fascinating world I had to write about. My workshop, though, would only last another couple of weeks—not nearly enough time to get to know these children well enough to do them justice on the page. So I decided to make the class my project and devote myself to teaching writing for the next three years. In the process, I'd get to know my students' lives and imaginations, and watch them grow as people and as writers. It was an exciting but risky proposition. I'd never written a book like this, and I had no idea how I'd support myself because no one would pay me for the two to five days each week I'd be teaching. But at least the research—the teaching—would be fun and rewarding, giving me the satisfaction of knowing I was doing something good and useful with my life. All in all, it was an arrangement that promised to benefit everyone, and it certainly benefited me: that fall, while I was having dinner with a friend, she asked me if I'd fallen in love. She said I was glowing.

Mrs. Duncan's production of *Peter Pan* was performed in the school auditorium before an audience of students and parents. She'd let the children choose their roles, as far as possible. Su Jung played Wendy, the girl-mother; Kemal was Captain Hook; Gary, the crocodile; and Allegra, Tinker Bell. Aaron wanted to be a pirate. Miguel said he'd be Peter Pan.

The production was sentimental and charming. The children flew to Neverland by dancing, arms extended, soaring through the sky, and when they sang, "I Won't Grow Up," I came close to tears. Miguel's best moment was the famous scene when Tinker Bell is dying and Peter Pan steps forward to beg the audience to clap to prove that we believe in fairies. Of course we did, and Tinker Bell was saved. Otherwise, I'm sorry to report, Miguel was too serious a Peter Pan, his performance lumbering and melancholy, but never mind—he knew his lines, projected well, and I was proud of him.

After the actors had taken their bows and the parents had hugged their kids and left, I helped to strike the set. Miguel was still wearing his green felt costume as he and I folded up the cardboard pirate ship that Simon and Gary had painted.

"Did your parents come?" I asked him.

"Yes."

"How many are in your family?"

"Um, six. My mom, my dad, and four boys."

"You have three brothers?"

"I'm the oldest."

"Three little brothers . . . wow."

"One of them was born at Sesame Street theme park. We were there and he came out by accident. So now he gets a free pass to Sesame Street forever."

"What a lucky way to start your life."

"Yeah!"

"Did your parents like the play?"

"My dad said I'd be punished."

"What?"

"I shouldn't have been in the play."

"But why?"

"It's against my religion."

"Being in a play is against your religion?"

"*This* play is."

"*Peter Pan* is against your religion? What religion?"

"Pentecostal."

All I knew about Pentecostals was that they were also called the Holy Rollers and spoke in tongues. I asked, "What's wrong with *Peter Pan*?"

"'Cause it has fairies."

"Fairies are bad?"

He nodded. "And dancing, too."

"Dancing is bad? What's wrong with dancing?"

"In my religion, there is a good way to dance, when you got the feeling of the Holy Spirit and your eyes are always closed and you're waving your hands. But other dancing, you're dancing to the devil, and then later when you die he's gonna tell you, 'You had fun dancing for me on earth. Now, dance for me here in the fire!'"

"And you knew all this when you rehearsed?"

"I was ashamed of myself. I should have just sat down and remembered that I can't do this. But I felt bad 'cause it's, like, fun, 'cause there is almost nothing that is good in this world, almost nothing. Nothing. So sometimes I feel that my religion is bad, 'cause it makes me mad that other religions, they can play with Batman, they can play with Power Rangers, they can go trick-or-treating and have Santa and all this stuff."

My childhood experience of church had been dramatically different. The services at our Presbyterian church were so pallid and boring I always fell asleep, so I was fascinated by Pentecostalism's ecstatic dancing, and could see how that would be exciting to a child. At the same time, I was horrified. If Miguel's father found *Peter Pan* sinful, so was childhood itself, and my heart went out to this poor kid whose need to be in a play was so strong he'd risked punishment for it. To show Miguel he had an ally, I lied, saying, "Well, *I* thought you were a great Peter Pan."

"Thanks, Mr. Swope."

I told this story to Mrs. Duncan, who explained that religion played a hugely important role in the lives of poor immigrant kids. She said the churches offered lots of activities, from academic classes to all-day Sunday worship that provided meals as well as socializing. Moreover, she told me, church gives immigrant families something familiar in an unfamiliar world, a chance to be with people who speak the same language and share a culture. "Religion is something poor kids can 'have,'" she said.

Imagination is something they can have, too, I thought. And in my class, Miguel's would be encouraged to run free. That was something I could give this kid.

A few days later, a Polaroid camera and two packs of film mysteriously appeared in Mrs. Duncan's mailbox. No note, no return address. A gift from the elves. "Strange," said Mrs. Duncan.

"Polaroids are magical," I said. "The kids will love this."

She handed me the camera, saying, "Go for it."

We divided the class into teams. Each team would think up a story, then stage and shoot three pictures, one to illustrate the story's beginning, one the middle, and one the end. Mrs. Duncan had a big box filled with costumes and props. The kids dug through it and came up with scenarios involving a masked robber, a giant bird, a knife-wielding murderer, and the Easter bunny. When the photos were done, I asked each team to pass their photos to another team. "Now write the story you see in the pictures," I said.

This turned out to be a terrible idea. Because I'd given no lesson in photography, the photos were a mess—badly framed and poorly staged. Only the kids who'd taken them could see what story the pictures told. So of course the written stories went in wildly different directions, and after Miguel heard the story written from his group's pictures, he said, "I didn't like that story. I mean, I liked it, but it was wrong."

"What do you mean 'wrong'?"

"Because it didn't tell the story the pictures said."

"That's the point. There's never just one story. Everyone looks at the same set of pictures and finds something different."

"But the pictures are the pictures," Miguel insisted, with all the determination of a fundamentalist who reads the Bible literally, "and the story they wrote wasn't the one we told."

"Since you feel so strongly about it, why don't you write your own version?"

"I will. But I want to write it with you."

This was an appealing thought, and I was eager for the chance to do something fun for Miguel. "Let's do it," I said. We went into the hall and sat at a desk pushed against the wall. I volunteered to act as scribe. We laid the photos out and studied them.

"Who are these characters?" I asked.

"Nicole is wearing a beret. She's a famous Japanese artist. Noelia is a movie star. That's why she's got a crown."

"What's the artist's name?"

"I don't know any Japanese names."

"Ummm, how about Kioshi? That sounds kind of Japanese, doesn't it?"

Miguel nodded, eager to move on.

I said, "Okay, I think we've got enough for a first sentence: Once there was an artist named Kioshi. Now let's show how famous Kioshi is. Finish this sentence: Kioshi was such a famous artist that . . ."

Miguel opened his mouth and a fully formed complex sentence flew out: "Kioshi was such a famous artist that every single one of her drawings were put in a gold frame and hung in the biggest and most important gallery in the museum."

"Whoa," I said. "You're good at this."

Miguel gestured impatiently for me to get writing, then leaned in close to watch. He pointed at the page and said, "Mr. Swope, you forgot to write 'and most important' gallery."

"Sorry," I said, making the correction. "What's next?"

"One day, Kioshi got bored with drawing. She said, 'If I ever even see another piece of drawing paper, I'll scream. I need a break.'"

"Good," I said.

"What are those?"

"Quotation marks. You use them to show the words a character is saying out loud."

"Cool!"

"What happens next?"

"So she got her special yellow feather—"

"From where?"

"From a magical bird. And then she went to play with her best friend, the movie star Estrella del Mundo—that's Spanish for 'star of the world'—and she had the same feather as Kioshi."

"The exact same feather?"

"Not the same same. Look at the picture, Mr. Swope! Estrella del Mundo's feather was *red*."

"I see. How did Estrella del Mundo get this red feather?"

Miguel paused. His eyes looked inward for a moment. Then he said, "One day, Estrella del Mundo was watching one of her movies, and the bird flew out of the screen and landed on top of Estrella del Mundo's crown."

"Brilliant."

"So when Kioshi came to play, Estrella del Mundo was so happy she couldn't stop weeping."

"Slow down. I can't write that fast."

But Miguel was on a roll. He spoke emphatically, like an orator, gesturing with both hands. "So to make Estrella del Mundo feel better, Kioshi said, 'Hey, tickle me!' Then Estrella del Mundo tickled Kioshi until Kioshi laughed. Then Kioshi said, 'Now it's my turn to tickle you.' And all that tickling made them exhausted and hungry, so they ordered in food."

"Pizza?"

"No, cold lemonade and chocolate-chip cookies. When they were finished eating, they tickled each other again, and then they laughed until they were ninety-nine years old."

"And then?"

"And then they died."

"How sad."

"Not really. 'Cause they died laughing."

That made *me* laugh. "Perfect," I said. "That's perfect."

We set about editing the story, moving sentences, changing verbs, adding details. Miguel paid attention to my every move, and after I handed him the finished text, he stared at it in silent amazement. Then he said, "This is a great story."

He was eager to read it to the class. As he did, his hands shook with excitement. When everyone clapped, Miguel was proud and swayed from foot to foot, as if in time to music. "When I grow up, I'm going to be a writer," he told me, and threw his arms around my waist.

 I tensed, lifting my hands in the air instinctively. It's dangerous for a teacher, especially a male teacher, to hug a child. Miguel hung from my waist as he looked up at me. "Be my papi. Papi!" he said in a baby voice.

"I'm not your father, Miguel."

He held me tighter. "Papi! Be my papi!"

I gently pried him loose, saying, "I'll be your teacher and your friend, but I can't be your papi."

Miguel often talked about his father, a man I never got to know because he rarely came to school, and anyway we didn't speak each other's language. My sense of him was shadowy, spun from things my student said: a smart man, a great athlete, a strict man, a man with a temper, a man who read the Bible to his children every night and who'd been married once before, in Ecuador, where he'd left behind two daughters years ago, and now was working as a handyman but mostly unemployed. Indeed, Miguel's family was often desperate for money and at times in danger of eviction, yet Miguel assured me that none of this was ever Papi's fault. He'd say his dad had hurt his knee, or been too busy volunteering for the church, or the boss had been unfair. There was always a good reason, just like all the reasons Miguel had when he came in without his homework, which was often.

Hunting for Stories

Helping Miguel write his story was so much fun I did the same with other kids. It was never hard to find a volunteer. I'd say, "Who wants to collaborate today?" and hands would fly. Each collaboration was a different experience, a different hunt in the forest. Some kids knew just what to do. They headed off into the woods with confidence and had an instinct where to look for good ideas. Others were reckless, charging blindly ahead, losing their way, wanting to put every little thing they found into their story. Many started out quite timidly. They needed to be taken by the hand—don't be scared, it's okay, the best ideas are off the path, just pick a direction, any direction, let's see where it goes—and in this way they learned they didn't need to be afraid.

I loved these hunts, but they were always tiring. Some were harder than others, for the forest didn't always offer up its treasures. Still, most everyone got lucky once, although some never did, and Fatma, for example, never volunteered to go into the woods with me at all.

Allegra, however, was eager. The only blue-eyed blond in the class, Allegra was part Croatian and part Bosnia-Herzegovinian, her parents refugees from the Balkan conflict. She had protruding front teeth, one recently lost, and was sweet, cute, and incorrigibly silly. Having the concentration of a rabbit, Allegra couldn't sit still to write, and it took her several days—*come on, Allegra, get back in your seat and write just one more sentence, please!*—to finish this intriguing story:

THE TOOTH ADVENTURE

Once there was a tooth who lost his sister in the woods. The next day he went back to the dark woods. He went in the woods with his friend, but his friend ran away and he went back home screaming his head off, "I want to go back home!" And then he heard a big BOO!

The next day he went back to the woods all by himself but he heard footsteps in back of him. It was his sister, Jane, and they went back home.

Once Jane and her brother went back to the woods to look for her friend because she was so anxious. So when they got there he was gone. They were furious and they were sad.

Hoping to encourage her, I asked her if she wanted to collaborate. "Okay!"

We sat at my hallway desk with my little tape recorder between us.

"You're taping me?"

"Yes. I tape everybody."

"Why?"

"So I'll remember what we said today. It's research for a book I want to write about working with you kids."

"Ohhhhhhhh," she cooed, pretending that she understood.

"What story should we write today, Allegra?"

Allegra smiled a goofy smile, flapped her arms in the air, and sang out, "I don't know!"

"A mystery? An adventure? A fairy tale?"

Again she threw her arms up. "I don't know!"

"How about an animal story? You like animals, don't you?"

"There's rats in my apartment."

"Really? Gosh. Really?"

"They only come at night."

"Oh, my. Would you like to write a story about a rat?"

"An elephant!" she said, and giggled.

"Oh, good. I love elephants. What other character should we have?"

Again the arms flew up, again she sang out, "I don't know!"

"Allegra, please stop saying 'I don't know.' What other character should we have?"

She rolled her eyes around and around like a dashboard doll. Then she said, "A scientist?"

"Excellent. What should we call him?"

"I don't know!"

"Well, let's see. You wrote that nice story about teeth. We could call him Dr. Dental. *Dental* means . . . well, how would you define *dental*? *Dental* means . . . it refers to teeth, like *dent*ist."

She gave me a blank look.

"You don't have any idea what I'm talking about, do you?"

"No."

"Doesn't matter. Do you like the name Dr. Dental?"

She nodded.

"Good. Now, how would you spell Dental?"

"D-E . . . D?"

"Sound out the word: Dennnnn . . . "

"N?"

"Excellent! Yes! Okay, what's next? Den*tull*: tuh."

"D?"

"Tuh, tuh."

"T?"

"Right again! Now: den*tul. Ul*."

"I?"

"Actually, it's A. A short *a*. Do you know what a short *a* is?"

She shook her head.

"Of course you don't. How could you?" There are so many things a child doesn't know! So many things to teach. But if we were going to finish the story, we had to move on. "Actually," I said, "since this is a name, we can spell Dental however we want. If you want to spell it with an *i*, we can. What do you think?"

She smiled yes.

"Brilliant choice. Okay: What does Dr. Dentil do with the elephant?"

Up went her arms. Out sang the voice: "I don't know!"

I had to stop her nonsense. I played the clown, leaned over, banged my forehead on the desk in frustration. "Stop, Allegra! Please, stop! I can't take it anymore!" Then I sat up, looked at her, and said, "Allegra, please. It's time to work now. You have to get a grip. Put your hands on your lap and keep them there. Concentrate: What does the scientist do with the elephant?"

She placed her hands nicely on her lap and we sat silently for a few moments. Then she stared at the ceiling and, without seeming to be conscious of what she was doing, slowly stuck five fingers in her mouth, like a giant pacifier. Or perhaps she was simulating an elephant trunk. Oh, Allegra, what was going on inside that silly little head? I waited patiently, but after a while I worried she'd drifted off into a dream. "Hello? Allegra? Anyone home?"

She took her hand from her mouth, tilted her head my way, and gave me a silly smile. "He chops off the elephant's trunk and sells it for money?"

Casual brutality comes naturally to the fantasies of children, and usually it's nothing to worry about. "What a wonderfully horrifying idea!" I said. "Let's play with that and see where we end up . . . " I figured that by this point we were home free, that the rest of the story would come easily, but I was wrong. Getting to the end of "Dr. Dentil" was like pulling teeth:

Dr. Dentil got back into his canoe, and ninety-nine days later, he landed in North America and walked straight to Macy's jewelry department. When he showed the trunk to the manager, the manager said, "Pretty nice stuff!" So the manager gave Dr. Dentil $3,000 and Dr. Dentil went straight to a store and bought lots of food so he would never be hungry again. Then he got married and had eight children. He was now a happy man, and he never went hunting again.

The Christmas Spirit

December brought tons of snow to Queens that winter. Cars were buried on the street, and plows made mountains twice the height of my students. I hadn't seen that much snow since childhood, and the magic of the white world and the presence of children in my life cast a Christmas spell on me. Like Scrooge on Christmas morning, I was giddily in love with life. God bless us everyone—the guy at the newsstand, the coffee vendor, the token clerk, each and every commuter, the crossing guard at school, the secretaries, the janitor, the principal. I felt warmly toward them all, for now I saw the child in each of them, the child they had once been, just like my students, eager-eyed and full of wonder.

But in school I had to keep a lid on. Because the children were Baha'is, Buddhists, Hindus, Muslims, Pentecostals, Sikhs, and Taoists as well as Catholics and Presbyterians, Mrs. Duncan didn't celebrate Christmas with trees and Santa Claus. Yet ignoring the holiday would have been absurd— Christmas is everywhere and inescapable, its cultural importance marked by a major school vacation. So Mrs. Duncan presented Christmas as a time to show love for family and friends with simple gifts.

On the day before vacation, we had a little party. The kids wrote poems to their families and made cards, Mrs. Duncan gave them each a book, and I gave everyone three different words—words I'd chosen just for them, big, fancy words they didn't know, words I'd written in calligraphy on little cards tied up with ribbon. (I'd see those words pop up from time to time in stories, but Miguel especially latched onto one of his, and *stalwart* was the adjective he'd often use for heroes in his stories.)

On the way to school that morning, I'd grabbed Hans Christian Andersen's "The Little Match Girl" from my bookshelf. I hadn't read it in years but thought the story of a poor girl looking through windows at the holiday happiness of others would resonate with my poor students. As I was reading it aloud to them, however, I wished I'd made a different choice. I hadn't remembered it as being quite so dreary and sentimental or so overtly Christian.

In the story, a barefoot waif huddles on a snowy street. She lights matches to keep warm, and in their brief flames she sees visions—of a stove, of a banquet table, of a Christmas tree, and finally of her beloved late grandmother, who lifts the girl up and carries her to a place "where there was no more cold, no hunger, and no pain—for they were with God." The next morning, the girl's body is found "with rosy cheeks and a smile on her face—dead."

"Reactions?" I asked.

As usual, Miguel had his hand up first. "I liked the part when she turned on the match, she had happiness, and when it turned off her niceness is gone."

Jessica, however, was confused. "How did she die?"

"Because of the cold?" said Su Jung.

"That's right. She froze to death."

"Her spirit left and went to heaven," said Simon.

"Because the girl really did need God," said Gary. "Because without him, she would die but she wouldn't get nothing."

MeiKai, a Taoist girl, said, "Yes, her spirit would be lost and she wouldn't be happy and she would have to go back over it all again and she would get cold."

"You mean she'd be reincarnated?" I said.

"Enh?" said MeiKai, confused by the word.

"When the little girl died," asked Carlos, "what did they do to her? Did they reincarnate her? Did they take her blood out?"

Rosie, who was Hindu, said, "In my religion, you burn the body and put it in the river."

"Does anyone know what *reincarnation* means?" I said.

A hand went up, and I called on Aliza, a Muslim, who tried her best to explain. "When my mother's father was about to die," she said, "at his funeral, my mother saw his spirit."

"That's not quite reincarnation," I said. "Anyone else? Noelia?"

Noelia, however, had something else on her mind and said, "I don't know why that little girl was smiling when she was dead!"

"She was so happy to be with her grandmother," said Su Jung.

"Yeah, she was happy she wouldn't have any more problems like be cold and walk on bare feet," said Miguel.

Then Okan wondered why the book didn't show an illustration of God, and I said, "That's an interesting observation. What does God look like?"

For a moment, no one spoke. Then Miguel said, "I don't really know how to describe it but he's in, like, robes and he doesn't have sandals, he just walks on his feet."

"My father told me God is not a he or a she," said Ibrahim. "He's just some spirit."

"Then why does God have a son?" asked Noelia.

"God's a man!" insisted Rafael. "I saw a Spanish movie and I think I saw God and he was wearing a cross on his chest."

Su Jung said, "I went to church and it said that Jesus died on the cross so others could live."

That struck a chord with many. "Yeah!"

Miguel said, "In my Bible it said that when Mary had the baby Jesus, he grew strong and healthy and when he went to heaven he had to see his father and his father commanded him to come to earth and die for us and forgive our sins."

But Ibrahim gently held his ground. "My God is not a he or a she," he said. "He, he, I mean . . . he's called Allah. In my religion, God never dies."

"My God is the same as Ibrahim," said Kemal. "My religion is true Muslim."

I could see Miguel was upset, his mind short-circuiting. How could it not? He'd been taught his God was the one true God and all other gods were false; he raised his hand, determined to set the record straight. I ignored his urgently waving hand, fearing a religious war, and instead called on Mateo.

"My cousin said that if God didn't die, then we would walk naked and we would never notice."

When his classmates and I giggled, Mrs. Duncan said, "It's wrong to laugh at anyone's religion, class. And I'm surprised at you, Mr. Swope." As the kids shot looks my way, I blanched, then blushed, shrinking down to eight years old again, but Mrs. Duncan wasn't really mad, and she deftly changed the subject by announcing, "And now, class, the time has come for: the grab bag!"

"Yay!"

Each kid had brought in an inexpensive gift and placed it in a communal brown paper grocery bag. They all lined up, waiting for their turn to grab a present. The gifts were modest: a coloring book, a box of crayons, a sheet of stickers, a plastic troll, a rubber ball. But the kids didn't care; they were out of their minds with happiness. Aaron got the gift I'd brought, but he didn't know what it was.

"It's an alphabet stencil," I explained. I could tell he wasn't impressed, so I said, "It's neater than it looks. See, you can use it to write out your name, or make signs."

But Aaron wasn't listening. His attention was focused on Kemal, who'd just pulled a large box wrapped in shiny blue paper from the grab bag.

We watched Kemal tear off the wrapping. "Wow!" he said as he examined his gift, a futuristic car that in a neat trick of design transformed into a superhero. It seemed unfair that Fate had given Kemal the most expensive gift. His family was one of the few in the class with money, or at least the promise of it. His father was soon to be a doctor and earn, as Kemal informed us with annoying frequency, "more money than the president of the United States!" Aaron told me, "That Transformer was supposed to be mine, but my mother said we were too poor to buy a grab bag gift, so I had to bring in my only Christmas present."

"Oh, Aaron. That was awfully nice of you."

As if things weren't bad enough, Kwan-Yin, Aaron's best friend, wouldn't be returning to school after the break. His family had found a larger apartment elsewhere in Queens. This population moves a lot, Mrs. Duncan told me, and children bounce from school to school. That day Aaron and Kwan-Yin wanted to collaborate on a final story. They sat side by side, writing with their arms around each other.

Courage

In January, Su Jung came to school with a bruise on her face. She said she'd fallen on the steps of her Presbyterian church, but Mrs. Duncan had her doubts. Since the holiday, she'd been concerned about Su Jung, who often arrived at school in tears. When Mrs. Duncan asked her what was wrong, however, Su Jung would not say a word.

"You don't think someone hit her, do you?" I said.

"I don't know what to think," she said. "It just seems like when a kid who comes to school crying, there must be something upsetting her before she gets here, at home or on the way. You won't believe this, but the other day Su Jung got in a fight with a boy in the lunchroom."

"A physical fight?"

"Yes, with a boy who lives in her building. But when I asked her what happened she wouldn't talk. So I've been trying to psychoanalyze her. Does any of this come out in her writing?"

"Nothing obvious," I said, and started looking through her writing folder. "Here's a story I kind of liked. It had a nice feeling of freedom."

I'M THE SNOOPY BALLOON

I'm all folded up in this dusty place. People come and clean the dust that's on me. I want to go outside and feel the wind.

I'm outside floating in the air. I hear screaming, babies crying, and laughing. I feel sooo grateful. When I look down all I see are people, people, people, people. I am high up in the air, feeling the cool breeze gently touching me. I'm so glad that I'm in the Macy's Thanksgiving Day Parade.

Now the parade is over. I have to go back to that dirty warehouse again. I wish the parade will start again.

"Hmmmmm," mused Mrs. Duncan. "There she goes with the dirt again. Anything else?"

"Not really. Here's one about a witch who's teased at school because of her looks, so she writes a story and somehow that makes her normal . . ."

"I read that one. I thought it showed good story development."

"Enh," I said. "I thought it was safe and predictable. I know she can do better. She hasn't written anything nearly as interesting as that first story, 'Living in the Jungle.' I get the feeling she's afraid of her imagination."

"I don't know what that means," said Mrs. Duncan.

That caught me off guard, made me think. Maybe I was talking nonsense, yet somehow it felt true, that Su Jung's imagination took her to scary places, places she didn't want to go. But even if I was right, what can a teacher do with that? How do you teach a kid to bravely follow her imagination, even when it's scary? And should you? I had no answers to these questions, but there wasn't time to sort things through. I had to teach my lesson.

I'd taken today's prompt from *Personal Fiction Writing,* a useful book by Meredith Sue Willis filled with creative-writing exercises. I told the class, "Take out a sheet of lined paper. At the top of one side, I want you to write this title: The Outside Me. Under that describe the way you look to others. Then turn the page over and write: The Inside Me. Under that, describe the you nobody sees, but you don't have to write anything private, unless you want to."

Under "The Outside Me," most kids gave a hint about what they thought of their looks. Kemal said, "My nose is big but it's nothing to laugh about." Noelia was sick of wearing braids. Rosie wrote, "My skin is brown (which does not matter)." But Su Jung's description of herself was strictly objective:

THE OUTSIDE ME

I have black hair and brown eyes. I always tie my hair before I come to school. I wear jeans almost every day. My skin color is peach. I am tall. I have short hair. I wear sneakers most of the time.

Under "The Inside Me," however, she'd written nothing. I said, "You have to write something, Su Jung. Look at how other kids approached this: Nicole wrote, 'On the inside I'm brave, but outside I'm shy.' Ashley wrote, 'Inside I am the wind of peace.' Aaron made a joke of his: 'The me nobody sees is my Batman underwear.' And here's Cesar's: 'Inside me I have a brain, a heart, stomach, guts, and blood.' So you see? Be inventive, but finish the assignment, okay?"

Su Jung pushed the paper aside and put her head on the desk, a puppet lying limp. I left her alone, but when the writing was collected that day, I saw that in the end she'd written something after all, six little words that broke my heart: "I am unhappy all the time."

I showed Mrs. Duncan, who straightaway asked a guidance counselor to see Su Jung. This was a lucky break. The counselor was gentleness itself, and once a week Su Jung went to her office.

"What do you do with her?" I asked the counselor.

"We play quiet games. Su Jung's a bright girl. She just needs tender loving care. And someone to speak to."

"What do you talk about?"

"Anything. Just talk."

"Does she ever talk about what's troubling her?"

"No. This is just a place for her to feel safe."

Su Jung wanted desperately to write a story with me. Often I'd pass her desk and she'd say, "Please collaborate with me, Mr. Swope!"

"But, Su Jung, each time we try, you never talk. I can't collaborate alone."

"Please!"

Sometimes I'd give in and say, "Okay, come on," and she'd smile, jump from her chair, and we'd go out into the hall. First, we'd chat a bit, which was nice. She told me things. She told me how she learned English by watching *Barney*. She told me her grandparents lived with her. She told me her uncle did, too, and that she liked him because he bought her things. She told me she slept in the living room with her grandmother and four-year-old brother. And I told her things. I told her how my cat once jumped from a third-story window and lived. I told her stories from my childhood. I told her how my friends and I once made a cemetery for birds only then we couldn't find enough dead ones to fill it up, so we plotted how to kill some, but we never did.

"You're strange, Mr. Swope."

"I guess. But isn't everyone? Anyway, let's get to work, shall we? What sort of story should we write today?"

Silence.

"Let's start with a location. Where should we set our story?"

Silence.

"It doesn't matter where, just name a place. Queens? Paris? Seoul?"

Silence.

"This isn't hard, Su Jung. Just pick one. Please, I can't collaborate alone."

Silence.

"Please speak, Su Jung. Just one word. Speak."

Silence.

"I don't have all day, Su Jung. There are other kids I have to see."

Silence.

And then I'd sigh and send her back and both of us would feel that we had failed. It was awful.

When Mrs. Duncan taught a unit on courage, I played my part. I told the kids, "Let's sketch a character called Courage. Imagine Courage as a human or an animal—but not a lion, that's too obvious. Think of something more surprising, like a bug. Or you might have a Courage with a thousand heads or with a body made of fire. It's up to you. But however you imagine Courage, you must make it somehow brave."

Su Jung wrote:

Courage is a rabbit with pink ears. When a lion told the rabbit to come to his house, the rabbit was afraid she was going to be eaten but the rabbit still bravely went to the lion's house.

I said, "Su Jung, is your rabbit showing courage or is it being stupid? If it were smart, wouldn't it just run away?"

"You didn't say that Courage must be smart. You only said it must be brave."

I met her father only once, at parent-teacher conference. He was quite tall, very thin, and spoke no English. Su Jung was there to translate. We sat around a low round table as if we were having tea and smiled at one another. Then I told her father, "Su Jung is very smart. She works quite hard, and shows some promise as a writer."

Su Jung smiled, pleased by my praise. As she translated, her father showed no expression. Then I mentioned Su Jung's silences, how she'd be part of a conversation in class then suddenly go silent, for no apparent reason. "It seems like she wants to talk, but she can't. Is there any light you can shed on this?"

Su Jung's face went hard as stone. I could see she felt betrayed, but I hadn't meant to tattle. I was hoping for some kind of breakthrough. I waited for her to translate, and though she said something to her father, I knew it wasn't what I'd said, and who could blame her? In her position, I'd have done the same.

As her father sat impassive, unaware, Su Jung and I had a private moment. I smiled to show I wasn't mad at her and in a teasing voice said, "You little sneak! What did you just tell him?"

Once she understood that she was safe, Su Jung grinned at me with playful defiance, pursed her lips, then zipped them shut with her fingers.

How to Kill the Parents

Rosie said, "Yo, Mr. Swope. Can I axe you a question?"

"Can you *ask* me a question."

"That's what I said!"

"No, you said 'axe,' which is one way to pronounce that word, but most people say 'ask.' Can you hear the difference?"

"Huh-unh."

"Say *ask*."

"Axe."

"Asss-kuh."

"Asss-kuh."

"You got it."

"So, Mr. Swope. Can I axe you a question?"

"Sure."

"How come you so red?"

Rosie was referring to my florid Irish skin. I shot back, "And how come you so brown?"

That made her laugh.

Rosie was one cool kid. She'd slouch into the classroom, hands slipped into the back pockets of her blue jeans and her long frizzy hair done up in a hundred braids covered with multicolored beads that clitter-clattered as she walked. I have a snapshot memory of her. One day at dismissal, I said good-bye to her outside school, then headed for the subway. At the corner, for some reason I felt compelled to turn around, and there was Rosie, standing where I'd left her, hands on hips, eyes fierce, *willing* me to look at her. I was sure she'd bewitched me, but who wouldn't want to be bewitched by such a charming little ball of fire? I smiled and gave a little wave; she glowed with triumph, then ran to catch her mother.

At first I thought Rosie was African American, but it turned out she was Indian, a Hindu from Gujarat. Her parents spoke heavily accented English, but her teenage brothers, like Rosie, learned their English in New York, and liked to speak the hip dialect of the inner city. Rosie called it "street talk."

During Black History Month, a fourth-grade class put on an assembly program on the life of Martin Luther King that mixed biography with break dancing, jazz, the blues, and Dr. King's words. It was an unforgettable production. These young immigrant kids, these multihued young Americans speaking King's famous words made me hear them as if for the first time. I dissolved in tears when four of them joined hands, stepped forward, and recited loud and clear:

> Something is happening in our world. The masses of people are rising up. And wherever they are assembled today, whether they are in Johannesburg, South Africa; Nairobi, Kenya; Accra, Ghana; New York City; Atlanta, Georgia; Jackson, Mississippi; or Memphis, Tennessee, the cry is always the same: "We want to be free."

I didn't cry alone. All the teachers were sniffling, and our tears were noticed by the kids. I think it scared them a bit; it isn't often that you see a teacher cry. I'd seen it only once, when I was in fourth grade and the principal came into the classroom to tell us that our president had been shot.

Before she saw that show, Rosie's hero was Mahatma Gandhi. That day, Dr. King became one, too. She'd experienced discrimination in kindergarten, she told me, when she lost a friend whose parents didn't want their daughter playing with a Hindu. Rosie was so moved by the King program she volunteered to write the thank-you note to the class who'd performed it:

> Your show reached out a hand and made me a part of that time when African-Americans were scorned. I imagined that I was above a crowd that wanted freedom and I said a speech like this, "God, send us here for peace and love, but not for any soul to be evil." I hope finally I reach to the stars. I promise I will. My dream is to have peace in the world and your performance showed me how.

I told Rosie, "You have to run for president one day, so I can vote for you."

Because Rosie was smart, ambitious, and willing to try anything, she was a delight to teach. Her writing folder was easy to spot in a stack because it was twice as thick as all the others. *If she does become a writer,* I remember thinking, *she'll be a novelist.* Her narratives were long, sometimes twenty handwritten pages, with twists and turns and subplots and stories within stories. I didn't mind that she rushed, never proofread, was impatient—her writing had passion, and her stories had a mysterious quality that reminded me of the brothers Grimm, so subterranean and dark.

My favorite Rosie story begins:

> Once upon a time, in the deep, creepy woods, there lived an ugly princess who died a long, long time ago. Her name was Menbell. When Menbell was alive, people used to want to marry her, but now nobody even wanted to look at her. So she lived all alone in her creepy castle. . . . All day Menbell just stared at the TV and happily giggled to herself.

Menbell, we learn, was covered in warts and never cleaned her castle, but then one night while she was walking in the woods a disembodied hand jumped onto her face, causing Menbell to scream "so loud she disturbed the forest's evil spirits." Princess Menbell took the hand as a sign that she must change her evil ways, and that very day she cleaned her home and took a shower, acts that restored her beauty and also returned her to life. Princess Menbell then left the forest and went into "the real world" to search for her father. With the help of a mysterious old man, she discovered her dad in the dungeon of the Leaning Tower of Pisa, lying in a coffin, dead, and brought him back to life.

The theme of Rosie's stories was almost always redemption, and their plots usually involved heroines who save their fathers, just as Rosie wanted to save hers.

As a boy growing up in India, Rosie's father had dreamed of becoming a doctor, but his family couldn't afford the schooling. After emigrating to America as a young man, he'd gone into business and now owned several candy shops. But his great dream was to have one of his children do what he'd never had a chance to do: go to Harvard. Since Rosie's older brothers didn't have the grades for that, the burden fell to Rosie, and she was determined not to let her father down. "My parents, they are my god," she said. "So I'll climb that mountain and go to Harvard, no matter what. . . . I mean to Harvard or, like, one of the top five schools."

At the same time, Rosie seemed to sense how steep the mountain was and how difficult her journey would be. After learning she was to play a pirate in *Peter Pan,* she wrote:

> I wanted to be a lost girl because I don't want to grow up and I'm not gonna grow up. I'm always gonna have fun and always I'll be my mom's and dad's girl no matter what happens and that is what I will do.

I encouraged the kids to ignore my assignments if they had something else they were dying to write, and I was pleased that Rosie always preferred to do her own thing. She was also game for a challenge. Once I suggested that—for a change—she write about a girl who was bad instead of good, and Rosie's face lit up.

She called her bad-girl story "The Ghost Party," and we met one day to discuss her first draft. Her antiheroine was Yanni, a nasty girl with "fat ugly legs" who got so mad at her parents she decided to kill them.

For half a second, I wondered if this fantasy was cause for concern. (After all, I'd suggested only that the girl be bad, not murderous.) But Rosie obviously wasn't a troubled kid, and if on some level she was working out a primal, Freudian urge, it seemed harmless. Besides, she wasn't the first writer who'd knocked off her protagonists' parents.

Most grown-ups are shocked to discover that children's classics are littered with orphans or kids who have lost at least one parent, usually the mother. A partial list includes *The Adventures of Huckleberry Finn, The Adventures of Tom Sawyer, Anne of Green Gables, Babe: The Gallant Pig, Bambi, Batman, The BFG, The Boxcar Children, Charlotte's Web,* "Cinderella," *Daddy-Long-Legs, David Copperfield,* "Hansel and Gretel," *Heidi, The Island of the Blue Dolphins, James and the Giant Peach, The Jungle Book,* "The Juniper Tree," *The Little Lame Prince,* "The Little Mermaid," *Little Orphan Annie, The Little Princess, Madeline, Oliver Twist, Peter Pan, Pippi Longstocking, Rebecca of Sunnybrook Farm,* "The Red Shoes," *The Secret Garden,* "Snow White," *Superman, Tarzan, Treasure Island, The Witches, The Witch of Blackbird Pond, The Wizard of Oz,* and recently, Lemony Snicket's *A Series of Unfortunate Events* and the Harry Potter books. Somehow, as we pass into adulthood we forget—a wand is waved over us, amnesia sets in, and we romanticize our childhood. We no longer remember youthful fantasies of being on our own or even, in angry moments, screaming at our parents (as I remember shrieking at my poor mother once), *"I wish you were dead!"*

Rosie's would-be orphan, her bad seed, is five years old, which was a good choice because it made the story so absurd. Yanni kills her parents with a time bomb.

"That's a little cartoony," I said. "Can't you think of some way for Yanni to kill her parents that a five-year-old could actually pull off?"

"Hmmmmm. Maybe she finds a snake in the woods. A poisonous snake and she put it in the shower."

"Good, good! Much better!" I started making notes: *finds snake, puts it in the shower.* "Okay, then what?"

"She was staying in the living room with her fingers inside her ears and waiting until her mother and father scream."

I'm writing fast: *fingers in ear, screams of agony.*

Rosie watched me write. She asked, "What's agony?"

"Pain and misery. Go on, what's next?"

"But Yanni doesn't hear screams of—what's that word?"

"Agony."

"Agony. Instead of agony her mother just calls her in for supper."

"Can Yanni hear her mother? Aren't her fingers plugging her ears?"

"Yeah, right. She can't hear. So her mother came and snatched her."

"I'm not sure *snatched* is the best word here."

"*Grabbed* her. 'Go take a shower!'"

Rosie liked this new plot so much she pointed to her first draft. "Can we cross out everything I wrote there?"

"Sure," I said, and with a flourish crossed out two whole pages. "Happy?"

"Yeah!" said Rosie, thrilled to see that a story could be remade so completely. "Then her mom picks her up and Yanni is screaming but her mom puts her in the shower . . . and her father helps her."

"Hang on, I can't write that fast."

"When I was little, Mr. Swope, my daddy took showers with me and my two brothers, all of us together. It was so fun!"

"Okay, so the parents are fighting with Yanni to get her in the shower. Then what?"

"The snake's in the shower, right?" asked Rosie.

"You're asking me? This is your story."

"Oh!" she said, delighted. "So Yanni's trying to go out of the shower but her mom is holding the door and her dad is kind of like pulling her back in and shampooing her hair." For dramatic effect, Rosie lowered her voice ominously and said, "Then the snake struck. And all three lay dead."

Imitating her voice, I added, ". . . as the shower sprayed their lifeless bodies."

"Wow," said Rosie. "That is so cool."

Your Child Is Wonderful

On the day of parent-teacher conferences, classes ended at noon. During the afternoon and evening, the parents came in. Except for our dinner break, it was nonstop. The good news was that every student but one (Rosie) had at least one parent come to school. The bad news was the same. Twenty-seven conferences, one after the other, boom, boom, boom, ten minutes each—which kid is yours?—and since everything said had to be translated, there was hardly time to talk about the child, let alone find out about the parent, and there was so much I was curious to know, so much my students were too young to understand or explain. What work had the parents done back home? What were the schools like? What did they eat? How did they pray? Why did they come to the United States? Did they miss their homelands? Was America what they'd hope it would be?

At the end of the night, I sat down to make notes but couldn't remember half the people I'd seen. Which parent was Amarjeet's? What had Cesar's mother said? It was mostly one big blur, but inevitably some things stood out.

Gary's father came in alone. He was a dignified man in middle age with a sun-wrinkled face. He'd nearly drowned when fleeing Cuba in a boat and now was a bellhop in a midtown Manhattan hotel. "A good job," he told me. I'd already met him, in the fall, when he'd come to school just to thank me for teaching his son. He understood my English quite well, but his accent was so thick I had trouble understanding him. He pronounced my name Meezer Thwope.

"Gary's wonderful," I said. "He's a smart, nice boy. Very polite. Eager to learn."

He asked me something, but I didn't understand.

"Excuse me?"

He repeated the question.

"I'm sorry?"

Again I didn't understand, and when I shrugged apologetically, he winced and his shoulders sagged in defeat.

"Gary has trouble telling stories," I said. "He can't hold on to a narrative. I don't understand this, because he's so bright. Maybe it's my fault. I tell the kids to make their stories unexpected, so Gary puts something unexpected in every sentence. I can't break him of it. It's just one crazy thing after another. There's never a story."

Gary's dad nodded, but he didn't know what to say.

"I'm not worried," I said. "He'll get better with practice."

"You no worried, Meezer Thwope?"

"No."

He accepted that with a nod.

"Are you reading to Gary?" I asked. "Do you read him Spanish stories?"

"No in English?"

"No, you should read to him in Spanish. The memory of a father's voice reading a story is a powerful one. Read in your native tongue."

MeiKai's mom, Mrs. Li, left Taiwan with her husband and son shortly before MeiKai's birth. She helped support the family by doing piecework sewing from her kitchen; her husband worked in a restaurant. MeiKai's mother spoke no English but had the warmest smile. I felt an immediate bond with her, one of those strange, inexplicable closenesses we sometimes feel with strangers, as if we had been siblings in a former life.

MeiKai had come with her mom and her teenage brother, Alan, who did the translating. I said, "MeiKai's a wonderful child. Very responsible. Very neat. She has trouble with paragraphs and is always forgetting to write her stories in the past tense, but that will come."

While her brother translated, MeiKai and I smiled at each other. Then I said, "The most remarkable thing about your daughter, though, is how happy she is. She's the happiest child I've ever known, and she makes everyone around her happy, too. It's a gift."

MeiKai's mother looked at MeiKai and nodded to say she understood: MeiKai's happiness amazed her, too. To teach MeiKai's mother an English word, I pointed at her daughter and said, "Happy."

Her mother said, "Happy."

"Happy."

All of us were smiling.

"Do you read to MeiKai in Chinese?" I said.

When she understood my question, MeiKai's mother looked at me, confused. "Enh?" she said.

Alan said to me, "Shouldn't she be learning English?"

"Tell her to read MeiKai stories in Chinese," I said. "It will make her a better writer. The memory of a mother's voice reading stories is a powerful one."

"Enh?" said MeiKai's mother.

Maya's father, who grew up working in the rice fields of Guyana, was so deferential and respectful of me as a teacher that I was embarrassed; he didn't know I was teaching by the seat of my pants.

"Mr. Swope, I want to extend my gratitude for giving of your time, your experience, your wisdom to teach Maya to write. As an expert in your field, Mr. Swope, whatever books you recommend as necessary, these I will buy her. The cost doesn't matter. I will sacrifice everything for Maya's education."

"She's lucky to have a father like you," I said, wishing that I had something wise to say about his daughter. But the truth was that I hadn't really tuned into Maya. She was quiet, did her work, and hadn't written anything that made her stand out one way or the other.

"Maya's a wonderful girl," I told him. "I'm pleased with her progress. The only thing is, she has a tendency to rush. She has to learn to slow down. Do you read to her?"

"Oh, Maya reads to herself a lot. She reads all the time."

"Yes, but you should be reading to her, too. The memory of a father's voice reading stories is a powerful one."

Fatma's father was from Pakistan. He had five children to support and looked so gaunt and haggard I worried that he was in the last stages of a terminal disease. Fatma, the girl who looked like a boy, was his youngest child. He hadn't brought her with him, but it was clear he had ambitions for his daughter. "Is Fatma the top writer?" he asked me.

I ignored the question, saying, "Her writing skills are excellent, the level of a much older child." I didn't tell the whole truth, didn't say that although Fatma wrote with more fluency than anyone in the class, her stories were repetitive, predictable, and so boring I dreaded reading them. (She favored realistic fiction, stories set at school or at home that were peopled with snide, sitcom characters.)

"The top student?" he asked again.

Again I ignored the question. "Fatma is quite independent. If I stop by her desk, she turns her page over. She doesn't want my help." When he looked concerned, I said, "But independence is a good thing in a writer. What is Fatma like at home?"

"She gets dark moods, but then comes out of them and is cheerful. We are living in a one-bedroom apartment. Sometimes to be alone she goes in the closet with a tape recorder. She talks into it, using many different voices."

"But that's wonderful!" I said, thrilled to see some evidence of an imaginative life. "I hope she can get some of those voices into her stories. Basically, what Fatma needs to learn is to let her imagination go."

"I'll have a talk with her," her father said, ominously.

I wanted to kick myself. Why did I have to go and say that? It wouldn't do any good, and it might do harm, make Fatma feel I'd ratted on her. I imagined him saying to her, "Mr. Swope is not happy with you, Fatma. You will never be the top student if you don't let your imagination go." And what would Fatma do with that? "I'm sorry I let you down, Father. I'll let my imagination go from now on, I promise."

Imagination isn't like learning to multiply. You can't learn how to have it and you can't will it. It either happens or it doesn't.

"Maybe she'll be a nonfiction writer," I said. "Do you read to her in—what language do you speak at home?"

"Urdu."

Miguel's mother was quite young, in her twenties, practically a girl herself. She had a round moon face and, as a Pentecostal, wore no jewelry or makeup and never cut her hair, which hung to her waist without a ribbon or barrette. Her dress was a simple cotton shift.

"Miguel talks about you all the time, Mr. Swope."

"He's a wonderful kid, incredibly smart," I said.

She was pleased to hear me confirm what she already knew. She was very smart herself. "I want Miguel to have what I didn't have," she told me. "I tell him I want him to be intelligent, to go to college before he gets married. I say to him, 'I want you to be in the math bee and the spelling bee. I want you to be in everything.' He tells me, 'Mom, you're pushing me too hard.'"

I saw in her an ally, and liked her immediately. I said, "Miguel's lucky to have a mother like you. It's good you're pushing him. He needs it. Because he's also lazy and sloppy and disorganized. He doesn't have discipline. His stories wander all over the place. I'm always telling him to cut to the chase, but he can't focus. Do you read to him in Spanish?"

"The Bible every night."

"Good."

"But it's hard for us, Mr. Swope."

"What's hard?"

There wasn't time. An announcement was being repeated on the public-address system and echoing through the hallways: "The building will close in five minutes. The building will close in five minutes."

I said, "Could we continue this conversation another day? After school, perhaps? And I'd love to interview you for my book."

Miguel's mother blushed, flattered. "You want to know about *me,* Mr. Swope?"

When I answered "Yes, absolutely," she invited me to their home the next day.

You Don't Got No Friends

Miguel Santiago lived three blocks from school in a dreary apartment building on a run-down block. The elevator wasn't working, so I went up the stairs. The hallways were clean but depressing—institutional tile and flickering fluorescent lights. Miguel's dad answered the door and greeted me politely. The apartment was neat and tidy and very small. Miguel and his younger brothers shared the bedroom; the parents slept behind a sheet that divided the narrow living room. Miguel's mom, whose name was Christina, said hello from the kitchen, which was little more than a closet. She was putting rice and beans on the stove for dinner.

Mr. Santiago offered me a folding chair at their dinner table, which doubled as a desk.

"*Gracias,*" I said.

"*De nada.*"

That was pretty much the extent of my Spanish. He and I smiled awkwardly at each other until Miguel came in and plopped on a chair opposite me—"Hi, Mr. Swope!"—at which point Mr. Santiago took his three younger sons to the bedroom, leaving me to talk with Miguel and his mom. At the parent-teacher conference I'd encouraged Mrs. Santiago to collaborate on a story with Miguel, and now she made a point of mentioning that they'd already done so. I could see her eagerness, so I asked to read it. Their story was a charming and odd retelling of "The Three Little Pigs" starring three little flames who were named Disaster, Dangerous, and Explosion; their wicked old wolf was a rain cloud. When I praised the story, Miguel's mother blushed with pride, and in that moment I saw her own ravenous hunger for an education.

I asked her to tell me how she'd come to this country.

"Well, Mr. Swope," she began, but I interrupted, asking her to call me Sam. She said she'd try, but she wasn't able to do so, because in some ways she considered me her teacher, too.

Christina Santiago was born in Ecuador. When she was two, her mother left her father and emigrated to New York, leaving Christina behind to live with her father. Five years later, at age seven, she was taken from Ecuador (and her father, whom she loved) to Queens, where she lived in a basement apartment with a mother she didn't remember, a stepfather she'd never met, and six siblings. She had no friends, knew no English, and did poorly in school. "I didn't have what Miguel has," she said, putting her arm around her son. "I didn't have no mother to sit with me and encourage and to help me, and so that's why I don't recall nothing that I learned." Then she smiled, trying to be positive, and said, "But now I'm learning a lot with Junior, 'cause I help him with his homework."

Miguel nodding, pleased with himself, said, "And I'm kind of like a German shepherd that takes care of her."

Mrs. Santiago's story got worse, reminding me of a folktale out of Grimm. When she was in tenth grade, her stepfather came home one night with a fellow worker. "I was watching TV," Christina told me. "I was laying on the floor, and when I saw my stepfather with somebody else, I ran inside the room because I was in my undergown. And my stepfather goes to me, 'Oh, sweetheart, come out in the living room.' And I go, 'No, I don't wanna go.' 'Well, come on, I brought somebody for you to meet.' And I go, 'I don't wanna meet nobody!' So my mother came and she told me the same thing, to come in. And then everything else happened," she said, glancing at Miguel. "And we had to get married."

Miguel said, "Mom, you picked the right man."

Because Mrs. Santiago was pregnant, she dropped out of school. The marriage got off to a rocky start. By the time Miguel was one, she and her husband were fighting regularly and ready to divorce. Then a friend paid a visit. "And he preached the word of God to us," Miguel's mom told me. "And that same day I accepted Jesus Christ as my savior, and my husband reconciled to Jesus, too, and since then, we have been under God's law. Seven years now. It's like a miracle."

I don't believe in God, but I wish I could. I envy others' deep belief, the strength and comfort they find in faith. Church, Mrs. Santiago said, was the center of their family life. They spent Saturdays as well as Sundays there, and when she told me Miguel had started preaching at church when he was four, I was amazed. She said, "Last week he preached, and everybody cried because the Holy Spirit got him. Everybody felt, like, goose bumps, chills."

Miguel tried not to smile, but he was proud. "Pentecostals have to be fishers of men," he explained. "We have to preach the word of God."

"What did you preach?"

"I said, 'I thank God because I didn't want to preach today, but my father pushed me, and if it wasn't because of my father, I wouldn't be here preaching because that's what Satan wants. He doesn't want me to preach!'"

When Miguel went off to do his homework, I mentioned something to his mother that was troubling me. I said, "Miguel doesn't have any friends at school."

She nodded, saying, "I tell my son, 'The only friends that you have is your father, your mother, God, and your brothers. 'Cause the other people, you may think they're your friends, but one day they'll get you in trouble. I know this from my own experience. So I go, 'You don't got no friends.'"

I left Miguel's home feeling sad, but I told myself it could be worse. His mother doted on him, at least, and the family was reading the Bible together every night. That was good; everyone, even nonbelievers, should read the Bible, if only as great literature. And his preaching, that was excellent public-speaking practice; he'd get a lot out of that. Although I would have chosen a different childhood for Miguel, I told myself, *If he does become a writer, he's going to have lots of great material.*

The Little Liar

One day Aaron and I got together to write a story. I asked him, "Who's going to be our main character?"

"A shark."

"No way. I've collaborated on three shark stories already and I'm sick of them."

"Aw, mannnnnnnnnn."

"Okay, okay. But if we have to have sharks, they have to be alien sharks on some faraway planet or something."

"The planet Zoid."

"Ooh, I like that," I said. "Tell me how the ocean on planet Zoid is different from Earth's oceans."

"It's hot like lava and it's pink like bubble gum. It even tastes like bubble gum."

"Excellent," I said as I started to write. "So what's our creature going to look like?"

"Exactly like a shark but it has a light bulb at the end of his tongue."

"Good," I said. "What's the light bulb for?"

"That's how it catches its dinner."

"Explain."

Aaron tucked his hands under his legs. "He buries himself under the sand with only the light bulb sticking up and then when a fish comes to see what is the light, he snatches the fish up in his mouth."

"Brilliant," I said, smiling.

Aaron didn't smile back, though. Like a born storyteller, he knew a smile would break the spell. But he couldn't hide the twinkle that lit up his eyes, and mine twinkled back, as if we were sharing a secret joke.

"What's this fish called?"

"Um, he's a popalok."

This was the name of a made-up animal in *The Araboolies of Liberty Street*. I never describe a popalok in the book, though; they're just mentioned in a list of the family's strange pets. I said to Aaron, "Tell me about popaloks."

Aaron explained that when a popalok is attacked by a merm, she gets so mad she lays two eggs, from which hatch baby popaloks reading books.

I was doubtful and said, "Really? Books?"

"Yep, books," said Aaron, giving me a look that said he knew it sounded strange, but that's the way it really happened.

"Okay. Books it is. What then?"

"Then the popalok shouts, 'Stop reading those damn books and help me catch that merm!'"

I don't know if Aaron understood the power and the danger of the imagination, how easy it is to get lost in the world of words while angry merms are circling, but an ambivalence toward language and imagination occurred often in his stories. In a short tale called "Who Am I?" a tiny crab says the word *funky,* which starts a series of terrifying events that only ends with the crab's promise never to say the word *funky* again. In "The Magic Eraser," four brothers are dying of cancer brought on from eating too much meat. Then they find a treasure chest that holds an eraser, the writer's tool, and it proceeds to erase not only the brothers, but the bathtub, the house, the neighborhood, the city, and finally the entire earth.

"Aaron, have you ever known anybody who died?"

"Two persons: my grandfather and my friend."

"What did your friend die of?"

"Cancer. His face was white."

"How old was he?"

"Six."

"You must have been sad when he died."

"That's why I didn't go to his funeral."

"What was his name?"

"I don't remember. George."

"And how did your grandfather die?"

"He died of cancer, too, because on television they say if you eat too much meat and not enough plants you get cancer."

The best nonfiction writers use the tools of fiction, a confusing distinction to children who have a hard time sorting out the real from the imaginary in the first place. When Aaron was working on a newspaper article about his father's life in South America, he wrote that his father's father died in an earthquake.

"Did a building crush him?"

"No," said Aaron. "He fell right in the crack of the earthquake."

I raised an eyebrow. "Really?"

"Yep."

"So, this is a different grandfather than the one who died of cancer, right?"

"No, it's the same one. He died of the earthquake and he died of cancer at the exact same moment."

What was Aaron thinking? Was he doing what all of us do, using his imagination to fill in the blanks as he searched for a plausible answer that reconciled conflicting facts? Or did he know he was making a wild guess that, with a little luck and a lot of chutzpah, he might get away with? If he could convince me, would that make it real?

"You're sure that's the way it happened, Aaron?"

"Yep, I am."

I thought of all the writers who'd imagined their way out of poverty, and fantasized that Aaron would be one of them. He had a wonderful narrative imagination, and it frustrated me that his written stories were so perfunctory, not much more than a series of scrawled grunts. Part of his problem was laziness—when I was standing over him, he added the details he knew I liked and was usually able to figure out where to put his periods and capitals. He also had a bad habit of writing with his hand twisted into a crook, so that he had to draw each letter backward and if he wrote for long his hand cramped. "Don't bend your wrist, Aaron," I'd say over and over again. "Don't clutch your pencil. Hold it gently, like it's an extension of your index finger. Sit up straight."

No matter how dashed off a first draft was, there'd always be something intriguing in it. When we wrote myths, his first draft was a video-game-inspired fight between a scorpion god and a dog god. "You write here that the scorpion kidnaps the dog's lady love and hides her," I said.

"Yep."

"But then you never talk about that again. Why is that?"

"I don't know."

"Do you know where the scorpion hides her?"

"Yep."

"Where?"

"In the dog god's brain."

This idea, I'm sure, just popped into his head, but I said, "That's fabulous, Aaron! You've got to work harder and get these great ideas on paper. Now, be sure to put that in your next draft, and I bet the story goes off in a more interesting direction than all this bang-bang stuff you've got now. Don't be lazy, okay?"

"When I write my next draft, Mr. Swope, it's going to be five whole pages long."

My heart sank when he handed in his assignment. He'd changed the spelling and the punctuation, but the only addition he'd made was a single sentence saying the scorpion hid the dog's lady love in the dog's brain. Otherwise, it was word for word the same story.

Using my sternest voice, I said, "I'm very disappointed, Aaron. You promised me five pages. And you still never tell what happens to the lady love after she's been put in the dog's brain. Does she stay there forever, or does she get out, or what?"

"She gets out."

"Do you know how?"

"Yep, she—"

"I don't want to hear it. I want to read it. Now, I want you to write this again, and I want you to promise me you'll write the best story you've ever written."

Aaron's third draft was neatly written, full of adjectives, fairly well punctuated, and more than five pages long. As he handed it to me he said proudly, "I've never written a story this long in my whole life!" I was delighted. Although his writing was stilted, his thinking was great: in this version, the treacherous scorpion agrees to return the dog's lady love, but when he removes her from the dog's head, he also snatches the dog's brain and sticks it in his pocket. In this *Twilight Zone* twist, the dog gets his lady love back, but he can't recognize her.

Is the scorpion a representation of Aaron himself? Isn't that what writers do, pocket brains?

That spring Mrs. Duncan brought live chameleons into the classroom for
a science project. Each team had a terrarium with leaves and a chameleon
that was fed with live crickets, and the children were excited to watch the
lizards swallow the insects whole in one quick gulp. When the supply of
crickets began to dwindle, Mrs. Duncan asked the children where they
thought more crickets could be found, and Aaron raised his hand. "My
grandmother has crickets in the fields behind her house on Long Island,"
he said. "I'll get some when we visit her this weekend." On Monday
morning Mrs. Duncan asked Aaron how the cricket hunt had gone, and
he said, "We caught one hundred crickets, but one died so now there's
only ninety-nine."

"That'll be plenty," said Mrs. Duncan. "Make a note in your homework pad to bring the crickets in tomorrow, because we're almost out,
and the chameleons are going to need more food."

On Tuesday Aaron came in empty-handed, and when Mrs. Duncan
asked for an explanation, he said, "We all overslept and were rushing
around like crazy and Mom forgot to give me the crickets."

"Your mother didn't promise to bring in the crickets, you did," said
Mrs. Duncan. "This is your responsibility, Aaron. The chameleons are
hungry. They are counting on you, the whole class is counting on you.
Don't forget again tomorrow."

Mrs. Duncan wasn't surprised when Aaron showed up cricketless on
Wednesday, and when she said, "Aaron, these crickets don't exist anywhere but in your mind, do they?," Aaron didn't answer.

Mrs. Duncan sighed, knowing she now had to take Aaron to task for
lying as well as starving the chameleons. But I was free to be amused by
his story. The detail of the single dead cricket delighted me, and I was
amazed by Aaron's confidence in the power of his mind to remake the
world.

Sometimes children's lies are calculated, but sometimes they just pop
right out, and for no particular advantage. It's as if kids' imaginations
suddenly turn on them just to get them into trouble. When I was nine and
traveling with my family by train, I insisted on sitting by myself several
rows back. By and by a woman sat down next to me. I had been warned
never to talk to strangers, and having one so close was both exciting and a

little scary. I watched her out of the corner of my eye. She took out a book and put on a pair of half-glasses. I had just started wearing glasses myself but had never seen strange glasses like hers. I forgot myself and turned to stare. Feeling my gaze, the woman looked down at me from over the top of her glasses, and I froze.

"Hello," she said. "Who are you?"

"I'm the prince of Czechoslovakia," I announced, shocking both of us.

"That's a long way from here," she said. "What brings you to America?"

Astonished that she believed me, my heart began to pound and my body tingled, excited by my power. I told her, "My whole family was killed. I had to flee for my life."

"You poor dear."

I nodded sadly and looked out the window.

"Tell me," she said. "Where in Czechoslovakia are you from?"

"Düsseldorf."

"Strange. I thought Düsseldorf was in Germany."

"It used to be, but then they moved it."

"Ah, I see," she said. She closed her book, took off her glasses, and asked me to tell her all about my life. As I spun my tale, I half-knew she understood I was making it up, but she was an attentive listener, and having her mind in my pocket was thrill enough for me.

When I told a friend this story, she said, "You stole that from *Catcher in the Rye*. Holden lies to a woman on the train, telling her he's got a brain tumor." I looked up the passage, and sure enough, Holden lies outrageously to a stranger on a train. I began to doubt my memory. Had I really met that woman on that train? Had I made it up, or elaborated that memory after reading *Catcher in the Rye*? Was I in Salinger's pocket and didn't even know it?

When I arrived at school late one April morning, Okan, a dreamy Turkish boy who was always thinking about airplanes, told me he felt sad.

"What makes you sad?"

"I feel sad because Aaron got mugged this morning."

I gasped and looked over at Aaron, who was hard at work on his multiplication problems, his red turtleneck pulled way up over his nose, as if he was trying to crawl into a shell and hide. He was so tiny and defenseless, and it made me angry that anyone would have harmed him.

When I asked Mrs. Duncan what had happened, she told me Aaron had come in that morning and announced that he'd been mugged, they'd stolen his backpack, and his mother had called the police. Muggings of children didn't happen often in that neighborhood, but they happened, and it was always traumatic.

"Is he all right?"

"He seems okay, but who knows what's going on inside his head? Still, I'm not sure what to do before I talk to his mother, because it also seems that all of Aaron's overdue homework was in his backpack when it was stolen."

"No!"

"Yes," she said. "But I don't have any choice. I have to take his story seriously. It's very upsetting."

Earlier in the year, Gary had brought in a Cuban story called "The Little Liar." In this apocalyptic version of "The Boy Who Cried Wolf," a boy twice tells his village that a flood is coming, and both times everyone runs for higher ground. When the flood really does come, no one believes the boy and the rushing waters kill everyone, including the little liar.

On the morning Aaron's backpack disappeared, I took him off for a collaboration. Before we began, though, I asked him what had happened.

"Well, I was walking down the street."

"What street?"

"I think, oh, yeah: near my neighborhood."

"Uh-huh, and then what happened?"

"Like, somebody just grabbed me from the back and put a gun in my cheek and they said, 'Give me your schoolbag.'"

"And what did you do?"

"I told them, 'I'd rather give you the schoolbag than waste my life,' and I gave them the schoolbag."

"That was the smart thing to do," I said. "So what did this guy look like?"

"Um, I couldn't see."

"Why not?"

"Because he was wearing a black mask."

"Um-hmmmm. Did he have a knife, too, maybe?"

"Yeah," said Aaron, wearing his poker face. "He had a knife and a gun. He put the gun on my cheek and put the knife across my throat."

"Did he have an accent?"

"He sounded kind of German, I think."

"I would have been terrified."

"It was the scariest thing that ever happened in my life, Mr. Swope."

"What did you do after you gave him your bag?"

"I ran back home and my mother called the police and I told them what happened."

"Did they catch him?"

"No."

"Well, I'm glad you're okay," I said.

I don't know whether Aaron sensed my disbelief or whether he knew his lie was spinning out of control and certain to catch up with him, but I didn't feel it was my place to call his bluff, so I changed the subject and asked him if he'd like to do a collaboration.

"Okay."

"What would you like this story to be about?"

"My life."

Aaron invented a story about a boy named Eric who goes to Mars, climbs into a floating castle, and finds an old, old man. When Eric touches him, the man crumbles to dust, but his eyeballs come after Eric and try to "munch" him up. To escape, Eric leaps out the window, surfs through space, and crashes into Earth, breaking it apart.

"Then what happens to Eric?"

"He lands on the tip of the moon. He yells, 'Help!' and then he got control of the whole universe, only he didn't get control of the universe alphabet."

"What's the universe alphabet?"

"There's twenty-six planets, and each one is named by a letter, and if he doesn't get control of the universe alphabet, the letters will come and get him."

"What will they do to him?"

"They'll make him into a letter so they can climb on him. That's why they want our galaxy, so there will be more letters."

"And what happens then?"

"When they get control of all the planets, God will become a letter tree, and then Eric will try and climb it because if he climbs it he'll be up in heaven and then he won't need to be a letter anymore."

"And what a relief that will be," I said.

"Yeah," said Aaron.

• • •

The next day, Mrs. Duncan summoned Aaron's mother to school and learned Aaron had come home without his backpack a couple of days before, having lost it—or tossed it?—at the playground. The conference made Mrs. Duncan angry with Aaron and annoyed with his mother, who'd been as amused by her son's audacity as I was, and had given him a smile that showed how adorably incorrigible she thought he was.

"At least his story shows Aaron has a strong imagination," I said.

"It shows he lied," said Mrs. Duncan. "Now I wonder about everything he ever said. Maybe he even made up that story about his Christmas present so we'd feel sorry for him. I feel manipulated and lied to, and because Aaron told me he got mugged, I had to worry. The children got worried. No, it's not okay to make up stories if other people are going to get hurt or upset."

I could see her point. "But aren't you just a little pleased that he tried to get out of his homework by telling such a daring lie?"

"Not at all."

"Isn't part of growing up learning to manipulate the system?" I said. "Sometimes con men are admirable."

Mrs. Duncan was shocked. "When are con men ever admirable?" she said.

"What about 'The Emperor's New Clothes'? Those tailors con everyone, and we love it that they lie."

Mrs. Duncan looked at me as if I were out of my mind. "But that's a story! This is real life."

All That Glitters Is Not Gold

I woke up one morning in May and immediately looked out the window, relieved to see the sun was shining bright. We were going on a field trip to the Metropolitan Museum of Art, and I wanted everything to be perfect.

The Met is a magical place. I knew the kids would love it. How could they not? The building itself, a massive stone palace stretching four blocks along Fifth Avenue, is awesome, and its galleries, corridors, and court-yards are varied and endless, pleasantly disorienting, maze within maze of paintings, prints, photographs, furniture, and bric-a-brac, precious odds and ends from many eras and cultures. We were going there to look at boxes—jewelry boxes, stationery boxes, music boxes, snuffboxes, tribal boxes, reliquaries, and sarcophaguses. It was research for the last major story the kids would write that year.

I'd told them, "Each of you is going to build a box, any kind of box you want. At the museum you'll see a range of possibilities. After you've built your box, you'll write a story about it. Then we'll make a book of your story, and that book will go inside your box for you to keep forever, so your children can one day find the box, open it, discover the book inside, which tells the story of the box that holds the book that tells—"

"—the story of the box that holds the book!" said Su Jung, smiling. She delighted in the circularity of that.

We called it the Box Project.

Before we went to the Met, we'd be making another stop, at my apart-ment. Mrs. Duncan wanted the kids to see where a "real writer" lived, and I liked the idea of having them in my home. I'd planned a surprise for them there, a surprise that involved two boxes. One box I'd wrapped in fancy paper and decorated with candies. The other was a cruddy old cardboard box I'd tied with twine.

Miguel wouldn't be coming with us. His father was punishing him because he hadn't defended his younger brother against a bully. "Miguel has to learn to protect his family," his mother told me. I begged his mom to reconsider, explained that the two events were unrelated, but she pointed out that when you're poor, there isn't much you can deprive a child of, and since Miguel was looking forward to the trip, this was something they could take away.

"This trip is not for fun," I argued. "It's an important part of his education." Although Mrs. Santiago was sympathetic, there was nothing she could do: once her husband made up his mind, there wasn't any changing it.

I sat with Miguel before we left that day. "I'm sorry you won't be coming with us. I'll miss you."

"I feel sad 'cause I won't get to see your house," he said.

"One day I'll invite you and your mom over. That's a promise."

I gave him a gift, a copy of my book *The Araboolies of Liberty Street*. He thanked me, smiled, and went off to another classroom while his classmates, in high spirits, headed for the subway.

My apartment, in a brownstone on Manhattan's Upper West Side, was a nice-sized single room with high ceilings and four windows overlooking the trees that lined my street. I had a Murphy bed, which cracked the kids up. And they were excited to meet my cat, Mike; she was hiding in plain sight on a high closet shelf.

"Hey, Mr. Swope," said Noelia. "If your cat's a girl cat, how come you named her Mike?"

"Yeah!" said Gary.

"Yeah!" said Jessica.

"Yeah!" "Yeah!" "Yeah!"

"Mike can be a female name," I told them. "My parents had a journalist friend named Mike and I liked her a lot."

"Ohhhh," they responded, without looking entirely convinced.

"Have some cookies," I said, passing a plate around.

Then I showed them my surprise. "Okay, guys, see these two boxes?" I held them both up. They oohed over the pretty box.

"Here's the deal," I said. "I'll give you whatever is inside one of these boxes, but only one. You have to choose." I paused to let that sink in. Then I said, "Okay, how many vote for the ugly box?"

Every hand went up.

That wasn't the answer I was looking for. They were supposed to choose the pretty box, and after they'd discovered it was empty, they'd be shocked and I would wisely say, "You see? Don't judge a book by its cover. All that glitters is not gold." Oh, I'd pictured everything, how they'd beg me to change my mind and let them have the ugly box, but I'd shake my head and tease them, saying, "No, no. You made your choice. You have to live with it." Finally I'd say, "Okay, all right," and I'd relent and open up the ugly box, which held a present for each one of them.

But it wouldn't work unless they chose the pretty box.

"I don't think you understand what's at stake here," I told them. "If you choose the ugly box, you don't get what's in the pretty box. You won't even get to *see* what's in the pretty box. Are you willing to take that chance? Think this over carefully, guys. Don't make a mistake."

A chant went up: "Ugly box! Ugly box!"

"Oh, come on, guys, stop. You're ruining my trick! How did you know? What gave it away?"

Kemal explained, "When you picked the pretty box up to show us, we could tell it was empty and knew it was a trick."

"You can't trick us, Mr. Swope," said Rosie. "We know whatever you say, the truth is always opposite."

"Well, rats," I said.

A deal is a deal, though, so I opened up the ugly box, which held a stack of *The Araboolies of Liberty Street,* donated by my publisher, and as the kids went out the door, I gave them each a copy.

We picnicked in Central Park before going to the Met. It was good to see the children on the grass, under trees. Su Jung sat with Mrs. Duncan and me. "Now that we know where you live, we can all come visit you when we grow up, Mr. Swope," she said.

"I hope you do," I said.

"And nothing is better than having *The Araboolies of Liberty Street.*"

"Thank you. That means a lot to me."

My book, I'd later learn, was not so welcome everywhere. That night Miguel's mother would tell him, "Your father's gonna be mad if he sees that book. You hide it. I think he's going to tear it apart."

When Miguel told me this news, I asked, "What's wrong with my book?"

"Stories are bad if you put witches or fairy godmothers, magic in it, 'cause when Jesus healed the sick, raised Lazarus from the dead, let Pedro go through the water without drowning, that wasn't magic, that was a miracle. So *The Araboolies of Liberty Street* is only half bad because it's just imaginative, not like with magic."

Out of deference to Miguel's religion, he was excused from certain tasks, like writing his own myth. However, I was never clear what sort of things he wasn't allowed to write, and sometimes the prohibitions took me by surprise. Once I asked the kids to write a story about a character with an obsession. "The obsession could be ice cream or basketball or books," I said. "But whatever it is, it must be reflected in every aspect of your character's life—home, clothes, job, food, everything."

The next day, Miguel's mother came in to tell me Miguel couldn't do that assignment. "If you're obsessed you're in Satan's power," she explained.

"Then what if we just say the character is very, very interested in something?"

"Oh, yes," she said, relieved. "That would be okay."

The conflict between what his religion taught and what I taught must have been confusing to Miguel. If *The Araboolies of Liberty Street* was half bad because it was imaginative, he was smart enough to know the stories he had written were also suspect, or even sinful, because some of them had magic.

One day he told me about a dream he'd had. He said, "After I said my prayers, I was falling to sleep, and I was very sleepy, and then, I had this dream. In the dream I lost my father, and when I saw two people that looked like my father, I said, 'Whoa! Oh, my God! Who am I going to pick? Who am I going to pick? Who's my father?' One man, he had chocolate, right? Hershey's. The other one had an ice-cream cone, like, strawberry. So I went to that man that has chocolate and he said, 'Oh, you think I'm your father? Well, bye-bye!' He wasn't my father! He was tricking me! And so I went to the other man, and he said, 'Why didn't you come to me, son? I'm your real father.' But I didn't know, Mr. Swope! I didn't know! I wanted to take that dream out of my mind. I didn't want it to continue. I tried to pray but the devil was saying these words like, 'Gagawaaaa.'"

Miguel's dream presented him with an impossible choice—the man with chocolate or the man with ice cream—as difficult as choosing between the heart's desire and salvation, between imaginative writing and the word of God, between a teacher and a father. Poor Miguel, I worried that I'd done him more harm than good.

"Then finally, I said the prayer," Miguel continued. "And I was with God and I saw everybody going to heaven, everybody that I didn't even know was going to go to heaven, like my teachers and all this stuff." As Miguel tried to sum up his dream, he got confused and stumbled on his words, but finally he landed safely, with a sermon, saying, "And I really do think that it's a proper belief to be a Pentecostal 'cause that way Jesus and all the other angels are with you."

For Miguel, the only way the conflict in his dream could be resolved, the only way his teachers and his classmates could come with him to heaven, was if we changed our beliefs, becoming Pentecostal. Miguel and I both knew that wasn't going to happen, though. His preaching didn't work. I thought of when he'd played Peter Pan, and begged the audience to clap for Tinker Bell to show her we believed in her, and everybody did and Tink was saved. But that, of course, was different. That was make-believe.

Sugar Plum Saves the Day

Noelia was Dominican. She had a huge Martha Raye smile and a laugh like Porky Pig's. When I asked her what she wanted to be when she grew up, she said, "A stand-up comic. That, or a joke-telling detective."

Her parents, young and beautiful, spoke no English. Both had jobs, he in a financial firm's mail room and she at JFK International Airport, where she cleaned planes between flights. They came to the parent-teacher conference dressed to the nines, in silks and satins and snazzy shoes. It was obvious they adored their daughter. When I told them Noelia was a hoot and had a wacky imagination but didn't always do her homework, they showered their lazy little girl with hugs and kisses.

A little chubby, Noelia wasn't a girlie girl into clothes, although she loved her Barbie doll and sometimes came to school in a fancy silver dress. That was more for theater than vanity, however; by year's end the dress no longer fit and the zipper strained so much at the seams I imagined her popping out of it, like a cartoon character.

After the kids had built their boxes, I met with them to hear the stories that they planned to write.

"Hey there, Noelia! How are you today?"

"Awful! Horrible! Terrible!" She spoke melodramatically, as if making a joke.

"And what is so awful, horrible, terrible?"

"My dad moved out."

"Oh, Noelia. Really? I'm so sorry. When?"

"Like two or three days ago."

My picture of her parents, happy and in love, suddenly turned dark. I didn't want to hear this, I didn't want to know this, I didn't want Noelia to be living this. What was amazing to me was how well she'd hidden it. If she hadn't said anything, I wouldn't have had a clue. How do kids deal with such awful stuff? She wasn't visibly traumatized, not knocked flat, like Su Jung, or intensely withdrawn, like Fatma. What can a teacher do at a time like this? What can you say?

"I'm really sorry, Noelia. That must be awful for you."

"It makes me feel like I'm dead."

"Your mom must be so sad."

"She's sick. She's going to the doctor to see if she has to go to the hospital. So I'm just trying to do something to make my mom feel better. I'm making her laugh all the time."

"You're good at that."

"I tell her jokes and she laughs like crazy at me."

"She's lucky to have you."

We looked at each other for a moment, saying nothing. I felt so sad I wanted to cry. Seeing my distress, Noelia said, "Hey, Mr. Swope. Wanna hear my story?"

"What a wonderful idea."

Noelia's box was a treasure chest. It kind of looked like her. She'd drawn a face with a smile on its rounded lid and had stuck lots of pipe cleaners from it, like a crazy hairdo.

"I love the pipe-cleaner hair," I said.

"That's not hair, Mr. Swope. Those are porcupine needles."

"A box with porcupine needles. Interesting. Do you have a title for your story?"

"Yes: How Sugar Plum Saves the Day."

"Tell me what happens."

"In a house in the clouds there lived two sisters, Sour Puss and Sugar Plum. Sour Puss was the yuckiest sister. She wore all her clothes inside out. Sugar Plum was the baby sister. She was also very chubby."

"What did she wear?"

"A little fat dress with petals. Then one day, Sour Puss was putting the finishing touches on her bomb."

"Excuse me, did you say 'bomb'?"

"Yes, a bomb. She's making a bomb. She goes, 'Put some sour cherry pits here, put some sour cherry pits there, put some pepper there. . . . Done! What an elegant bomb! Now I'm ready to destroy the heavens!'"

Noelia cackled like a witch, then continued, "All of a sudden, a box landed on the floor with a bump out of nowhere, just like that! 'Ouch!' said the box."

"This is a talking box?"

"Yes."

"Okay. Go on."

"Then Sour Puss goes, 'Hey, that's my box! I've got to get it back!' Then the box started to hop as fast as she could. It wants to get away from Sour Puss. It hopped to Sugar Plum and jumped to her."

"Into Sugar Plum's arms?"

"Yeah."

"That must have hurt."

"No, Mr. Swope, it didn't. Sugar Plum hugged the part without needles."

"Whew."

"And the box goes, 'Make sure that mad girl doesn't get me!' So Sugar Plum goes, 'Okay, I'll help you.' And Sugar Plum goes, 'I know, I'll pull the needles out, one by one. It's coming loose, it's coming loose, okay, they're all coming loose. Ouch! I need a Band-Aid!'" Noelia shook her finger as if it had been pricked. "Then, after five hours, Sugar Plum finally finished getting rid of the needles and then she opened the box and found out Sour Puss's heart was in there."

"How does she know it's Sour Puss's heart?"

"It's green. She never had a red heart."

"What does Sugar Plum do?"

"She says to the box, 'Let's put the heart back in her chest where it belongs.' And then she snuck into Sour Puss's room and opened her chest."

"How does she open her chest?"

"With a key."

"There's a key? Where does Sugar Plum get the key?"

(What a stupid question. Honestly, when I listen to the tapes of these story conferences, I'm embarrassed. I often asked the most ridiculous questions, questions that had nothing to do with the story the child was trying to tell, questions that sometimes derailed a plot and sent it off in a direction it wasn't meant to take.)

Noelia said, "Sugar Plum had the key since she was born."

"I see," I said, although I didn't. "Go on."

"So Sugar Plum put the heart back in Sour Puss's chest, and Sour Puss was kind again and everything was back to normal."

"Is that the end?"

"No. The end is: So then Sugar Plum and the box became good friends. That's how I want to end it."

"I like that. That's going to be a nice story, Noelia."

"They were good friends. That's how I end it."

Kindness and Doom

Each box was as unique as a fingerprint. Gary's was shaped like a red sports car and belonged to the devil. Okan's held ghosts and other "horrors of all horrors." Mateo made a coffin. Nicole's contained the four seasons, and Simon had an entire city inside his.

Miguel's box reflected the Apocalypse, so central to his Pentecostal faith, and was a kind of hell. A Satanic character had locked "everyone in the world" inside of it except a "stalwart boy" (named Miguel) who acts as savior, breaking the box open and setting the people free.

I'd never seen Su Jung happier than on the day she made her box. She'd decided to use papier-mâché, which was wonderfully messy, and Mrs. Duncan gave her a garbage bag to wear over her clothes. Su Jung's box was simple and elegant. She painted it yellow, and in the center of the lid she put a single rose.

When Su Jung and I met for her story conference, we had the classroom to ourselves. (The conferences were taking longer than I'd thought, so Su Jung had volunteered to come back early from lunch.) We sat at the low round table at the back of the room. She told me she was going to call her story "Kindness and Doom."

"Wow. That's a powerful title. What's the plot?"

"There's a king in the Kingdom of Kindness. And he sends a woman to an island to get a box."

"What's in the box?

"He doesn't know what's in it?" she asked.

"What are you asking me for? You're the writer, you decide. Why does he want the box?"

"He just wants what's in it?"

"Why?"

"Because he's curious?"

"No, that's not good enough. If you're king, you're not just going to sit around and say, 'Oh, I wonder what's in a box.'"

"The box is a gold box."

"Ah, well, now that makes more sense. Go on."

"Well, see, when the woman goes, because she's a kind woman, she finds the gold box and brings it to the king and then he sends the man there . . ."

"Where?"

"To the place."

"Why?"

"To see if there's more. To see if he gets the gold, right? So the box knows that."

I was having trouble following her, but she was talking so easily, I didn't want to interrupt.

"When the man opens the box, keeps on smaller boxes inside, and then the last box, he opens it, and then he got a sign that says you got tricked by the cover."

"What do you mean by the cover? The outside of the box? The box looks pretty outside, but inside it's empty?"

"Yeah."

"And then what happens?"

"And then he just goes back and the king thinks that he just kept the gold, so he sends the man to the Kingdom of Doom."

"He banishes him. Do you know the word *banish*? It means to send someone far away as punishment."

"And then he's trying to pay back to the king."

"You mean, get revenge?"

"Yeah."

"Okay, let's stop for a moment. If you were writing a novel, this would be fine, but your plot is too complicated for a short story. Why don't you start your story after the banishment, and just make it a revenge story. So you'd begin with the King of Kindness and the King of Doom. What do you think?"

"Okay."

I said, "Now, tell me about the Kingdom of Doom. *Doom* is a funny-sounding word, isn't it? What does it mean exactly?"

"I think I know what *doom* means, but I can't explain it."

"Same here. Get your dictionary and we'll look it up, okay?"

She fetched the dictionary, found the word, but her eyes stayed glued to the page.

"Su Jung? Are you going to read it to me?"

Silence.

"Oh, no," I groaned melodramatically, trying to make a joke of it. "Please don't do the quiet thing, Su Jung. Not today! I've got too many other kids to work with. Please just read it."

She looked at me with that miserable, trapped expression, wanting to talk but unable.

I tried to bribe her. I reached into my pocket and pulled out some change. "Here: if you read the definition of *doom,* all this money is yours."

Silence.

I said, "All right, then. I can keep quiet, too, you know. So when you're ready, let me know. I'll just sit here and wait." I folded my arms patiently, as if we were in a friendly contest.

Silence.

I tried emotional manipulation, saying, "Would it be easier for you to work with Mrs. Duncan? Because I don't know how to help you. And that makes me very sad. I'm sorry. But this just isn't working."

Silence.

Finally, I tried tough love, hoping to force her to break through her silence. I said, "Okay, we're done. This is a total waste of my time, and it's a total waste of your time. You've got a good beginning and lots of good stuff. Go work on your story by yourself." I waved her away. She picked up her dictionary and returned to her seat, banished. Her back was to me. She made no attempt to write. The air was charged with our unhappiness. I felt weak, childish. Why, with all my love for her, was I unable to help? I went to her desk.

I said, "What's happening here, Su Jung? I'm so confused."

"Me, too."

"So why don't you read it out loud? What's the big deal?"

"I don't know."

"Please read it."

Su Jung picked up the dictionary. "'Doom,'" she read. "'Something that cannot be escaped, especially pain, ruin, or death.'"

"Thank you," I said. "Thank you, thank you, thank you. Okay: pain, ruin, and death. So the King of Doom wants what?"

"Revenge."

"And the King of Kindness wants . . ."

"Kindness."

"How does the King of Doom get revenge?"

"Puts a potion of doom in a bottle and saying it's kindness?"

"Excellent. What color bottle?"

"Blue?"

"Don't be so unsure of yourself. Blue is the perfect color for that bottle."

The rest came easy; we were home free. I helped her shape her plot, and then she wrote three drafts. In the end, she was proud and I was, too. This was her story:

KINDNESS AND DOOM

Once on different continents on Mars there was a Kingdom of Kindness and a Kingdom of Doom. Surrounding the Kingdom of Kindness were statues of cupids and angels. On the other side of the planet, surrounding the Kingdom of Doom, was dark black smoke. King Free ruled the Kingdom of Kindness and King Sheets ruled the Kingdom of Doom. In between them was a deserted island named Parade Island. No one lived on that island. There were only trees and flowers there, and it was so tropical you could hardly stand it.

The King of Doom wanted revenge because a long time ago the King of Kindness had banished him and ever since the King of Doom's heart was full of only pain, ruin, and death. For years and years, King Sheets kept on thinking how he would get even, and finally he came up with an idea. He would have a golden box made and inside it he would put a blue bottle labeled "Kindness." But the bottle would really contain a potion of doom. Then he would bury the box under a tree on Parade Island.

When he had done this, King Sheets sent his prettiest servant to King Free. She was wearing a white gown and fake wings and pretended to be an angel. She said to King Free, "There is a box under the middle tree on Parade Island and inside it is a potion of kindness. Wherever you spread the potion, that thing or place will turn into kindness." King Free said, "Prepare for action!" and the king and all his servants went to the island.

They quickly found the tree, and the king dug the box up. It was so beautiful. It was gold with a flower on the lid. . . . The King of Kindness spread the potion all over the world. But instead of kindness, the world became doom. The sun turned black. . . . King Sheets was happy with laughter. He had tricked King Free!

But King Free was clever and killed a swan, the most beautiful one, and mixed the swan's heart with the leftover potion. He started spreading it, and when the first drop of the new potion touched the ground, the whole world became normal again. . . .

They made a party for the King of Kindness, but before they did, they drowned the King of Doom and his servants and they never saw them again and the King of Kindness (and his servants) lived happily on the deserted island.

A World without Story

It was the last day of school.

Mrs. Duncan had warned me to remember that the children were my students, not my friends, but I hadn't listened. I wanted to be pals with them and now that we were parting for the summer, I was sad. I'd miss hearing about their lives. I'd miss their stories. I'd miss the way they smiled when I walked into the room.

The class had a surprise for me. It was Mrs. Duncan's idea. She'd found a pewter box from Thailand, and in it each kid had placed a tiny envelope. Mrs. Duncan had told them, "Put something in the envelope that doesn't cost any money and has special significance for you and Mr. Swope."

Aaron, Noelia, and Mateo had drawn characters from stories we'd written together. Knowing I was interested in her religion, Rosie gave me a portrait of the Hindu god Ganesh. Miguel included a picture of the Ecuadorian flag with a note from his mom that said, "God bless you!" Su Jung, who'd never let me take her photo, gave me her school picture. And MeiKai wrote this poem:

> *A world without*
> *story is like a*
> *dynamite blowing*
> *the whole world.*
> *No writing, no story.*
> *There is*
> *nothing in this world*
> *without story.*

None of the children were as openly sentimental as I was. They were happy it would be vacation. I went around the room, child to child, to say a personal good-bye—to some, forever. Allegra was moving to Brooklyn. Kemal was moving to Mississippi, where his father would have his first job as a doctor. Ibrahim was returning to Egypt because his parents didn't like to see him becoming so American.

"Hi, MeiKai. I love your poem "A World without Story." Wow. Where'd you get the idea?"

"I just wrote it."

"I'm so impressed. Because there really is no world without story. Story is how we know the world."

"That's why I said that."

"Are you going anywhere this summer?"

"No."

"What will you do all day?"

"Sleep. Be annoyed by my brother."

"Well, you've earned some rest. You worked hard this year. Send me a letter, if you can, would you? I'd love to hear from you."

"Okay, Mr. Swope!"

"Hi, Ashley. Thanks for the Thai coin. That was very thoughtful. It was really fun teaching you this year. I'll always remember your "Mad Gonzulla" story. Are you going anywhere this summer?"

"No."

"Well, read a lot of books, and only write when you really, really feel like it, okay?"

"Okay."

"Promise?"

"Okay."

"But I'd love to get a letter, if you have the time. Have a good summer and please say hi to your parents for me."

Few of them had plans for a family vacation. It dawned on me slowly that most would be spending their summer days inside their apartments, unable to go outside and play. This was upsetting; children should spend their summers barefoot and outside. They should run through meadows, explore woods, splash in streams.

Cesar was one of the lucky ones. He'd be making his first trip to Ecuador.

"That's so exciting, Cesar! Will you be in a city or the country?"

"Like a farm, I think."

"With cows and chickens and stuff?"

"Yeah."

"Will you get to milk a cow?"

"No way!"

"You have to milk a cow if you get the chance!"

"That's gross, Mr. Swope."

"No, it's not. It's natural. Will you send me a postcard?"

"Okay!"

"Promise?"

"Promise."

I didn't know what to say to Fatma. We'd never made a connection, although I'd tried. She only ever spoke to me in grudging monosyllables. Her moods seemed awfully dark; when I passed her desk sometimes I'd get a chill. Mostly, I left her alone, but sometimes I forced myself on her to teach a writing trick I knew she'd appreciate, like how to use parentheses.

I expected more from Fatma because words came to her so easily, but I blamed myself for not inspiring her. I hadn't figured out a way to reach her. She had, though, written one authentic thing that year:

THE OUTSIDE ME

The outside of me is that I'm very shy and I'm very quiet. I don't really get along with people. I don't want to butt into people's business, and if I need information, I don't directly (or automatically) go to a person who has alot of info. about what I want. Someone has to convince me or practically brainwash me to get info. from someone.

THE SECRET ME (INSIDE)

The secret of me is that I am *very* athletic (I play b-ball or baseball every day) and I'm not shy at all. Hard to believe, eh? I am very open-minded and I say whatever comes in my mind. (No wonder I get in trouble lots of times.) My father thinks I am tomboy because of the way I act. (Everyone in school who does not know me thinks I'm a boy.) I can take out weird voices and do things that boys do. (No wonder I don't get along with girls my age so much.)

Because Fatma was terribly asthmatic and physically awkward, I found it hard to believe that she was all that athletic, but for a child, to say a wish aloud is enough to make it true. "You did an excellent job on this assignment," I'd told her at the time, to which she'd sneered, "You *always* say that."

This was true. I was lavish with praise, but I had my reasons. The most helpful comment I'd ever gotten from teachers on my writing was: Great job, Sam! Still, I'd been especially cautious in my marginal comments to Fatma. She seemed so fragile.

In truth, I was a little frightened of her.

Her gift to me had been three words, the same gift I'd given out at Christmas. The words she'd chosen for me were: *aesthetic* (relating to beauty and art); *amative* (full of love); and *epithalamium* (a poem written for a wedding).

I knelt beside her desk. She was reading, hunched over a paperback copy of Louise Fitzhugh's *Harriet the Spy*. Harriet is a character ferocious in her desire to be a writer. As part of her self-imposed training, she spies on family, friends, and neighbors, taking notes (often unkind) on their behavior. Fatma had a lot in common with Harriet. Both were tomboys and good with words. Both were moody, misunderstood, intelligent, and secretive.

"Hi, Fatma. How are you enjoying *Harriet the Spy*?"

She gave a nod but didn't look up.

"Thank you for the three words you gave me. They're all beautiful. I especially like *epithalamium*—it's so much fun to say."

She didn't look up.

"And I'll always remember your outside/inside pieces. You wrote about yourself honestly and well."

She didn't look up.

"It's been a pleasure teaching you."

At last she said something, but with her nose in the book, I couldn't hear what.

"I'm sorry. I didn't hear."

"I hate you."

I think I went unconscious for a second. Gary and Jessica were sitting nearby and I could see their shock that Fatma would speak so disrespect-fully to a teacher. They watched me closely, wondering what I'd do. Somehow I managed to say, "I'm sorry you feel that way, Fatma. I cer-tainly don't hate you. I hope you have a good summer. Good-bye."

I don't remember what I did next. Probably ran for Cesar or MeiKai or Noelia, a child I could count on to show me some love. I knew I shouldn't take Fatma's hateful words personally, but I did. I wanted to be univer-sally adored, a dangerous weakness in a teacher.

Fatma may or may not have had a crush on me, but in my heart I knew she had good reason to despise me: I didn't like her writing. I'd tried to hide the fact, but kids have keener instincts than you sometimes think. Surely she'd picked up on that, the way one always does.

The rest of the day I tried to look happy, but inside, I was devastated. I couldn't unburden myself to Mrs. Duncan until the children had gone— *Good-bye, Gary! Good-bye, Jessica! See you in the fall!*—and when Mrs. Duncan heard what Fatma had said, she was angry. I could see she planned to give Fatma a talking-to but then remembered that Fatma was no longer her student, no longer hers to reprimand. There was nothing to be done. With a rueful smile and a tinge of dread, Mrs. Duncan told me, "They're becoming fourth graders."

The Island Project

❅   ❉   ❀

All about Me

After giving Mrs. Melvern, my students' new teacher, a few weeks to get acquainted with her new class, I made an appointment to meet with her during lunch to discuss how we might work together. Although I wouldn't be teaching the kids on my first day back, I was eager to lay eyes on them. I'd missed them during the summer, and often wondered what they were doing at any given instant. My summer was spent preparing lessons and reading books about teaching. I had lots of plans.

I arrived at school early and waited outside their new classroom, listening to Mrs. Melvern teach. She was reading aloud from Emma Lazarus's famous poem "The New Colossus," written for the Statue of Liberty. She told the class, "When the poem says, 'Send me your huddled masses,' that means, 'Send me all the people you don't want.' That's what it's saying, the poem. Okay? Do you understand what I'm saying?"

Knowing the kids were just inside the door was too much of a temptation. I had to peek. So as not to be seen, I stepped back into the hallway shadows, then leaned my head in bit by bit until a wedge of the room came into view: There they were! There was Nicole! Amarjeet! Rafael! There was Miguel! Noelia! Mateo! There they were! I was shocked to see how changed they were, not just taller but morphed, stretched and pulled like creatures in a fun house mirror, everything out of proportion, noses too big for faces, heads too big for bodies. Some were fatter, some had pimples, some had breasts. Simon had a teenage hairdo, lots of gel. Elena was wearing lipstick. There they were! Then Maya laid her head down on her desk and behind her was Su Jung.

Su Jung!

I'd received a letter from her during the summer telling me she'd cried because she missed me so. By the end of third grade, Su Jung and I had grown quite close, close enough that she confided to me her parents had divorced and that her mother had moved out at Christmastime last year.

So that was it, her mother had left, she had been abandoned. That was why Su Jung was so unhappy all the time.

"I didn't know," I said to her back then. "I'm so sorry. That must be painful for you. Where is your mother now? Korea?"

"Yes."

"Do you ever hear from her?"

"No."

"She never calls? She never writes?"

Su Jung looked anxious, but said nothing.

Neither of us spoke, but I thought I should say something, so I fell back on a speech I'd heard in various movies, and said, "Su Jung, I want you to listen to me. Because what I am about to say is the most important thing I'm ever going to tell you. Are you listening? It isn't your fault your mother left. Do you understand me? It isn't your fault! There must have been something wrong with her. No mother in her right mind would leave a wonderful daughter like you. And you *are* wonderful, Su Jung. Do you believe that? Because it's true."

She looked at me silently, her face inscrutable.

"Then I'll say it again and again and again until you do believe it: Su Jung is wonderful, Su Jung is wonderful, Su Jung is wonderful, Su Jung is wonderful . . ."

That coaxed a smile from her. She said, "My grandmother said my mother's going to go to hell."

Months had passed since that conversation. Su Jung was a fourth grader now. I leaned in from the corridor to study her face. Did she look happy? I didn't think so, but maybe she was only bored.

Mrs. Melvern was saying, "Just because an immigrant comes here doesn't mean they get to stay automatically. We can send them back if they don't have the right papers. Suppose they have an illness and we didn't have the medicine? There could be an epidemic and everyone will die!"

Cesar's hand went up. So did Najiyah's. I was curious to hear what they had to say; all these kids had immigration stories. Why didn't Mrs. Melvern stop talking and call on them? Then someone else's hand went up, but I couldn't see who it belonged to. When I leaned in closer for a better view, Jessica spotted me and cried out, "Mr. Swope!"

I jumped from sight, but it was too late. The class was out of control.

"It's Mr. Swope!"

"Where?"

"He was just there, in the hall!"

"Mr. Swope!"

Mrs. Melvern stuck her head out the door. She was pretty, and young enough to be Mrs. Duncan's daughter. I smiled sheepishly and apologized for the disruption. "Don't worry about it," she said. "Come on in. They've been so excited you were coming."

I entered the room, the kids burst into cheers, and then I did a little dance to show them I was happy, too. "Hi, guys!" I said. "I missed you so much! How were your summers?"

Hands waved like flags in a parade.

"Mr. Swope!"

"Mr. Swope!"

"Mr. Swope!"

"Whoa, whoa, whoa! Not all at once!"

Some had gone away, to Boston, Niagara Falls, Philadelphia, Long Island. Both Nicole and Cesar had been to Ecuador. Most of them hadn't gone anywhere, though, and it broke my heart when Miguel described with great excitement his only outing of the summer, a day trip with his church to a state park.

It was time for the children to go to lunch. Mrs. Melvern asked me to wait while she took the class to the cafeteria. The kids filed past me out the door and I felt like a general inspecting his troops. Some of them were new, replacing kids who'd moved away. "See you soon, guys," I told them all. "Sharpen those pencils! We've got a lot of work to do this year!" As Su Jung walked by, she slipped a folded-up sheet of paper into my hand.

Once they were gone, I perched on a desk, startled to find it taller than the third-grade desks had been. The chairs were bigger, too. I unfolded Su Jung's piece of paper. It was a story, dedicated to me.

POOR CINDERLOCKS

One day there was a girl named Cinderlocks, and she lived with her old father. There was a farmer who owned the whole town. One day the father went up the hill to the farmer who had run out of hay for his cows . . . and said, "My daughter can turn leaves to hay." . . . The farmer said, "Bring her at once!" and so he did.

When Cinderlocks reached the farmer's barn, the farmer said, "I'll give you only one chance to turn the leaves into hay. It better be by sunrise. If you don't, I'll kill you." And he locked Cinderlocks up. Cinderlocks started to cry. Soon it was sunrise, and poor Cinderlocks died.

Several times the year before, Su Jung and I had tried to collaborate on a retelling of Rumpelstiltskin, but we'd never finished because she'd always ended up unable to talk. That she'd written this retelling by herself was progress, I supposed, but what a depressing story: poor Cinderlocks, indeed. And poor Su Jung: if a child cannot imagine happy endings, can she have one?

I sighed, put her story in my knapsack, and had a look around. I don't like empty classrooms. They make me sad—too many echoes, too many ghosts of childhoods gone. Unlike Mrs. Duncan's room, which was sunny and overlooked the playground and its trees, Mrs. Melvern's looked out on an interior courtyard and had no view of anything. It wasn't as cheerfully decorated as Mrs. Duncan's had been, either, or as organized.

I noticed pages of student writing thumbtacked to the board. They were essays the kids had written on the first day of school, and each was titled "All about Me." Few mentioned anything intimately personal, although I was pleased to see that Su Jung was strong enough to write that her parents were divorced. For the most part, their essays stated random facts about their lives—their age, their birthday, a scattershot list of favorite things. Noelia's was typical:

My name is Noelia. My hobbies are rock collecting, reading, and drawing. My favorite sports are football and baseball. But my most favorite sport is volleyball. I like hamburgers, chicken, and French fries. My favorite school subject is social studies. This past summer I went to Orlando. I saw Mickey Mouse, Snow White, and Belle. I also went to Universal Studios. The End

Although these "All about Me" essays weren't all about *me*, I searched for evidence of my effect on the kids and was disappointed to find writing mentioned only twice. Even at that, MeiKai merely mentioned it in passing. Just one kid expressed the kind of passion I wanted all of them to have:

The thing I am obsessed with the most is writing. I love writing. Writing is part of my life. So when I grow up I'll be a gynecologist and a part-time writer. My favorite genre in writing is horror. My birthday is on April 2. I like to read horror, mystery, and realistic fiction. My favorite authors are Judy Blume, Beverly Cleary, Roald Dahl, Christopher Pike, Nicholas Pine, Louise Fitzhugh, Norton Juster, and E. L. Konigsburg. My favorite book of all times is *Harriet the Spy*!

That was written by Fatma.

Mr. Swope Redefined

"I'm not the sort of teacher who plans in advance," Mrs. Melvern told me over lunch. "Because what's the point? You're never going to be able to do what you planned, anyway."

Mrs. Melvern's parents had emigrated from Germany, but she'd been born in Queens and had gone to parochial schools. She hadn't been teaching long, and didn't seem to like it much. This class, she said, drove her up the wall. She complained that they caught on to things too fast, got their lessons done so quickly she couldn't keep up. She complained that their faces never lit up with "Ah, I got it!" She also freely admitted that a lot of the kids, including Miguel, Okan, Najiyah, Rafael, and Noelia, got under her skin, rubbed her the wrong way; she just didn't like them. To make matters worse, Mrs. Melvern was pregnant with her first child, and that, naturally, would be her priority for the year. As a result, the kids weren't challenged, discipline suffered, and half the class stopped doing homework.

This was heartbreaking. My only comfort was the thought that all of us have had bad teachers in our lives, and all teachers have bad years. Nevertheless, I didn't like being in Mrs. Melvern's classroom. I hated its chaotic atmosphere, didn't like the way she encouraged the kids to tattle on one another, and was depressed to see the children spend so much time not learning.

Moreover, my own teaching suffered. I hadn't realized how much Mrs. Duncan had made me look good. When I presented a new project to the class, she was always there, gently making sure all the kids understood what was going on. I was like a kid who thinks he's riding a bike brilliantly, unaware that his parent is holding him up, and once Mrs. Duncan's guiding hand was gone, I crashed. My lessons were all over the place; I'd have to learn how to teach on my own.

Much of the fall was spent in chaos, confusion, and frustration. In desperation, I asked the principal if I could use the book storage room for an office. After she said yes, I was no longer a constant presence in my students' classroom. I still worked with the whole class for several periods a week, but the rest of the time I met with kids in small groups and individually.

The book storage room wasn't big, but once I'd reorganized it there was space for two tables and eight chairs. It had a window, but that was mostly obscured by stacks of dusty, beat-up boxes filled with old books. The kids thought my office looked like an attic in a haunted house, so I shouldn't have been surprised when, during a group conference close to Halloween, Gary asked to see my teeth.

"What?"

"Can I see your teeth?"

"Why?"

"No reason," he said, exchanging conspiratorial glances with the others.

I played along and bared my teeth, at which the three of them gasped, then giggled.

"What's so funny?"

Maya said, "Someone in the class noticed you have pointy side teeth."

That was true; my incisors are pretty pointy.

"And this person also noticed how your office is always dark."

"And your point is?"

They only giggled, wouldn't talk.

"What?" I said. "What?"

Rosie blurted out, "Fatma says you're a vampire! Is that true?"

"Yes," I said. "Any other questions?"

They squealed with delight and raced in mock terror from my office.

Poetry 101

I sometimes had the children memorize poems, and now I wish I'd done more of that. Nothing gets the beauty of a language into your bloodstream more than verses learned by heart. I selected poems that were strong on meter and rhyme, which children love and make a poem easier to memorize. It was fun selecting particular poems for particular kids: Poe's "El Dorado" for Aaron; Durston's "The Wolf" for Miguel; Frost's "Stopping by Woods on a Snowy Evening" for MeiKai; Hoffmann's "Story of Little Suck-a-Thumb" for Cesar; Yeats's "The Lake Isle of Innisfree" for Su Jung; Lear's "The Owl and the Pussy-Cat" for Noelia; Hughes's "Dream Variations" for Rosie.

Writing poetry was something I would do with the entire class, saving prose for smaller groups. In a single period, I could give an assignment and the class would write at least one poem, often more. They were poems only in the loosest sense, the freest sort of verse, mostly unstructured and unrhymed. Unlike fiction, these poems gave the kids a way to express a complete thought quickly, and because they didn't have to worry about grammar and punctuation, their minds were free to play with language and images in ways they never did in prose.

For my first poetry lesson, I wrote METAPHOR on the board.

"Anyone know what this word means?" I asked.

No hands. That wasn't a surprise. But even if they didn't know the name for it, I knew they understood the concept. Everyone does. Metaphors are everywhere.

"Let me give you an example," I said. "When I say, 'Wow, Nicole, your story blew me away,'" does that mean this?" I mimed being blown backward by a strong wind, my arms flailing until I slammed against the blackboard, where I crumpled to the floor and played dead. I opened my eyes and looked up at Nicole, a tiny, quiet child with large, timid eyes. "Is that what 'being blown away' means, Nicole?" Her face registered panic, so I stood up, dusted off my trousers, and called on someone else. "Is that what it means, Su Jung?"

No answer.

"Oh, come on, Su Jung. You know this."

No answer.

"Rosie?"

"It means you liked it."

"'Liked' it?" I said. "Being 'blown away' means I only 'liked' it?"

"Okay, loved it."

"Yes, loved it, adored it, was transported, the way a strong wind transports the body. You see? That's what metaphor does, it makes a point by showing what two completely different things have in common. Let me give you another example: Mr. Swope is a big fat pig." A few kids giggled, mostly Noelia and the boys. I could always count on them for a cheap laugh. "Does that mean I'm a real pig? Nicole?"

She understood the game now. "Noooo," she said, her voice barely above a whisper.

"That's right. But what does it mean I am?"

"Greeeeeeeedy."

"Right! So 'Mr. Swope is a pig' is a metaphor that compares the eating habits of a pig with the eating habits of Mr. Swope. Got it?"

Were they with me? Did they understand?

"Let's brainstorm some metaphors of our own. Think of something that in some way reminds you of yourself. It could be anything—a piece of chewing gum enjoyed for a while and then abandoned under a desk, a mitten that thought it was forgotten but then winter came around again, an eraser that is overworked. Any ideas?"

MeiKai said, "I'm like a sticker."

"How?"

"'Cause I like them!"

"You're not supposed to pick something you like. You're supposed to pick something that's somehow like *you*. Any other ideas?"

Miguel said, "I'm a bolt of lightning."

"Why?"

"Because I don't let nothing stop me."

"Good! Any others?"

Maya said, "I'm like a book with lots of stories in it."

Jorge said, "I'm like a TV 'cause sometimes I'm the Comedy Channel. Sometimes I'm the Sports Channel, the Learning Channel . . ."

"Now you're catching on," I said. "Okay, let's give it a try. Write a sentence or two saying what you are and why you're like it. If you get inspired to write more than one metaphor, go for it."

While the kids were writing, I walked around the room. Not all of them had fully grasped the lesson, but Su Jung had. And when the class was finished writing, I wrote her metaphor on the board: "I'm a puzzle because I don't say much and I'm hard to figure out."

I said, "Now I'll show how to turn a sentence into a poem by breaking it up into poetic lines. Using Su Jung's words in the exact same order, make three different poems from her sentence. One poem should have three lines, another four, and another five."

The results were all over the place, but this was the version I told the kids I thought worked best:

> I'm a puzzle
> because I don't say much
> and I'm hard to figure out.

Then I asked the class to turn their own sentences into poems. Here's what Noelia came up with on her first go-round:

> I'm
> a pogo
> stick.
> Very energetic.
> Jumping up and
> down.
> People are
> always looking
> at me, trying
> to
> calm
> me down.
> But I'll always be energetic
> and active.

Understanding line breaks wouldn't come quickly, and I often intervened, acting as editor, making suggestions they were free to accept or reject. But what impressed me about the exercise was how many found a metaphor that caught something essential about themselves:

> I'm a chalkboard.
> Oh, I'm scratched by chalk and just . . .
> just used, controlled, never appreciated.
> Words and some other drawings are written on me.
> Sometimes even the wrong things are written on me.
> And when they wash me,
> I have little joy
> except that I'm going to be written on
> all over again.
>
> MATTHEW

> I am not one, but many
> tales in a book,
> with something to tell always.
> When you open me up,
> you keep on reading,
> because I never stop telling tales.
> I may look thin,
> but I am a book filled with stories
> for all eternity.
> I can do anything in my stories,
> and I mean anything!
> No one can stop me.
>
> MAYA

> I am a shoe!
> Stomp, stomp, stomp
> "Ow!" I say. "That
> hurts!"
> Every day
> me and my sister
> step in puddles,
> mud and lots of
> other disgusting

stuff.
Then my owner puts me
on a shelf.
When we're
rotten we get
thrown away.

NAJIYAH

If I'm a broken branch
on the ground,
I get walked on.
People tease me by callng me skinny
and saying I'm too long.
But one thing is my friend the tree.
It keeps me up so nobody can bother me.
And the leaves keep me warm.

NAZUK

I'm a big red 75.
I'm also a math score
ready to be seen
and get yelled at.
But I don't care
because I feel good
being a big red 75
on a math
test.

MEIKAI

And then there was Jessica's:

I'm a desk
as neat as
can be

"But, Jessica, you aren't neat," I said. "Just look at your desk! It's a disaster. The point is to pick something that expresses the way you really are, not how you'd like to be."

Jessica lived in a sunny, plant-filled apartment on an upper floor of a dreary, soulless brick building with her parents and two siblings. Her family was enviably close. A middle child, Jessica said she adored her older brother, who greeted her after school each day with a kiss, and that the whole family ate dinner together every night "like the Italians do."

Jessica's father was short, slight, and full of life. He wore an earring and had an impish smile. Although he'd been to college in Ecuador, where he'd studied engineering and languages, he now worked (when there was work) as a carpenter and house painter. He didn't complain. "No matter what job you do," he told me, "I don't care if you shine shoes—do it with all your heart!" He'd come to America looking for opportunity, he said, then smiled ruefully. "I had an idea of New York City from pictures. That it was a nice place, clean, no homeless, no poverty, a perfect place."

It took him twelve years to get his green card. "All those years I had no rights," he told me. "I didn't know English. I didn't know the law. I was afraid of everything. It's hard to be poor in the United States. In Ecuador, you can be poor with dignity." Ecuador was also safer than New York, he said, and the communities there were more tightly knit, the schools better. "At eleven, I was reading El Cid, Dostoevsky, *Hamlet*. Here? No."

"Why didn't you go back?"

"I came here, got stuck. I don't know why I didn't go back. I always ask myself that."

Jessica's mother had grown up in a large, well-to-do family in Guayaquil. She'd met her future husband while on a vacation in New York; they fell in love, got married, and started a family. When I asked her if she missed Ecuador, where most of her family still lived, her eyes filled with tears.

Jessica's stories often involved a character who looked for happiness in another world and failed to find it. In one, "The Magic Mirror," the protagonist enters the world inside her bedroom mirror, which is deceptively appealing: "My room in the mirror world was neat and clean, not messy like my room on the other side. My books were good as new, my bed was neatly made, and my radio got excellent reception!" In another, titled "The Wishing Tree," the protagonist leaves his farm to make his fortune in the city. In the process, he loses his soul but eventually is saved by the love of a good woman and returns to the farm, where he finds true happiness.

Jessica was a Baha'i. This young religion, founded in nineteenth-century Persia, today has five million adherents worldwide. The Baha'i faith is Utopian and progressive, emphasizing good citizenship, tolerance, sexual equality, the elimination of extreme wealth and poverty, and education for all. For the Baha'i, all gods are one, and humanity is but a single race—a fact that, once understood by the peoples of the world, will lead to the creation of a peaceful, global society.

"What else could you use as a metaphor for yourself besides a desk?" I asked Jessica.

"A flower?"

"How are you like a flower?"

"'Cause I'm blooming, growing."

"Be careful with the hearts and flowers stuff. You know how I hate it when you get sappy. Think of something else."

"Like what?"

"You're a smart girl. Look around the room. You'll come up with something."

And within moments, she did:

> *I am a pencil*
> *ready to write*
> *my life*

The Animal in Miguel

The cafeteria was a dreadful place in the basement. Hundreds of kids at a time ate there, kids who'd spent all morning having to be quiet and sit still. Because of the room's low ceilings and hard surfaces, the sound bounced all over the place, creating a din, a roar so deafening you had to scream to be heard. It was a madhouse, the Hades of the school, a place where the Furies all ran wild.

A day or so before Thanksgiving, I arrived at their classroom after lunch to find Mrs. Melvern berating Miguel in the hallway. "I want you to hear this, Mr. Swope," she said, and told me Miguel had been acting like some kind of animal in the cafeteria, crawling on the lunch table, lifting his shirt, and exposing his stomach to the girls.

Humiliated, Miguel began to cry, his shoulders jerking up and down as he said it wasn't his fault, the girls were picking on him, Mateo had taken his stuff. . . . All the while Mrs. Melvern looked at me, her eyes saying, "Can you believe this garbage?"

"You might as well stop crying," she told Miguel. "Because tears don't work with me. I won't feel sorry for you." But Miguel couldn't stop, so Mrs. Melvern said, "I have had it with you," and sailed into the classroom, leaving him with me.

I puffed up my cheeks and let the air out slowly. I said, "What are we going to do with you, Miguel?"

He looked at me and snorted back his tears.

"Get your writing folder," I said. "Let's go to my office."

Once downstairs, Miguel sat opposite me, hands folded on his lap, shoulders slumped.

"What's going on, Miguel?"

He looked down.

"How's your asthma?"

"Better."

"How are things at home?"

"So-so."

"Why so-so?"

"I don't know. 'Cause, like, there's, like, in the bank we need to add money but we have to pay for the bill more than six thousand dollars, and my father can't get a job. But the thing he's very good at and that he could get a lot of money is a mechanic, but now the doctor, they told him that he's allergic to dust, and he can't work in that. So my father has been only working now in painting, but they don't give him enough money. And so I gave them my allowance. I have twenty-seven dollars, so I gave them all of it and I just kept two dollars."

"Oh, Miguel," I said, my heart melting. "That was awfully nice of you."

He said his parents had had a big fight. "My dad said that my mom doesn't help him and that's not true but he just got mad and he just left."

I told him it's hard for kids when their parents aren't getting along. I said marriage is difficult, that parents sometimes fight. He nodded, showing that he understood, but understanding didn't make it easier for him to bear. I told him I was worried about him, and when I said that kids had told me he could sometimes be a bully, he opened his mouth to defend himself, but I locked my eyes onto his and raised my eyebrows, silencing him.

"I'm just saying that's what other people say about you, Miguel. I don't know what the truth is. But you should think about this, okay? You probably frightened the girls at lunch. You don't want to end up a bully, do you?"

He shook his head.

"All right, then," I said, and let it go at that. Because I didn't know what else to do for him, I asked if he wanted to collaborate on a story.

He nodded, and I got out my pen and some paper.

"Who's the main character going to be?"

"A girl."

"What's her name?"

"Her name is Tasia. She lives by herself."

"Why?"

As always, he plunged right in, no notion where he was headed.

"She lives by herself 'cause she's an orphan."

"What happened to her parents?"

"Her parents were having a fight 'cause the woman had a job and the man always took the money to buy cigarettes and alcohol. And then 'cause all the complaints she made, he like beats her up, like gets her black and blue, and is kicking her. And then the man like picks her up and then like throws her and then she's, like, dead. And then he takes her money, and he goes to a store, and he's drunk, and people kill him."

This was a troubling opening. How much did it say about Miguel's home life? I was under the impression that his father didn't smoke or drink, and although Miguel's mom had said they used to fight, I'd believed her when she'd told me that her troubled marriage had been saved since they'd found God.

What's the best way for a teacher to handle the graphic violence of a child's imagination? You can outlaw it, make a rule that says no fighting in a story, and every now and then I'd do that. But I also sometimes let imagination take its course, hoping that would help a kid get it out of his system. With Miguel I often tried to take a middle road, but at any given moment there was no way of knowing if I'd made the right choice.

I asked Miguel, "Where is Tasia when her parents die?"

"She's at school."

"And when she comes home she finds out that—"

"That nobody's there."

"And that her parents are dead."

"Yes."

"So, what does she do?"

"She has to find a place to live. So she found a little stable where there were horses, and she took some straw and made a pillow, and she went asleep."

Miguel's stories always had animals. Sometimes they were horses, but mostly they were predators. When I asked him why, he said, "I put wild animals in my stories because that's what I'm going to be in the future, a tamer of wild animals." Miguel's interest in animals was intense. He avidly watched animal documentaries and read nonfiction books about them. Yet he'd had little direct experience with animals, having never had a pet or been to the zoo, and the wildlife in his neighborhood offered little more than pigeons, sparrows, starlings, rats, and the occasional feral cat. Once, though, he told me he'd been playing in front of his building and had caught a cockroach, which he put in a little jar he'd found on the sidewalk. When he brought his new pet home, his mother got upset, partly because she didn't want a cockroach in her apartment, and partly because the jar was a discarded cocaine vial.

It took almost an hour to finish our collaboration. As usual, Miguel's mind wandered all over the place, and wrestling his imaginings into a narrative took all my concentration. When we finished, I asked him to write the story up for homework. He winced at the prospect, and I backed off immediately. He was right, the story was much too ambitious. He'd never get it all down. "But you have to write something for me, Miguel. You haven't done a single second draft this year."

I looked through his writing folder. It was depressingly skimpy, but I found a first draft of a story I'd liked and had already edited. It was called "Marzolo the Red Fox." Marzolo is a boy who eats contaminated meat, which causes him to turn into a fox by night. This pleases Marzolo, who sneaks into the nighttime world alone, having adventures and returning to his bed before dawn. When his father also eats contaminated meat, the two go out together, having fun. I'd found the ending sweet and hoped it said something good about Miguel and his dad.

"What about this Marzolo story?" I said. "I liked this one. And it's not too long."

"Yeah, I like that one, too!" He said he'd do his second draft over the Thanksgiving vacation.

"Promise?"

"Promise."

"Shake," I said.

He gave me his hand, but the moment we touched I withdrew mine and made a face. "Ech," I said, shaking my hand as if it had something gross on it. "Your hand feels like a dead fish. A handshake should be firm, Miguel. You should look me in the eye. Try again."

His grip was a bit firmer this time, and he looked me in the eye.

"That's better," I said. "Now, go back to class and ask Amarjeet to come down, okay?"

"She's in India."

"What?!" This was a shock. Amarjeet had been in class just yesterday, and had never said a thing!

Miguel said, "It was a surprise to Mrs. Melvern, too."

"Did she go for a visit or forever? Is she coming back?"

Miguel shrugged.

"All right, then. Send down Rafael, Aaron, and Jorge." This group was working on comic strips.

"Can I stay and make comic strips, Mr. Swope?" Miguel asked. "'Cause that's what I want to be when I grow up."

"Not today. Do a good job on your story and we'll talk."

His face fell, but he managed a smile, said, "Thanks, Mr. Swope," and left.

✠   ✠   ✠

Surprise!

At the end of the fall term, I was in the classroom and about to give a lesson when I noticed something odd. A length of string had been tied to the window lock, then snaked out the open window, its other end below and out of sight.

"What's this all about?" I asked the class.

They shook their heads.

I gave the string a tug and could tell something was on its other end. "What the heck?" I said. I pulled the string in hand over hand, and before long hauled in a manila envelope. On the outside was written: *For Mr. Swope's students.*

"What do you think it could be?" I asked.

"Open it! Open it!" they cried.

"Okay," I said. Inside was a stack of papers. I examined them, my face momentarily puzzled, but then I looked up at the kids in surprise. "Well, what do you know!" I said. "It's a test!"

It took a second for the class to put two and two together and realize they'd been tricked.

"Aw, mannnnnnnnn!" they said.

WRITING ASSESSMENT

You are walking with your parent down a busy street. Slowly, your parent begins to change shape. You watch in amazement and alarm. Describe this moment, tell what your parent changes into, and then tell what happens next.

You are to write a three paragraph story with a beginning, middle, and end.

Each paragraph must be at least six sentences long. Pay attention to periods and commas and paragraphing. Be specific, give lots of details, and be surprising.

You have fifty minutes. Remember: have fun.

For this assessment, I'd come up with a prompt that wasn't open-ended, that handed the kids a plot so they could relax a bit and concentrate on showing off their writing skills. Certainly the word "assessment" added some stress to the exercise, but judging from their stories, which were lighthearted and funny, the kids enjoyed themselves. Most featured mothers who got turned into aliens or monsters, but several kids came up with something more interesting—Su Jung turned her father into the planet Pluto, Aliza's mom became a leaf, and Nicole transformed her mother into "a notebook with bunny ears." All the stories ended happily, with the parents restored to their proper selves, and all were clearly told except for the ones written by Simon and Gary.

I never would have given them a test if it hadn't been for Mrs. Duncan. At the end of third grade, she'd wanted to see what they'd do when faced with a formal writing assessment in which the stakes were higher. I was reluctant. I told her I hated tests and that I wanted the students to have a positive experience with writing. But Mrs. Duncan insisted, and because I would have lain down in front of a truck for her, I agreed. Based on the excellent results of that assessment, I'd decided to give this one in fourth grade, as well.

What did these assessments demonstrate? In terms of original narrative, not much—they were all variations on the plot I'd given. What did impress me, though, was how much better the students' grammar was in the assessment than in a first draft written for me. Given that pressure, they called on all the skills they'd learned. Moreover, the experience didn't seem to give them the sort of psychic scars I'd feared.

So in a sense, the surprise was on me, because I'd never thought I'd ever say something good about a test.

The Queen Mother of the West

Several weeks after the Christmas break, I walked from the subway up the hill toward school. It was a gray and dreary winter morning. Lights were on in the classrooms, making the windows warm and bright, but I wouldn't be attending school that day. MeiKai, the happy Chinese girl, and her teenage brother, Alan, were waiting for me in the playground, sitting on the jungle gym. They'd be playing hooky, too, along with lots of other students in the school. Today was Chinese New Year, and MeiKai's mom had invited me to her home for the festivities.

As we walked the several blocks to their apartment, the children told me they'd stayed up late the night before and opened their windows to allow the old year to leave, then made noise to frighten away the New Year's dragon so it wouldn't come to eat them.

"That must have been fun," I said. "This is the year of the ox, right?"

They thought so.

"What's the significance of that?"

They didn't know.

"What's going to happen today?" I asked. "How do you celebrate Chinese New Years?"

"Sit around," said Alan. "Eat."

"And get money!" said MeiKai.

Alan laughed. "Yeah: money!"

Indeed, money is a major part of the holiday. Kids get cash sealed in small red envelopes, red for good fortune.

The Li home sat at the end of a mixed-use street that fed into the commercial boulevard beneath the elevated subway. When the train roared by, the sidewalk trembled. Their apartment was the ground floor of what was once a tiny two-story house. Mrs. Li greeted me at the door with many bows. She was happy to see me; her smile covered half her face. (Her husband was at work—Chinese New Year is a big day for Chinese restaurants, so none of the cooks got the day off.)

The front door of MeiKai's apartment opened into a small kitchen, which housed a large sewing machine on which Mrs. Li did piecework for a clothing manufacturer. There were three other rooms, all of them immaculate, and all of them small. The bedroom was closely packed with single beds for the grown-ups, a bunk bed for the kids, and a small desk for Alan's computer. Their living room had two cheap sofas facing each other and was so narrow it reminded me of a subway car. The only decoration was a fish tank that sat atop a crude, homemade table built of two-by-fours. It held several fish, including a pugnacious black one named Mike Tyson.

Mrs. Li was eager to show me the fourth room, which she'd only recently turned into a shrine to Xiwangmu, the Queen Mother of the West, the foremost female immortal in the Taoist pantheon. In the center of the room, atop a table draped in red cloth, sat a statue of Xiwangmu. Her expression was remote, peaceful, Buddha-like, and she wore an elaborately embroidered gown and a fantastic headdress festooned with pompoms. MeiKai told me, "Very expensive!"

I was full of questions, but Mrs. Li and I didn't share a language, so MeiKai, with a child's grasp of Chinese and English, had to interpret, and what she said often confused me.

Upon being introduced to the Queen Mother of the West, I asked MeiKai, "Am I supposed to say something to the goddess? What do I do?"

MeiKai conferred with her mother, then told me, "Tell her your name and address."

"What do you mean, my address?"

"You know: street, city, zip code blah blah blah."

"Really? Why does she want to know that?"

"So she know where you from!"

"Okay," I answered, and turned toward the statue. "Happy New Year, Queen Mother of the West," I said, and I gave my name and mailing address. Then I bowed, Chinese style, because it seemed the thing to do.

Mrs. Li smiled approvingly and handed me three incense sticks to light. After that was done, she decided more were needed. In all, I lit nine sticks and placed them in a semicircle around the Queen Mother of the West.

"Where did the Queen Mother of the West come from originally?" I asked MeiKai's mother, who answered through MeiKai.

"It's, like, back before there were humans? When the cosmos was just gas? The Queen Mother of the West was just a tiny bit of light. Then the light landed on top of the mountain and turned into the Queen Mother of the West."

Within the past few months, Mrs. Li had decided to become what MeiKai called a "priest" in order to help people. It involved a great deal of studying. MeiKai said her mother's education included much study of Lao-tzu's *Tao Te Ching*, the Tao bible, and also intensive calligraphy practice, the art of which takes years to master. As MeiKai told it, Mrs. Li's education was directed by the Queen Mother of the West, who would appear to MeiKai's mother in dreams.

MeiKai's mother asked if I wanted the Queen Mother of the West to tell me about my past lives.

"Yes," I said. "That would be very interesting. Thank you."

MeiKai and I sat in the living room so Mrs. Li could be alone with the goddess, but I watched out of the corner of my eye as she knelt before the statue and prayed intensely. Her eyes were closed tight and her lips moved quickly, her voice a murmur. From time to time she'd go silent and tilt her head slightly, as if listening, then she'd speak again, as if asking a question.

"Is your mother talking with the goddess now?" I asked MeiKai.

"I think so, yeah!" said MeiKai.

"But how?"

"I'm not sure how to say," MeiKai said. "I think it's, like, called third eye?"

While MeiKai's mother was occupied, I gave the kids their New Year presents. Alan got a crisp new bill I'd put in a red envelope the local Citibank had had on hand for the holiday. But I hadn't wanted to give MeiKai money; that wouldn't have felt right. Instead, I gave her an anthology of poetry. When she unwrapped it, she gasped and hugged it to her chest like a treasured teddy bear. MeiKai liked to read, as did a number of kids in the class. Because their parents couldn't afford books (or didn't know what books to buy), I don't know what these kids would have done without their local library. I hadn't appreciated how vital a public library is to our immigrant population, or to our culture. Though terribly underfunded, that small Queens library was always packed with adults and children speaking any one of dozens of languages and looking for help. For my students, it was a lifeline to their adopted country's literary heritage, giving them access to the great children's books, books they wouldn't have read otherwise, books that are now part of who they are.

Eventually, Mrs. Li emerged from the shrine, looking exhausted. It hadn't gone too well, I guess. She said the Queen Mother of the West was very busy that day and had only had time to tell her that in my most recent past life I'd worked in a fabric factory, and in my first past life, I was a guard to a god.

"What sort of god?" I asked MeiKai.

MeiKai said, "I don't really know how to say in English."

"To say *it* in English."

"Enh?"

"You can't say: to say *in* English. You have to say: to say *it* in English."

"Say *it* in English!" said MeiKai, smiling, thinking her job as translator was done.

I said, "MeiKai, don't get lazy on me. Even if you aren't sure how to say it in English, you have to *try*."

"Enh?"

"Find other words to say the thing you don't know how to say. Talk around it."

"Hmmmmm," she said, thinking hard. "Something like a god responsible for things happen on earth?"

"What sort of things?"

"Anything!"

"What, a God of Earthly Matters? Something like that?"

"Yeah!" she said, pleased to have a word for it. "God of Earthly Matters! That's it!"

I was dubious. "You don't even know what 'earthly matters' means, do you?"

"Not really," she said with a happy shrug.

Legend has it that the Queen Mother of the West tends the peach trees that bear fruit once each three thousand years and confer immortality on anyone who eats them. Another myth involves the Emperor Mu, who explored the regions beyond his realm. In the far-off, rugged Kunlun Mountains, he came upon Xiwangmu's garden paradise. The goddess entertained the emperor so pleasantly that he promised to return, but events intervened, and he died without seeing her again.

This melancholy story must have resonated with Mrs. Li, who had also traveled far and longed to see her home again. Born in mainland China, Mrs. Li was just a few weeks old when her family had to flee their village at a moment's notice to escape Mao's approaching army. In a scene of panic, they boarded a boat for Taiwan. Because the boat was dangerously crowded, an uncle wanted to throw the infant Mrs. Li overboard, but then a soldier intervened, sacrificing his place, and MeiKai's mother's life was saved.

The family settled in Taiwan and was very poor. At a certain point Mrs. Li's father fell seriously ill, and she went to a local temple to the Queen Mother of the West and prayed for him, promising to worship the goddess if her father recovered, which he did. Eventually, MeiKai's mother married, and when she and her husband got seriously in debt, the only way to pay off their creditors was to come to America, where MeiKai was born (her real Chinese name means "star born in a foreign land").

To celebrate the New Year, the Lis were having an open house, and Mrs. Li had prepared a traditional feast. There were lots of dishes, all of them vegetarian, as well as platters heaped with oranges, candy, and dried sweet fruit. The party went on all day, and guests came and went. It was an interesting assortment of people, well-to-do and poor, and some of MeiKai's classmates stopped by, too. Because Koreans (as well as Vietnamese) also celebrate the lunar New Year, Su Jung made an appearance. So did Ashley, whose mother was Chinese and whose father was Thai. And when Ella, who was born in Hong Kong, arrived, she and MeiKai huddled in a corner, comparing their take for the day. From what I could see, they'd cleaned up, getting at least a couple hundred bucks each.

Everyone was happy. In fact, being happy on New Year's is practically obligatory because your mood that day is said to set the tone for the rest of the year. This wasn't a problem for MeiKai, though. Chinese New Year was the perfect holiday for a child so infectiously happy.

Eventually, the apartment was so thick with incense smoke my eyes were burning, so I said good-bye, and Mrs. Li sent me off with an English translation of her bible, the *Tao Te Ching*; a calligraphy brush; and a bag of oranges. The *Tao Te Ching* was short enough to finish on the subway ride home, but I was hard put to see how it related to the Queen Mother of the West. Nowhere in the book is there any mention made of gods, nor are there any stories or parables. Much of the *Tao Te Ching* is poetic and bafflingly mystical:

> The Tao is abstract,
> and therefore has no form,
> it is neither bright in rising,
> nor dark in sinking,
> cannot be grasped, and makes no sound.

The book is also sprinkled with aphorisms that express an appealing philosophy urging one to lead a simple life, be in harmony with nature, and struggle against pride, cunning, and profit. It says:

> Retain the mind like that of a child,
> which flows like running water.

The Fantastic Binomial

On Valentine's Day, Cesar gave Mrs. Melvern and each girl in the class a rose. Cesar had a heart as big as his tummy, which was pretty large.

"I need some nouns," I told the class. "Cesar, give me a noun."

"Um, let me see," said Cesar, his face confused. "Noun, noun, noun . . . I know I know that. Run?"

Gosh, I thought I'd tossed him a slow ball.

"That's a verb," I said. "I need a noun."

"Green?"

"No, that's an adjective. Can anyone give me a noun?"

No hands went up.

"Oh, come on, guys. Someone must know what a noun is . . ."

I shouldn't have been surprised. We'd gone over basic grammar the year before, but not often. I couldn't see the point. The kids were writing well enough without being able to identify the parts of speech, the same way they were able to sing without knowing music theory. Of course they made lots of mistakes, but it was easier to teach them copyediting symbols so they'd understand my corrections, then have them rewrite the piece correctly. This was tedious rote work for them, but I was heartless. Sometimes learning must be tedious. It can't all be fun, fun, fun.

Gradually, most of kids got the hang of grammar, although a few, like Cesar, still didn't grasp the concept of a sentence. Even without the help of periods or capitals, though, Cesar had written some charming stories, and one had made him famous in our class. It starred President Clinton, who, along with New York's Governor Pataki and Mayor Giuliani, were often cast as buffoons in the children's stories. This is his second, corrected draft:

THE GHOST WHO FELL IN LOVE WITH BILL CLINTON

Once upon a sunny and strange day, a lady named Jackie was hit by a Coca-Cola truck. The truck was brown and its front end was as pointy as a bird's beak. Jackie died on the spot and suddenly her spirit came out of her body and flew to the White House where Bill Clinton was dancing the polka with his maid who was about ninety-five years old and so weak she couldn't lift a rat. Jackie fell in love with Bill Clinton. Then he left in his great, big, golden limousine and went to Discovery Zone and spent so much time jumping and running he almost fell asleep. Jackie appeared and tried to kiss him, but Bill Clinton gave her a kick that almost broke apart her lip.

Then he said, "What do you want?" "I want to marry you." "No way! I'm not going to get married with a short spirit that is like a ghost!" "Oh, yes, you are!" Then she got a gun and tried to shoot him so he would be a spirit and marry her once and for all. But Bill Clinton called the army and it was Bill Clinton vs. Jackie.

Jackie and Bill Clinton threw bombs at each other. Then a time bomb hit Bill Clinton and his last words were, "Give me clothes!" because while the war was going on Bill Clinton's fell off and he was fighting naked.

Then Jackie was waiting for Bill Clinton's spirit to come out but it didn't. It went straight to heaven. She was very, very sad. And as she went flying around Washington D.C., she saw George Pataki. And guess what? She fell in love with George Pataki and it all started again.

We'd acted that story out to great hilarity. Cesar cast himself as the president and asked his teacher to play the ghost. She gamely obliged, and to show the ghost's love for the president, she put her hands together and held them to her heart, like the swooning belle in a melodrama.

When I congratulated Cesar on his successful story, he blushed and said he was a little ashamed of what he'd written. "It's not nice to make fun of somebody," he explained. "Especially the president."

Eager to get past grammar and on to writing, I said, "Come on, guys! Someone must know what a noun is."

Miguel gave it a shot. "I'm not really sure, but isn't a noun like, something real?"

"That's an interesting way of putting it. What we usually say is: A noun is a person, place, or thing. So 'Miguel,' who is a person, is a noun. And 'New York City,' which is a place, is a noun. And 'book,' which is a thing, is also a noun."

I looked around the class. Had they gotten it?

"Do you understand, Cesar?"

"Yeah, I know it now!"

"Okay, good. Give me a noun."

"Read?"

"No, that's a verb."

I'd gotten off track, glanced at my watch.

"Someone else? A noun? Okan?"

Whatever word popped into Okan's mind made him laugh so much he couldn't spit it out.

"Okan, get a grip."

At last he blurted, "Doo-doo!" which also cracked Gary and Rafael up, and now the three of them were doubled over.

"Okay, okay, very funny. Yes, 'doo-doo' is a noun. Someone else?"

"School."

"Good. Another?"

"Chair."

"Good. Another? Something less common?"

I kept the kids naming nouns, waiting for ones that weren't so everyday. This was in preparation for a writing exercise I'd found in a book of essays called *The Grammar of Fantasy* by Gianni Rodari, an Italian writer and teacher. He called this exercise the "fantastic binomial," and for it to work, you need nouns that aren't ordinarily found together. So I didn't write *school* or *chair* on the board, but I did write down *broccoli, rainbow, clarinet, wristwatch, baby,* and *duck.*

I told the kids, "Choose two words from this list and make up a title for a story. Be as wacky as you want."

"Can we use more than two words on the list?"

"No."

"Can we use a word that's not on the list?"

"Yes, but the title's two most important words must be from the list."

Soon the kids had written several titles each, and I asked them to read their favorite title out loud.

"The Duck Who Stole My Wristwatch!"

"The Broccoli Rainbow!"

"The Baby Who Played the Clarinet at Carnegie Hall!"

"The Duck Who Ate the Baby!"

"Great titles!" I cried. "Gosh, I'd really like to read those stories, wouldn't you?"

"Yeah!"

"So let's do it!"

"Huh?"

"Write the story that goes with your title!"

"Aw, mannnnnnnnnn!"

The point of Rodari's exercise is to jolt the writer into unexpected trains of thought, and many of my students, Cesar especially, needed that. When free to write whatever he wanted, Cesar wrote endless versions of the same story about an astronaut sent into space by the mayor of New York City to battle various aliens. Once I'd told Cesar to shake things up, try something different, and his face lit up with inspiration. "I'm gonna do that, Mr. Swope!" he said. "This time I'll have the *president* send the astronaut on a mission!"

At least one children's classic was inspired by a challenge similar to the fantastic binomial. *Green Eggs and Ham* was written when Dr. Seuss's editor bet him he couldn't write a book using only fifty words. But Cesar, too, rose to the occasion with a story starring a bunch of broccoli as loyal and big-hearted as Cesar himself.

BROCCOLI AND CLARINET

"It's cold in here!" said Broccoli as he slowly opened the refrigerator door. Broccoli stepped out of the refrigerator and tripped over something. It was a clarinet. "That stupid clarinet!" he said. "Should I play it? Sure, why not?"

Broccoli opened the case and started playing. His playing sounded so beautiful that the boy who owned it went upstairs fast and told his parents. They did not believe him until they heard it. When they heard the sound themselves, they liked it so much they sent Broccoli to the Make Your Sound Company. The company loved it, too!

Broccoli became famous and so did the clarinet. He played jazz songs and also rock 'n roll. The famous pair traveled to Miami, Orlando, and Hollywood. Broccoli made lots of money and he gave it all to the family because he didn't need it. He just made money for fun.

One day when Broccoli was taping a record, he started turning brown. Parts of him fell down and dropped. "Come on," said the boy. "Record your record or we will be poor." So they patched him up with masking and Scotch tapes. "Okay," said Broccoli in a weak voice. He played and played until he couldn't play anymore. He fell apart, but the family did not care. They were rich. They threw him in the trash.

The Great Tribulation

"If I die before the Great Tribulation comes," Miguel explained in his sweetest voice, "I'm going to wait, and when God calls me with his trumpet, I'm going to go to heaven. If I didn't behave well in life, I might go to hell, which I don't really like 'cause I've heard that in the Bible it says that the monsters of the devil's gonna scratch your face and cut your head off and make you into a monster and you're not gonna ever die when they try to eat you, so I don't really want to go down there and have that pain."

Like Miguel, I was raised a Christian, but my Presbyterian Sunday school gave me conceptions of God, Jesus, and the devil that were radically different from his. As a child, I thought of God as merciful and kind; Jesus, meek and mild; and the devil as a kind of bogeyman, not really real. For Miguel, God was severe and wrathful; Jesus, a sword-wielding judge; and the devil, an actual threat.

Miguel told me, "God right now he's videotaping what I'm saying to you so when we go to heaven, when it's time at the Great Tribulation, when God is showing us all our movies, first he'll show the good part, then the bad part. While that's happening, the devil gets prepared with his monsters to come out, 'cause the monsters are locked up, right now. They're, like, chained."

Mrs. Melvern had given up on Miguel. When I made excuses for him, she dismissed them, saying, "The only reason Miguel doesn't do his homework is because he wants the attention. I've gotten to the point that I just look at him and say, 'I'm not bothering with you anymore. If you don't care, I don't care.'"

I was worried about Miguel's future. For poor kids like him, good grades are the only ticket to the better high schools and to college scholarships. So I called his mom, asked if I could stop by to see if we could figure out a way to turn Miguel's school performance around.

I sat on the sofa, Mrs. Santiago sat on a chair, and her husband, who couldn't understand our English, hovered nearby in their closet of a kitchen. Miguel's baby brother was in bed sick, and Miguel and his two other brothers were shooed off to the bedroom to keep the sick one company. They went without fuss; even the three-year-old seemed to understand that something serious was going on.

I asked Mrs. Santiago why she thought Miguel wasn't doing his homework.

"I don't know what's going on with Miguel," she told me. "I try to check has he done them, but he lies to me. I asked him, 'What's going on? Are you testing us or what is it?' He goes, 'No, Mommy. I don't know.'"

She said it took Miguel hours to do the simplest assignments. As in school, he had trouble concentrating, but at home he also had the distraction of his younger brothers. I suggested that Mrs. Santiago give Miguel a spot in the apartment all his own. "And when he's sitting there, make it a rule: he's not allowed to talk to the boys and they're not allowed to talk to him. Tell them there's an invisible force field around Miguel." She said that wouldn't work; I didn't know her headstrong boys—no matter what she told them, the second her back was turned, they'd be bothering Miguel.

I said, "Then maybe you could reconsider and let Miguel go to the after-school program? They make the kids do their homework first, but then they play. And that would be good for Miguel. He needs to socialize. He needs to play with kids his own age."

She shook her head, said she was afraid he'd say he'd gone to the after-school program but hang out on the streets instead. She said, "The thing is, Mr. Swope, that I'm a worried mother. See, like life is? My husband's niece has a son, Miguel's age, and they let him be all day out and the parents doesn't even know where he's at. He's always on the street. He goes by himself, he buys stuff. Miguel wants that freedom, but I cannot give it to him. I can't."

"What about his father? Does he get involved in the children's homework?"

"I have told him, but he hasn't done nothing about it. He's just, like, letting it go. Except today he told Miguel, 'If Mr. Swope comes and tells me you're not doing your homework, you're going to get it. I'm not letting this one pass by.'"

I groaned. "Oh, please don't tell your husband that's why I came. I don't want Miguel to get it because of me."

"I think you go too easy on him, Mr. Swope. He knows you don't get mad with him, so he thinks, Why do Mr. Swope's homework?"

"It's true," I sighed. "I don't get mad at him. But I don't want to make writing a punishment. I want him to enjoy it."

She smiled gently, understanding my quandary. She, too, indulged Miguel, and knew she babied him. "But what can I do, Mr. Swope? He's my firstborn."

"How are things between Miguel and his dad?" I asked.

"They don't have much of a relationship. Miguel cannot talk to his father. Sometimes I have to tell my husband, 'Talk to him, so Miguel sees that you have an attention to him, 'cause he doesn't hardly see you. You're always in a hurry. You're always doing church work.'"

What did Miguel have that was positive in his life? What did he enjoy? Maybe there was a way to capitalize on that. When I asked if he was still preaching at his church, she said no. "You see, Mr. Swope, the children only preach on Saturday, and my husband works for the church on Thursday and Friday and the whole family goes on Sunday, so going Saturday, too, is too much for him. My husband gets tired."

Then Mrs. Santiago told me Miguel had started misbehaving in Sunday school and was also getting rough with her. "We play and everything, but now he raises his hand to me. We're playing, but he hits hard. And my husband comes home and he has to hit him! I want Miguel to be the boy that he used to be. He's nine years old. He's changing. Every day."

Given Mrs. Santiago's loveless childhood and troubled marriage, it's not surprising she wanted Miguel to stay young. Miguel was probably her first experience of unconditional love, and now that he was growing older and withdrawing, she must have been feeling it keenly. But as far as the homework problem went, we weren't getting anywhere. I suggested we bring Miguel into the conversation.

Miguel slunk into the room and took a chair beside his mother with his shoulders hunched, his head bowed. He was nervous, which I didn't think was a bad thing. Maybe that would help.

I said, "Miguel, we've been trying to figure out how to help you do your homework, and we wanted to hear what you think the problem is."

He didn't look up.

Mrs. Santiago gently placed a hand on Miguel's knee. "What's going on, Junior?"

Silence.

"Why you not doing your homework?"

Silence.

"Why, Junior? How many times I have spoke to you? Why aren't you concentrating? What do you have in your mind that's bugging you? Why?"

Miguel hugged his stomach, turned away. He had no words, could only moan.

I said, "Miguel, doing homework shouldn't be such a big deal. I understand that most of it is stupid, but you'd get us all off your back if you'd just play the game a little. You're really smart, Miguel, but your grades aren't showing that."

"Yes, you're very talent!" cried his mother. "You have a lot of things! But you're seeing all the misbehave students, so you're dragging that from them. I don't know why. What else do you want, Miguel?"

Silence.

One of Miguel's younger brothers roared out of the bedroom and headed for his mother, crying, "Mama! Mama!"

"*Vaya, Daniel! Vaya!*" she answered with an intensity that so startled the little boy, he turned around and ran away.

Mrs. Santiago stroked Miguel's hand. "What is bothering you?" she repeated. "You know you're losing grades. Do you know that? That's what you want? You wanna be in another class that is not the best class?"

Silence.

"Is that what you want?"

Miguel shook his head and whimpered, "I'm not smart. I'm stupid," at which Mrs. Santiago grew alarmed. She leaned in close, grabbed Miguel's chin with her hand, forced him to look at her, and spoke urgently, as if she was trying to wake him up: "Miguel! Remember the preacher yesterday, what he said? You have to be a winner! Who's telling you you're a loser? Who's saying that to you?"

Miguel's head fell back, his eyes went shut.

"Miguel! Who's saying that?"

Silence.

"Who? Who?"

Miguel answered in a tiny voice, "The devil."

"That's right! The devil!"

Mrs. Santiago gathered her arms around her son and he collapsed against her chest. Sobbing, he crawled onto her lap and as she stroked his head, she told him, "Fight the devil, Junior. Cast him out."

Shaken and disturbed, I gathered my things, nodded good-bye, and let myself out the door.

On the subway home, though, I decided to be hopeful. There's more than one way to reach a child, I thought. Who knows? Given Miguel's world, maybe what I'd just witnessed was a breakthrough. Maybe something had cracked. Maybe now he'd do his homework.

The Case of the Missing Report Cards

"I'm sick of it," Mrs. Melvern told me. "Fifteen kids didn't do their homework last night. I get less work out of these tops than I did with my bottoms."

The school was "tracked," grouping students according to ability—bottom, middle, and top. My students were in the grade's top class, and I'd noticed that tracking fostered elitism, making it hard for the children not to think of themselves as better than the other kids in their grade. Then again, I could appreciate Mrs. Duncan's point of view. In her experience, classes of mixed ability were good for slower kids but not so good for brighter ones, who got bored. Given large classes, it's awfully tough to challenge each child according to their academic needs when the range in ability is great.

It's basically a question of social goals versus academic ones, and in a nod to the former, Mrs. Duncan never used the word *top* in her classroom and referred parents with questions about their child's rank to the administration. Mrs. Melvern, however, had no such compunctions. Class rankings were an integral part of her strategy for motivating students. She told me, "I said to them, 'Oh, Noelia: I guess you want to meet new friends next year, because you won't be in the top class unless you do your homework.' I said, 'Oh, Miguel. I guess you don't want to stay with your friends, because that's what's going to happen to you.' I said the same things to Aliza, Rafael, Najiyah, Okan, and the others. This is what I'm reduced to: threats."

Although Mrs. Malvern's threats did not result in improved performance, they did increase the children's anxiety as report card day approached. Some of them had parents who pushed them hard; bad grades would spell trouble at home. I'd left early the day before, when report cards were to be handed out, and as I walked into the classroom the morning after, the kids were way too quiet and Mrs. Melvern was at her desk, scowling. Something was clearly up, but I didn't guess that a crime had been committed.

I crossed the room and whispered to Mrs. Melvern, "What happened?"

"Someone stole the report cards."

My mouth dropped in shock, but inside I felt a naughty thrill. I imagined some kid—Rafael maybe? Miguel?—rashly committing this daring, if futile act.

"Do you have any idea who did it?"

"I can't prove it," she said, her eyes narrowing into little slits, "but I'm sure it was Noelia."

"No!" I gasped. Impossible! Giggly, gentle Noelia could never be a thief!

Or could she?

"What makes you think it was Noelia?"

Pure intuition, it turned out. But Mrs. Melvern quickly added that she wasn't alone; others suspected it was Noelia, too. Ella, for instance, had guessed that Noelia did it because Mrs. Melvern had yelled at Noelia just the day before and told her that when the report cards came out Noelia would be kicked out of the band.

"Which was true, I did say that," Mrs. Melvern told me. "So there's a motive."

I was appalled at Ella's treachery. "She said this with Noelia right there in the room?"

"No, this was today, and Noelia is absent. Which I also find suspicious. Like she's afraid."

To further bolster a weak case, Mrs. Melvern handed me a note marked PRIVATE. It said: "I don't know who did it but I think Noelia did it but I don't really know." The note wasn't signed, but I recognized the handwriting: Et tu, Jessica!

It wasn't as if Noelia were some stuck-up, bossy child the other kids were eager to take down a peg. She was well liked. The only way I could explain this nasty finger-pointing was to think that Mrs. Melvern had—unconsciously, perhaps—imposed her own suspicions on the class. This isn't hard to do with kids—a telling glance, some subtle innuendo, and their imaginations quickly connect the dots, transforming speculation into fact. This happened in Salem with the witches. It happened in California in the 1980s during the McMartin day-care scandal.

I said, "But no one actually saw Noelia steal the report cards?"

"Someone must have seen," Mrs. Melvern insisted. "Kids don't miss a thing. So far, though, no one's talking."

This gave me hope.

Mrs. Melvern said she'd turned the classroom inside out, searched every book bag, even dug into the bathroom trash. But the cards were nowhere to be found.

Wow, I thought. If Noelia did it, I was impressed. This showed imagination as well as chutzpah. Give that girl an A!

Mrs. Melvern said, "And if they don't turn up today, I'll have to do them all again. Do you have any idea how long it takes to fill out twenty-eight report cards?"

I shook my head in sympathy and hid the smile that would have said, "It serves you right."

Later that day, a frowning assistant principal appeared in the doorway, and the room went hush. Everyone knew why he was there. I'd known Mr. Ziegler only as a friendly, mild-mannered fellow with a combover, so I was shocked to see him play the heavy. His performance began calmly, reasonably, solemnly. He told the class that the administration was deeply disappointed, that this theft betrayed the trust of family, teachers, school, and country. Then he told the children it was their duty to report anything they'd seen or heard. When no one responded, he added a touch of anger to his voice, told the kids no stone would go unturned, the truth would out; he vowed he'd find the culprit—it was only a question of time! When this brought no one forward, he pumped up the volume. His face turned red, the veins in his neck bulged, and he wagged a finger in the air and shouted, "I'm not through with this investigation, not by a long shot! And if any of you know anything, you better come tell me, privately, in private, because they're going to be in a lot of trouble, *a lot of trouble!*"

This confusing threat frightened everyone. As it hung in the air, Mr. Ziegler went silent and, in a particularly effective touch, let his spotlight glare move searchingly from child to child. By this point, every heart was pounding, every palm was wet. Even I felt guilty. But if the kids knew anything, they didn't rat, and I was proud.

The next day, I came to school first thing, hoping to find Noelia, wanting her to know, no matter what, that I, at least, was on her side. The air in the classroom was still tense. Eager not to be noticed, the kids were at their desks and hard at work. Noelia was there, coloring with crayons. Her frizzy hair was twisted in a bun positioned cutely to the side of her head, and she was wearing small hoop earrings, blue jeans, and a soft pink pullover with a lacy collar. When I knelt beside her desk and asked if she wanted to come to my office and collaborate on a story, she was so desperate to flee the room that she grabbed her writing folder and darted out the door.

In my office, she did something strange. She climbed on the table and started crawling around in circles. Round and round and round she went.

"What are you doing?"

"I like to crawl on tables, Mr. Swope. Some people just don't have imagination for table crawling."

"Got ants in your pants today, huh?"

"I sure do, Mr. Swope."

Was she being clownish, like the stand-up comic that she hoped one day to be? Or was this a display of nerves? If so, did it suggest she was guilty? Or that she knew that others thought she was? Or was something else bothering her? Last year she'd told me her father had moved out, but when her parents had come to the parent-teacher conference together this year, they'd been so lovey-dovey that I wondered if Noelia had exaggerated the problem. (A teacher once told me she makes a deal with parents: If you'll believe fifty percent of what your kid says happens in school, I'll believe fifty percent of what she says happens at home.)

"How are things with your family, Noelia?"

"Fine."

"Where's your dad living now?"

"He's living with us again."

"How's that?"

"Pretty good."

"He's getting along with your mom?"

"Umm, there have been a few problems," she said, still circling round and round. Then she added, "Lots of problems, if I do say so myself."

"Like what?"

"They were fighting about where my sister and I were going to go next summer. My dad says, 'Why don't we take them to the Dominican Republic?' and my mother says, 'Hey, I want to see what Miami looks like.' I don't know when that's gonna get straightened out."

"That sounds pretty normal. Everything else is fine?"

"Yeah, everything else," she said cheerfully.

As she continued making her circles, I said as casually as I could, "I heard there was some excitement in class the other day."

"Yeah, the report cards got lost," Noelia told me. "Mrs. Melvern just put them down and then the next minute they're gone. Whoever could have taken them must need a brain transplant or something. Who would ever take a report card? I ask you. Who?"

"Stop going in circles, Noelia. You're driving me crazy."

She climbed off the table, took a seat, and looked at me with an adorable smirk that showed several missing teeth.

I asked, "Why do you think someone might have taken them?"

"Somebody might have got a bad grade," suggested Noelia. "I got two of them! Two U's: 'Completes Work on Time' and 'Homework.' My mom's gonna ground me for life."

Hmmmmm. If she was guilty, this was a pretty clever answer. You wouldn't expect the culprit to point out her own motive. Then again, how could she know she'd gotten two "unsatisfactory" marks if she hadn't seen her report card? Maybe Mrs. Melvern had told her in advance. That was possible, but as I tried to puzzle the mystery out, I suddenly felt guilty and decided not to pursue my investigation. I didn't like playing games with Noelia. And anyway, suppose she did confess? Would I have to report her? And if I didn't, would I get in trouble with the school? It was better not to know.

Still, I was worried for Noelia. If she didn't shape up, Mrs. Melvern might fail her.

"Why is it you don't do your homework, Noelia?"

"The little homework monster has been eating my papers, going, 'Ew, homework! Yum!'"

I rolled my eyes.

"But it's gonna get better, Mr. Swope. It's gonna get better."

"Noelia, this isn't good. You're always in trouble with Mrs. Melvern. Bad grades have consequences."

"I'll flunk."

"Yeah!"

She could see I was upset (much more upset than she was), and she tried to cheer me up. "I'm not worried about it, Mr. Swope. I know how to stop it. Every time I hear my Bad Conscience, I'm gonna just ignore it."

I said, "You know, Noelia, that's an interesting idea for a story: a girl who has a Good Conscience and a Bad Conscience—"

"I know. I'm gonna write a story about that."

"Want to work on it now?"

"Okay."

"Same deal as usual, right? You talk, I take notes, then you write the story up for homework, right?"

"Okay."

"Who's going to be the lead character?"

"A little girl. Her name is, um, Maxie."

"Good name. Where does Maxie live?"

"She lives on a foreign planet in a private house. It's white with pink polka dots all over it. She always wears a pink polka-dotted dress with blue."

"What's her school like?"

"It's a big ten-story building. Maxie's class is on the first floor. Her teacher's very strict. They study vomit. They have vomit tests, vomit classes, and every time Maxie vomits, it comes up the same thing, just a little piece of spit comes out."

"Very nice!" I said. "I like that! But don't forget she has these conscience characters, right?"

"Right."

"Are they invisible or visible?"

"Only Maxie can see them. The Bad Conscience always tells Maxie she doesn't have to vomit, she doesn't have to do anything. Then the Good Conscience goes, 'Don't listen to him! He's trying to get you in trouble!' Then the Bad Conscience goes—"

"I get the idea. I love this. You've got a terrific setup. What's the plot? I know! Maybe there's a big test coming up, and if Maxie doesn't pass it something terrible will happen to her. So she has to study." I consciously steered the narrative in the foolish hope that this would help Noelia understand the consequences of not doing her schoolwork.

Noelia was willing to play with that idea. She said, "And then the night before the test her Consciences come out. And the bad one says, 'Forget about studying! Enjoy life!' And the good one says, 'He's a big fat liar!' And Maxie's going crazy and then she tells them to shut up! She stuffs them back in her ear, she closes them up, she plugs them up. Then they come out again and they start arguing again and they get Maxie so irritated she grabs them both and swallows them. Now they're living in her tummy."

"And then?"

"She doesn't have to worry about them, anymore." Noelia sat there, happy, thinking she was finished.

"But Noelia," I persisted, intent upon my moral. "What happens with the vomit test?!"

"Oh, yeah. She gets to school. She vomits just a tiny piece of spit and the Bad Conscience comes out with it. So she grabs the Bad Conscience, throws him out the window. And then the piece of spit turns into a gigantic puddle of vomit that fills up the whole school."

This story had just gushed out of her, and I was so delighted by it that I abandoned my didactic scheme. What a miracle this Noelia was, her imagination a force of nature that would not, could not be directed.

"I love that, Noelia! Maxie triumphs in the end!"

"Yeah."

"It's absolutely brilliant. And so wonderfully gross."

"I know," she said, with a modest shrug.

Noelia left my office with my notes to write the story up for homework, but she didn't do it. She had no burning need to have it down on paper for the world to see. But I did. So I hounded her, and then she turned a little something in, a rush job, just a scribbled page or two. So I hounded her again, and then again, till finally she got the plot down, more or less, enough so we could act it out in class. And boy, was Noelia happy then. What a show! "Maxie's Story" was a big fat hit, the kids were rolling on the floor, and Noelia was a star.

As for the report cards, they were never found. All the other teachers were baffled. No one could believe a kid could pull it off. Where could they have stashed the cards? There was speculation that Mrs. Melvern might have absentmindedly misplaced them, which was plausible—she was pretty disorganized.

Ever since that episode, I've toyed with the idea of writing a short story I'd call "The Case of the Missing Report Cards." The only problem is I can't decide which approach to take.

Sometimes I think I'll steal a page from *Murder on the Orient Express* and gradually reveal that the entire class was in cahoots and planned the theft together.

Other times, I think I'll tell the story in flashback, start with Noelia all grown up and a successful stand-up comic. As she tucks her daughter, Maxie, into bed, Maxie says, "Mommy, tell me again about the time you stole all those report cards."

Then again, maybe it would be best to tell the story more or less the way it really happened, except with one last twist. I wouldn't let the reader know until the very end that the culprit was in fact the children's writing teacher, Mr. Swope.

La Vieja

One happy day in spring, Mrs. Melvern told me she had had a change of plans and would be starting her maternity leave before her baby arrived. This meant she'd be gone the last four weeks of school.

My first reaction was unkind: Ding dong, the witch is dead!

My second reaction was unexpected: Now that Mrs. Melvern had one foot out the door, I started to like her.

My third reaction was worry: Who would be the substitute?

With a lousy sub, things could go from bad to worse, and there were some pretty peculiar people subbing in that school, like the guy with a toupee who made the kids spend the day copying definitions out of the dictionary or the woman who spoke only in a shriek and wore so much makeup she looked like Bette Davis in *Whatever Happened to Baby Jane?* I wanted to salvage something from the year for the kids, so I rushed to see Mrs. Scalise, the principal, to beg for the best substitute she had.

In her seventies, Mrs. Scalise was short and stout and wore her long, fine blond hair gathered loosely atop her head. Age had taken its toll on her legs, which were swollen, making it difficult for her to walk without a cane. But in her day, I'd heard, she'd danced on the tabletops at the Christmas parties, a story easily believed. She was still full of life, had a ready laugh, and liked to flirt.

Mrs. Scalise, who spoke classic Queens, had immigrated from "It'ly" to New York when she was just a toddler, after the First World War. Her mother was "illit'rit" and her father's education had stopped at the third grade.

"Why did your family come to America?" I asked.

"Poverty. Starvation."

The immigrants her family settled among in Queens were poor. In those days, immigrants in Queens were predominantly European, and Mrs. Scalise's neighbors were Irish, German, Italian, and Jewish. Mrs. Scalise's father worked in a candle factory. Then, as now, immigrant life wasn't easy, but it was better than what they'd left. Mrs. Scalise knew exactly what her students were up against, and she fought for them tooth and nail.

Mrs. Scalise's job as principal was gigantic. The school had more than sixteen hundred children from dozens of different countries speaking many different languages, and every year enrollment went up. She had too few teachers, too few aides, and not enough supplies or classrooms. Moreover, she was hampered by union rules that made it almost impossible to fire incompetent teachers, and low salaries that made it difficult to hire good ones.

She didn't speak highly of her teaching staff. In her judgment, most of the teachers were merely "adequate," and those who weren't totally devoted to their students, who didn't give their all, she held in contempt. In her estimation, only a handful of her teachers were exceptional, and Mrs. Duncan was "the best of the best."

Mrs. Scalise had her defenders, but many, if not most of the teachers, found her stubborn, capricious, and authoritarian. Behind her back, some called her La Vieja (the old woman) while others just called her the Bitch. Not that Mrs. Scalise cared. That woman had skin made of titanium. "You can't run a school this size and not make enemies," she told me. "I'm not in a popularity contest here. Everything I do, every battle I fight, is for the children."

Of course that's what every embattled educator says—it's for the children!—but the problem is that everyone has a different idea of what sort of education the children need. Mrs. Scalise believed that students needed to master basic academic skills, of course, but she was absolute in her determination to offer them Art. She went after grants, squeezed her budget tight, and somehow found the money to have an art teacher, a music teacher, a chorus, and a band. Moreover, at least some classes took part in dance, opera, drama, and creative-writing programs, and each student got a copy of the annual literature and art journal.

By order of Mrs. Scalise, every class had to present an assembly program, which usually took the form of a play with homemade sets, costumes, and preferably music, too. Some, like Mrs. Duncan's *Peter Pan* the year before, were fairly elaborate.

I asked Mrs. Scalise what she looked for in these shows.

"Perfection."

On Assembly Day, every child was supposed to wear blue pants or skirt, a white shirt, and a red tie. The assembly program began in a ritualized, martial manner. With the music teacher pounding out a march on the piano, the student standard-bearers entered the auditorium, solemnly carrying flags. Then the rest of the kids followed, lined up two by two and marching in unison: right, left, right, left. Upon reaching their seats, the children recited the Pledge of Allegiance and sang "America the Beautiful."

"This is all to instill pride," Mrs. Scalise explained.

Teachers complained it took weeks to get these mandatory plays ready, weeks that would be better spent on lessons to bring up the school's repeated dreadful showings on standardized tests. But Mrs. Scalise dismissed that as a red herring, pointing out the extra time wouldn't help a poor teacher improve test scores. "A good teacher, a teacher like Mrs. Duncan, can cover everything," she said. "Besides, you have to realize that assembly programs include language arts, visual art, planning, public speaking. All of which are terribly important. And I'm a firm believer that talent's innate. Unless you give it a chance to show itself, you'll waste it. So you want to grab it. You have to expose children to everything because we don't know who might respond."

The biggest Scalise extravaganza of the year was the Multicultural Festival. Held toward year's end, the festival involved the whole school as well as the neighborhood. The festival lasted all day, and it was a joyful event. Kids dressed up in native costumes, their parents cooked native foods, and each class had a multiethnic feast. Another high point was the parade, in which sixteen hundred kids marched through their neighborhood streets, waving to families and friends, many of whom also wore ethnic dress. The parade concluded in front of bleachers, where, before an audience of thousands, each grade performed a different ethnic folk dance. (Because Pentecostals forbid dancing, Miguel had to stay home on festival days, and one year Fatma was kept home, too, because the costume given to the girls for that year's Swedish dance included a very short skirt offensive to a Muslim girl's modesty.)

During the dance performance, Mrs. Scalise always sat front and center, her cane tapping out the rhythm as she watched closely, making sure the dances were perfectly executed.

Mrs. Scalise told me, "Teachers say these students don't need these so-called extras. They say what these kids need is basics. But what are the basics? How many teachers, how many people, live without music or art? None! Art is all around us, but these teachers don't understand that. The creative arts aren't 'extra.' They're a part of life. They're what make life bearable."

If you love the arts, this is self-evident. Many grown-ups, alas, don't remember—or never had a chance to find out—how naturally creative childhood can be. (For many of us, it's the most creative time we'll ever know.) The plays we were in as children, the dances we learned, the paintings we painted, these constitute some of our most vivid memories, and they opened a door to Art for us.

I begged, practically on my knees, for Mrs. Scalise to give the class her best substitute, but she offered no assurances. "Do you have any idea how hard it is to find a good substitute?" she said. "And then I also have to think about all the other children in this school. If your kids get a good substitute, other kids, kids who may need it more, get a bad one."

"But my class has to have a sub for a whole month," I argued.

"It isn't easy," she said. "The whole situation is infuriating. It's not what should be, but that's the way it is."

They Go All the Way Down

As I sat on the subway, headed for school on the first day of Mrs. Melvern's maternity leave, I was giddy with happiness, like a character from a Victorian novel about to be reunited with his long-lost, long-suffering children. The tide had turned, Mrs. Melvern was gone, and we'd be together again, just like old times.

Mrs. Scalise had assigned the class a lovely substitute, a young Italian who'd married a man from Queens. Although Mrs. Frilicci had no teaching experience, she was smart and kind and didn't dislike any of the students. This in itself made a world of difference.

Through trial and error, that year I'd learned a simple lesson. To teach well, I had to be prepared and keep my lessons focused. From the moment Mrs. Melvern told me she'd be leaving, I'd begun to plan. I wanted to do a major project in this last month, something similar to the Box Project, something fun, something that involved both writing and art.

But what?

For several anxious, even anguished days, no ideas came to me, and I was as miserable and irritable as I am when my writing isn't going well. But finally I landed on a theme—the island—which proved so fertile that ideas grew thick and fast, making it hard for me to fall asleep. Then once I had, more ideas would drag me back awake. The island seemed to offer possibilities for everything, and I devised lessons that encompassed art, math, reading, science, social studies, and writing. I'd never get to all of them, I knew, but I was happy to have extra lessons up my sleeve, in case one failed.

When the Island Project's opening day arrived, I was ready, and I walked into the classroom confidently, eager to reclaim the class.

"Hi, guys," I said.

"Good-morrrrrrning-Mister-Swoooooope."

"I hate it when you do that," I said. "You sound like a bunch of robots. Just shout out a hi if you feel like it, but not altogether, okay?"

"Yo!"

"Hey, man! Wuz happenin'?"

"Much better. Thank you."

I picked up a piece of chalk and drew a cartoon desert island with a single palm tree.

"What's that?" I asked.

The answer was so obvious that the kids suspected a trick.

"Nicole, what's this?"

Her lips moved, but I couldn't hear her.

"Louder, please."

"An island?"

"Right! And what is an island?"

"Land all surrounded by water," said Simon.

"Right again," I said and grabbed the eraser. As I went to rub away my island, though, I paused, suddenly puzzled. "Huh," I said. "That's interesting."

The class looked at me, waiting.

"What do you suppose keeps an island from floating away like a raft?"

I looked out on a sea of puzzled faces. They studied my drawing in silence. Then Ella raised her hand. "Maybe islands *do* float," she said.

Others agreed—yeah, maybe they do!

"But Queens is on Long Island," I said. "Are we floating? What keeps us from drifting out to sea?"

"Ropes?" said Maya.

"Anchors?" said Gary.

Ella thought perhaps Long Island was too heavy, so it couldn't float.

"But if it was heavy, wouldn't it sink?"

That got them thinking.

"Fishes!" cried Noelia, bouncing up and down. "Fishes and turtles and dolphins and mermaids keep it up!"

"In old stories maybe," I said. "But what about real life?"

Then Okan said, "Maybe the water beneath Long Island is shallow, so it drags on the bottom."

"Possible," I said. "But what about islands in the ocean where the water is a mile deep? What keeps them afloat?"

Okan frowned thoughtfully. He was a light-skinned boy from Turkey, with blue-gray eyes that reminded his mother of her beloved, much missed Adriatic Sea. Okan's parents were artists, which might explain why he was such a dreamer, often off in his own world. He was very interested in science and fascinated by all things mechanical, especially airplanes and fire trucks, which he drew with precision. After thinking hard about the puzzle of an island, he ventured an answer, but he wasn't confident because his thought seemed so improbable: "Maybe they go all the way down?"

"Yes!"

This was the moment I was waiting for, a realization from my own childhood that had been so thrilling and profound it had constituted a revelation. I don't recall the circumstance, can't remember which teacher taught me islands or how her lesson demonstrated that the sea is just the top of it, that islands go, as Okan said, the whole way down and are attached, connected, mute heralds of a vast and hidden underwater world. But to this day the thought of islands gives me goose bumps, and they are a central metaphor for how I think about the world: we cannot draw conclusions by appearances, there's always more than meets the eye, whole worlds exist that are invisible. In this sense, islands also shaped the way I thought about this class, this archipelago of children, each one the visible face of unseen, mysterious worlds I tried to fathom.

I took the chalk and drew the world beneath my cartoon island, gave it slopes that reached the ocean floor. Then I drew other mountains, tall but not quite tall enough to reach out of the sea. I drew a school of fish, a shark, a sunken ship. Above, up in the sky, I drew a cloud, a bird, a plane.

I studied my students' faces. If anyone was having an epiphany, it wasn't obvious. There was no swelling music, as there would be in a movie, no close-up zooms of faces filled with awe. The most I could say was that I had their full attention—or, more accurately, that islands did. I seized the moment. In a quiet voice, so as not to break the spell, I said, "Take out a sheet of paper, please. I'd like you each to write a poem. Make your first line: 'If I were an island . . .' Then go on to describe an island you might be. Would you be deserted? Would there be animals? Magic? Strange, sweet music? Would it have—"

CLANG CLANG CLANG.

Damn damn damn: A fire drill.

CLANG CLANG CLANG.

In frustration, I gently banged my forehead on the blackboard, Charlie Brown style.

"Quickly, children. Shhhhh! No talking," said Mrs. Frilicci.

CLANG CLANG CLANG.

The kids knew the routine. They stood, pushed their chairs under their desks, and got in line at the door. When I looked up, resigned, Ella noticed a chalky island smudge on my forehead. "Look at Mr. Swope!" she whispered to MeiKai, who glanced over her shoulder at me and giggled as they walked into the corridor, heading for outside.

The Island Project

Some kids gave reports about the islands they had known. Ella talked about Hong Kong, where she was born. Noelia spoke about the Dominican Republic; Lucinda told us about Puerto Rico; Gary, Cuba; MeiKai, Taiwan. Okan gave a report on Easter Island, which intrigued him, and after Aaron took us on a tour of his native Ecuador's Galapagos Islands, I gave lessons on Darwin, natural selection, and volcanic islands.

As it happened, Mrs. Melvern, who had excellent taste in books, had had the class read *The Island of the Blue Dolphins* and *The Black Stallion,* both of which feature islands. I tracked down other island passages to read to them, including John Donne's "No man is an island" meditation. As with boxes, once I started looking for islands, I found them everywhere. Literary islands, I discovered, are usually exotic but dangerous havens for the shipwrecked. Sometimes the islands are realistic, like the islands on which Robinson Crusoe, Melville's shipmates, the Swiss Family Robinson, *The Cay*'s Philip and Thomas, and William Steig's mouse Abel struggle to survive. Elsewhere, they're fantastical, as Homer's Odysseus, Shakespeare's Prospero, Swift's Gulliver, Barrie's Peter Pan, and Collodi's Pinocchio discovered.

And then, of course, there's Gilligan.

The inspiration for our final writing project came to me while reading Robert Louis Stevenson's *Treasure Island*. I was at home at the time, my cat in my lap, and when I read in my edition's preface that Stevenson got the inspiration for his book while looking at a map of an imaginary island he'd sketched, I got so excited I cried, "That's it!" which startled Mike, who leapt from my lap with a *"Meow!"*

• • •

Before the children made their own imaginary islands, we studied maps. I brought in books with reproductions of ancient, fantastical, and modern maps. We made a list of geographical terms—coves and bays and inlets, peninsulas and plains and plateaus, forests and mountains and deserts—and compared the different symbols cartographers used to designate them. The children learned to measure distance and read a key, discovered that north is always at the top, and were taught to find their native countries using latitude and longitude.

I gave everyone a five-by-three-foot piece of paper that was red or blue or yellow. I asked them to lie down on it and get themselves into an island shape so that their partners could then trace their bodies' outlines. This would be their island's shape. The sheets of paper were so large, however, that the project had to spill into the hallway, and before I'd found a spot for everyone to work, Noelia, Miguel, Rosie, and Najiyah were already done, their islands drawn, but each one was the same—a corpse-pose island with the body on its back and arms and legs slightly apart. I threw up my hands in frustration and said, "What were you guys thinking? Why did you all do the same thing?"

"You didn't tell us we had to be different!" said Rosie.

"I've been telling you to be different for two years!" I cried. "Haven't you learned *anything*? Now, turn your papers over and make another island, but this time think about the sort of island shape you want. Be original. Be unique."

Kids curled, stretched, twisted, draped their hair or spread it out, sat cross-legged, knelt, then changed their minds and tried another position.

Much better, guys!

The island outlines were quickly done. Because these maps were so large and unwieldy, we reduced them. Using yardsticks, the kids drew grids on their large pieces of paper. Using rulers, they next drew proportionate grids on nine-by-eleven-inch drawing paper. After lettering the columns and numbering the rows in both grids, the kids could easily copy the coastlines of their islands square by square onto the smaller paper, thereby making exact, but smaller, copies. I was pleased. This lesson was not only fun but offered the kids a skill they might one day use.

Then I handed out the Magic Markers and said, "Let's make islands." Each child worked at a different pace, some passionate and careless, some cautious and methodical; some stayed within the lines, some didn't. More than half used vibrant primary colors, but a fair number chose deeper, earthier tones, and a few used hardly any color at all. Some islands were delicately rendered, some were bold, some tentative, but all the kids were happy in their work. The room was full of chatter, and I was hopeful they'd find stories that would come from somewhere deep inside themselves.

Okan chortled to himself and worked intensely. He'd had a rough year. He was one of the ones Mrs. Melvern hadn't liked, and he hadn't much liked her. He complained that she taught them lessons they already knew. He told me he was bored. An only, latchkey child, Okan would go home from school and be alone for several hours, worried about the violent, crazy man who lived across the hall. Okan said, "Once the police came and took him away and he was screaming and all wrapped up in white cloth." That spring, though, the man returned, and not long after jumped from his window to his death.

From a distance, Okan's island was unnerving: a body on its side, arms akimbo, the sort of silhouette police chalk leaves around a body that has fallen from a great height. Inside his island's borders, Okan had so much detail it looked as if he'd drawn his body's nervous system and then tied it up with blue rope, the zigs and zags of which I thought were waterways.

"Wow," I said. "Look at all those rivers!"

"Those aren't rivers," Okan explained. "Those are highways."

"Highways?" I said. "Your island has *highways*?"

"Mmmm-hmmmm."

"Really? You want traffic on your island?"

"Mmmm-hmmmm."

I bent over to look more closely at his map and was upset to find he'd smothered his body with commercial outlets: Dunkin' Donuts, McDonald's, Burger King, Pizza Hut, Kentucky Fried Chicken, Chinese restaurants, a Pepsi fountain, a Radio Shack . . .

I thought, *Okan, how could you! This wasn't what I wanted! I wanted Nature, Fantasy, Adventure, Mystery, Myth!*

I was disappointed, even angry. Was this why I was working so hard? To help these kids along so they could grow up to be real estate lawyers and developers, writing contracts, leases, franchises, letters of agreement, so they could be a part of all that's ugly in the world?

I wasn't being fair, I know, but really! Such a depressing island— overdeveloped and cram-packed, not a waterfall or a snowcapped mountain or a buried treasure in sight! I tried my best to hide my irritation, though, and asked, "Do you have an idea for a story yet?"

"Not really."

"Well, let's see if we can find someplace interesting to start."

I squinted and scoured his island, looking for something that might form the basis of a story Okan would want to write and I could bear to read. At last I found a castle in the northern reaches of his island. This was promising—Okan had told me once that the thing he remembered most about Turkey were the castles.

I said, "Hey, what's with this orange castle? It's kind of cool."

"Actually, that castle is not supposed to be orange," Okan said. "It's supposed to be white."

"Interesting. Okay. So what happens in this white castle?"

"They sell hamburgers."

Blubber Island

I asked the kids to come to their initial story conference with a story idea, but few did, and I couldn't blame them. Stories didn't emerge as naturally as I'd hoped; not all their islands easily suggested narratives. Some kids created islands that were all about design and color. Others made mish-mashes, a swamp here, a desert there, a mountain range, a castle, then a racetrack and a spa and a Cockroach River, a Belly Beach, a Foot Forest, and a Booger Hill. Maya's island was towered over by a gigantic evil tree. It was easiest to find a story when the island had a theme, like Noelia's Messy Island, Lucinda's Disgusting Island, and Rosie's Island of Screams.

Cesar's island's theme was food. He had the Chocolate River, the Hamburger Lake, the Ice-Cream Cone Mountains, and the Marshmallow Clouds. His island was oddly shaped, though, because he'd gotten confused when he'd reduced it and had screwed up the grids. In the end, his island's silhouette was not so much a body as a blob.

He told me, "Elena said my island looks like it's a stomach and it's fat, like me."

Elena was a pretty girl, and a number of kids, both boys and girls, had crushes on her. I wondered if Cesar did, too. I said, "Elena shouldn't call you fat. That's mean."

"It's okay," he shrugged good-naturedly. "I'm fat, anyway. I have to face it."

"You don't mind being called fat?"

"No."

"Really?"

"I love my tummy!" he told me, and to prove his point, he looked down at his bulging belly and squeezed it in his hands. "Hi there, blubber!" he said.

"Tell me about your island, Cesar."

"It's called Blubber Island. It's a fat boy's paradise. See that fat statue there? That's me, King Cesar."

"Do you have an idea for your island story?"

"Yeah."

"Who's going to be your main character?"

"Elena."

"What's going to happen to her?"

"She's gonna die," he said sweetly.

"Why?"

"'Cause she's gonna eat too much."

"How does she get on this island?"

"I haven't figured that out yet."

"Let's just make it up."

He was stumped.

"Well, you like space-travel stories," I suggested. "She could be in a rocket—"

"Yeah!"

"So how would that play out?"

"She's in space and she wants to get down where there's food and water, right, so she falls down on my island and she lands on the Chocolate River."

"What happens then?"

"She thinks it's a wonderful island but it's not . . ."

"Why?"

"'Cause she eats too much?" asked Cesar. "She gets fat? She explodes?"

"Don't be so insecure. Those are wonderful ideas. You've got a great start." As I jotted down his story outline, I asked, "Do you feel ready to write a first draft?"

"Yeah."

"Good," I said. "Excellent work. Thank you. When you get back to the class, send Fatma down, would you?"

"She's absent."

"Again?"

Fatma had been absent nearly forty days this year. At one point, an asthma attack had put her in the hospital, where she'd read lots of books multiple times. Sickly childhoods aren't uncommon among writers; some credit their careers to the fact that they spent so much time in bed reading and dreaming. Wouldn't it be just like life, I thought, if Fatma, the one I couldn't seem to reach, ended up a writer?

Whose Story Is It, Anyway?

Like the child herself, Nicole's island was shy and tentative, most of it white, empty space, just a tiny feature here and there. Unlike some kids, Nicole hadn't found her voice as a writer, and I was anxious for her to do this, but I feared that wasn't likely to happen today. Her island didn't offer promising terrain.

I'd asked Rosie to join us, hoping that would put Nicole more at ease, and the three of us sat in my office, studying her map.

"What a fun island!" I lied. "Tell me about it, would you?"

"Lots of crazy things going on," said Nicole.

"Such as?"

Silence.

"What's this in the middle of Grassy Park?"

"A little spring."

"Aha. Anything special about that spring?"

Silence.

"How about Ugly Lake? What makes it ugly?"

"They throw garbage in there?"

"I hate it when people litter, don't you?" I said. "Is that what your story's going to be about, litter or pollution?"

Silence.

"What's this?"

"A cave maze."

"Interesting! What's inside?"

"There's lots of stairs."

"Oooh, that's good. Do they go up or down or both?"

"Both."

"And what happens if you go up the stairs?"

Silence.

"Then what happens if you *down* the stairs?"

"You might get out of this cave?"

Because the cave had only led us back to the island, I moved on, asking, "What about Sing Lake? Why is it called that?"

"'Cause when you go over there, you always hear the lake sing."

I was thrilled. "That's terrific, Nicole," I said. "So poetic, like a myth. There's an idea for a story: 'How Sing Lake Got Its Name.'"

Silence.

"What kind of songs does the lake sing? Sad songs? Happy songs? Pretty songs? Rap songs?"

Silence.

"Hello?"

Nicole said, "Well, when the weather is, like, nice, it sings happy songs. When the weather is bad, it sings sad songs."

"Okay. But why? How did Sing Lake come to be?"

Silence.

I worried I was pushing her in a direction she didn't want to go. I said, "Do you have any other ideas for a story?"

Silence.

"Any ideas at all?"

Silence.

"Maybe Sing Lake was once a person," I suggested. "What do you think?"

Silence.

"Nicole?"

She was a tiny child with great big watery eyes that made her look as if she was about to cry even when she was happy. Because she was so shy, I didn't get to know Nicole well. Back in third grade, Mrs. Duncan had told me that Nicole reminded her of herself when she was young and timid. For that reason, I felt a special tenderness for Nicole, and because she wanted to be a teacher, I liked to think that I was helping her grow into Mrs. Duncan.

I said to the girls, "Why don't the two of you figure out how Sing Lake came to be. It could be anything, you decide. I'll sit here and read my *New York Times*."

To give them a sense of privacy, I lifted the paper and opened it wide, making a wall between us. But I wasn't reading, I was listening, eager to hear about Sing Lake.

Rosie asked, "Do you want the lake to have been, like, a lady or a man?"

"A lady," said Nicole.

"Of course," said Rosie, businesslike.

This was followed by silence. I peeked around the paper; Rosie was studying Nicole's island. She said, "This cave maze is *really* cool. What happens there?"

"The cave is if you wanna die and then you wanna see the world again," said Nicole.

"So it's like a suicide place?" said Rosie.

"Yeah."

At that moment I was so focused on Sing Lake that this bit of dialogue flew right by me. Much later, when listening to my tape recording of the conference, I did a double take. What was that Nicole had said? I hit the rewind button and again listened to her tiny voice saying, "The cave is if you wanna die and then you wanna see the world again."

Was that why she'd told me her cave had two sets of stairs? Because one led to death, the other back out of the cave and into life? How could I have missed that! And if I've interpreted her idea rightly, where did it come from? What drums do children hear? Narratives about a hero who travels to the underworld and then returns occur in many cultures, and there's a chance Nicole borrowed the idea from one of those. But it's also possible that she'd found it on her own. Maybe I romanticize childhood, but it often seemed that the children's minds had access to the primal sea of stories, stories so fundamental to the human condition that they are inescapable, inevitable, perhaps even innate.

It made sense that Rosie would inspire cave thoughts from Nicole when I could not. Nicole knew Rosie's stories; we all did. They were intense tales, set in forests and dungeons, often peopled by anguished ghosts. It's possible that Nicole's imagination was inspired by Rosie's, or maybe Nicole was only trying to please her friend. It's hard to know.

I've taught writing to kindergarteners and graduate students, and helping anyone find a story is a tricky business. You try to guide, shape, ask for elaboration, more details, but the urge to take over the narrative is strong. My imagination was so excited by the singing lake—I already had a vision for the story—that as Nicole and Rosie discussed the cave I only heard them getting off the track and put a stop to it.

KH

77. Headings used for the first time
    Field: a1001 |aCosentini, John W
    Indexed as AUTHOR: cosentini john w
    Preceded by "b": cosell howard 1918
    Followed by "b": coser lewis a 1913
    From: b12931597 Cosentini, John W Font
    Cosentini
    Catalog Date: Nov 15, 2005 Group: 0
    3:39:50 PM

78. Headings used for the first time
    Field: a1001 |aCoutinho, Afrânio
    Indexed as AUTHOR: coutinho afranio
    Preceded by "b": coutin susan bibler
    Followed by "b": coutts brian e
    From: b12931640 Coutinho, Afrânio Intr
    Catalog Date: Nov 15, 2005 Group: 0
    3:39:57 PM

Still hiding behind my newspaper, I said in a deep Wizard of Oz voice: *"Stay focused on Sing Lake."*

The girls fell silent. In my mind's eye I saw them look at the newspaper, then look at each other, smiling at my silliness. They waited a moment to see if I'd speak again; then Rosie got back to work, abandoning the cave I hadn't let them enter. "How about this idea, then?" she said to Nicole. "The lady got, like, this punishment to become a lake. She was really good at singing, so she became a lake."

Silence.

Rosie said, "You got any other ideas?"

Silence.

But I thought Rosie's idea was worth pursuing, and when Nicole didn't respond, I looked over the top of my paper and asked, "What was the lady punished for, Rosie?"

"I was thinking maybe she was trespassing," said Rosie. "But it's not my story."

"You're absolutely right," I said, chagrined. "I shouldn't have interrupted. You two figure it out. If I say anything else, ignore me."

I made such a clownish show of retreating behind the newspaper that Nicole got the giggles, which gave Rosie the giggles, too, which made Nicole giggle more, till both were having fits, which made me smile behind my newspaper.

Rosie got a grip first. "Just tell me, Nicole. Why does the lady sing?"

"'Cause she just likes to sing. 'Cause her job was to sing."

"How does she turn into a lake?" asked Rosie. "Was she drowned in there?"

"No. She drank too much water and she spitted it out and her voice got in there."

"Really good!" said Rosie.

There it was—Nicole had her story. The rest was just details. To speed things up, I put my paper down and made some notes for Nicole to use in her first draft.

"Tell me, Nicole. Why did the lady drink so much water?"

"She was so thirsty 'cause she was in the sea and just found this island. She goes to the Grassy Park and finds a spring there and she is sooooo thirsty she drinks for two or three days and she was so full of water she spit it out and her voice got in there."

I loved this idea so much I was tempted to write the story myself. Somehow, though, that felt like stealing. Yet how much did the idea belong to Nicole alone? If I hadn't been there, she wouldn't have had it, and if Rosie hadn't been there, it would have been different. And probably Noelia should get credit, too. I didn't see this at the time, but looking back, I doubt Nicole's singer would have spit her voice out with the water if Noelia's Maxie hadn't spit her conscience out with vomit earlier that year. Yet I would never accuse Nicole of stealing from Noelia's "Maxie's Story"; she'd transformed the idea so much she'd made it all her own.

In a sense, all writing is collaborative, more than most of us, even writers, think. Our stories are like islands, connected to people and events and other narratives in ways we cannot always see. "Excellent job, you two," I said. "This is going to be a beautiful story, Nicole. Your best yet. I'm very proud of you. Could you send Fatma down next?"

"She's absent."

Miguel's Island

When Miguel showed me his map, I had trouble making sense of the shape.

"Where's your head?"

He pointed to a peninsula that looked like a squashed banana.

"That's your *head?*" I cried.

He giggled, saying, "I know!"

"Who traced your body?"

"Noelia."

That figured; Noelia doing her usual slapdash job.

Miguel said, "And look here: she made one fat sneaker and one skinny one!"

"Doesn't matter. Okay, who lives on your island?"

"Only me and sixty wolves."

"So it must be kind of lonely there?"

"No."

"Not lonely at all?"

"I don't speak any language."

"You can't be lonely if you don't speak language?"

"No."

"All right. Interesting. How long have you been on the island?"

"When I was five, I went with my family on a trip to Ecuador and we got in a terrible storm and we didn't have no shelter—"

"— any shelter—"

"—any shelter and we just swam onto the island and then my family left me here."

"Who's in your character's family?"

"It's my family! My father, my mom, and my three brothers, and they told me they was gonna go back and wait for a boat to take them back to New York and bring them over here."

"That doesn't make sense. Why would they leave one kid behind? It's too complicated. The point is, somehow you have to end up alone on the island. So: you're on a boat."

"Yeah."

"There's a storm."

"Yeah."

"The boat sinks."

"Yeah."

"You don't know what happens to your parents, you get separated in the storm. You land on this island."

"Yeah."

"Then what happens?"

"And then I meet these wolves and they take care of me. It would be like a parent showing me what to do and how to live. What to eat. How to hunt. And I've forgotten about everything human, I just eat raw meat and everything. I forget how to speak English and I'm acting like a wolf. I forgot everything about me."

"Wonderful! When does your story take place, Miguel? What time period?"

"It could take place on the date of my birthday."

"What is it with you and your birthday?" I said. "You use that a lot in your stories."

"Hey, yeah! I don't know why I do that."

It was interesting to see Miguel develop themes from earlier stories. His island story was to my mind a real advance, an evolution, quite mature and more believable. In his story about Tasia, the orphan who ran away with horses to live in the forest, her role was parental; Miguel's island-story hero, named Miguel, lived with wolves who parented him. And while Miguel's earlier character Marzolo magically turned into a red fox by night, his current hero acts like a wolf but remains human.

When the children wrote their island stories, I put Miguel at a table off to the side I called his "office," saying, "You're like me, Miguel. You can't write with lots of distractions around." He worked hard on his island story, which was long and had echoes of *The Island of the Blue Dolphins,* which he'd recently read. When Miguel told me his idea for an ending, I said, "That's brilliant!" and encouraged him to write it, even though I knew that it would make his mother sad. It did—"a little sad," she told me.

One day, I saw a small boat land on shore. Five people got off. Some memory of the past told me that they were friendly and would not harm me. The wolves were going to attack but I stopped them. When the five people saw me, they said, "Have you seen a man about twenty-years-old?" I just growled. The oldest human examined me and found that I had similarities with them.

They saw I was a man that looked the age of twenty, so they took me as their son. "Son," said my mom and dad, "we missed you so much! This is your brother Samuel, as you know, and here are Daniel and David who were born while you were stranded." I howled at them, unable to speak English.

They were going to take me but I turned my back and refused to go. But then they left me because they knew I wanted to stay on this island with my wolf pack and we continued having our adventures.

The Ludicrous Girl

A heat wave descended on New York with such humidity that everything was soggy, including my mind. The world seemed to move in slow motion, as if I were drugged. Because the school had no air-conditioning, I'd bought a fan for my office, which helped a little. I'd had story conferences all morning. Each lasted twenty minutes to an hour, and it was very hard work. As the morning dragged on, it was a struggle to stay awake. But the kids were at lunch now, so I put my head on the table, closed my eyes, and listened to the muffled sound of children in the class next door practicing their recorders in such slow and halting fashion that they turned "Twinkle, Twinkle, Little Star" into a dirge. I dozed off.

A knock at the door startled me awake. I shot up, shook myself, wiped the drool from my chin, and said, "Come in!"

It was Fatma.

"Fatma, at last! It's so good to see you back in school. You've been sick so much I haven't had a chance to congratulate you on winning the school spelling bee. Although I wasn't at all surprised."

"Thanks."

Though she was adept with language, Fatma's writing folder was even skimpier than Miguel's. But I knew she was writing. Like Harriet in *Harriet the Spy*, the book she loved so much, Fatma often scribbled in a notebook. Yet when I'd ask to see what she'd written, she'd slam the book shut and turn away, and so I kept my distance. She was very private.

On the day the children had written metaphors of themselves, Fatma had come up with two:

I'm like a folder,
all shut up
and only opened during a test,
to guard my master's papers from outsiders.
I feel like one of those red coats
in the Revolutionary War,
trying to guard my master and his side.

I'm a book
and my cover is ripped
and my back is dirty.
But the beauty of my pages
and the story is still there.
No one reads me,
even though my story is still there,
just because the cover is ripped
and my back is dirty.
As they all say,
"You can't judge a book by its cover."
But the problem is,
no one follows that moral.

As her poems suggest, Fatma kept the world at arm's length, then blamed the world for staying away. Perhaps it was this psychological dynamic that made sarcasm her natural mode of discourse: sneering as a mode of self-protection. Or maybe it was just the fact that Fatma had four teenage siblings and got her sarcasm from them. She produced her best story of the year when I asked the kids to write a story with a Fool. For the rest of the class, this lesson was a disaster. Creating a Fool was much harder than I'd thought. But it suited Fatma to a tee.

THE LUDICROUS GIRL

"Mom, Dad, I've got terrible news," said Lindsay Kay. Lindsay was a fourth grader. She was nine-years-old. She was a rather ridiculous girl. . . .
"M-m-m-my caa-n-n-ndy wr-wr-wr-ap-p-p-per d-d-died!" Lindsay managed to say, crying.
"What?! Your candy wrapper died? How can it die?" . . .
Adam and Chris, Lindsay's brothers, fell on the floor in helpless laughter. . . .

"Everyone follow me," said Lindsay.

She led them through the kitchen and the living room, and into their backyard. There she did the most ridiculous thing of all. "We are going to have a funeral for my Bubblegum Candy Wrapper," she said.

"Oh, all right, all right," everyone agreed nastily.

Then Lindsay went back in the house and five minutes later returned with a Styrofoam tombstone.

"She's lost her mind," said Adam.

The tombstone said:

> Here lies Bubblegum Candy Wrapper,
> My beloved sweet Bubblegum,
> She was my best Bubblegum
> And now that she's gone,
> I do not have any Candy Wrapper,
> I loved her so very much.

. . . Lindsay dug a little hole for Bubblegum Candy Wrapper. "I loved that Candy Wrapper," she said. "She was the best thing in the store."

Then she put some flowers around it and said, "Chris, I want you to say something nice about Bubblegum."

"Well, uh," Chris kept laughing here and there. "Bubblegum was very, uh, well . . . exotic. That is all I have to say."

"Mom, you go next," Lindsay said.

"Uh, well, I really didn't know Bubblegum, but I suppose she would have been nice."

"Adam, next."

"All I have to say is that, um, um . . . well, she was a very good candy wrapper."

"Dad, you go last," Lindsay said.

"Uh, Bubblegum was very, uh, useful. You could've wrapped up anything in her."

"Very well. And now this funeral of Bubblegum Candy Wrapper has ended." As Lindsay was saying this, her parents and her brothers fell on the grass laughing very hard. . . . "Well, I never!" cried Lindsay, and ran away.

Fatma's island map had almost no details. She'd roughly colored in her body island by pressing very hard with dark blue marker. It didn't look like a map so much as a silhouette. I asked if she had an idea for an island story.

She said, "Um, I've been thinking about it, but I'm not really sure."

"Who's the hero of your story going to be?"

"I don't know. A scientist."

"Okay, good. What's he or she like?"

"Mmmmm . . . kinda weird. He could be a Native American. And uh, he's kind of crazy, right, so he's kind of like a mad scientist who wants to blow up the world and everything."

I had the feeling she'd come up with this idea not because she wanted to tell that story but because she wanted to be shocking. Fatma seemed so troubled, so subterranean, as if there were volcanic rumblings inside her, waiting to explode. I often felt that she was toying with me, a puppeteer tugging the strings of her teacher marionette, keeping him off balance. I proceeded cautiously and said, "Um, okay, sure, why not? A scientist blowing up the world. . . . Why does he do this?"

"Because he hates all the white settlers that came. They sort of ruined the earth because they polluted, you know, and like trashed and everything and so he wants to blow up the world."

"All right. . . . But I think you need another character, don't you?"

She shrugged.

"Suppose the scientist has a child," I suggested. "How would the kid feel about his or her father blowing up the world?"

Now it was my turn to be manipulative. I wanted her to give the scientist a child not for the story's sake, but for Fatma's. I wanted her to imagine a child who would be the voice of reason and morality, a child who'd want to grow up, be happy, have a family, reach a ripe old age, and would beg her father not to bomb the planet. I wanted Fatma to imagine a character who would bring the scientist to the light, in the hope that that would bring Fatma to the light.

"If I were the kid," Fatma replied, "I'd be excited. I would *want* him to blow up the world."

"Why? You don't like the world?"

"It would be cool."

Who was this girl? How much of my idea of her was fed by my own fantasies? To what extent had I invented Fatma, based on how she'd hurt me? When I told friends she'd told me, "I hate you," they laughed and said, "Oh, Sam. It's obvious she has a crush on you." Maybe so, I guess, but still: Who wants to be loved like that?

I didn't like the way the conference was going. This story wasn't about a scientist, not really; it was about something else, something I couldn't see or understand. I tried to gain the upper hand by playing to Fatma's strong suit. I said, "I know what you could do! You could write a really funny island story, a story like 'The Ludicrous Girl.' It could be about a bumbling scientist whose attempts to destroy the world backfire in ridiculous ways." I looked at her, hoping to see her face light up. "What do you think?"

"I like it," she said, nodding unenthusiastically.

"Good," I said, then quickly added, "but you could also write something else entirely. It's up to you."

In the end, Fatma wrote something, but it was only a paragraph long. I returned it to her, saying, "I'm sure you know this wasn't your best effort. But don't worry. This happens to writers all the time. When your heart's not in it, it's hard to write well." I suggested she start over, write a new island story, or even write a story with no island at all. But she insisted she was going to rewrite the one she'd started. Later, when I asked her for her second draft, she said she hadn't been able to do it because she'd lost her first draft and her island map, as well. I didn't believe her. I figured she'd thrown them in the trash.

At the time, I thought Fatma was being lazy. But now I wonder if there wasn't something else going on. Had I been like the white settlers on her island? Had I taken over Fatma's story, poked around in ways she didn't want, made suggestions that she didn't like, and so ruined everything that she'd decided just to blow the whole thing up?

The Black Plain

"What a wonderful shape you made for your island, Su Jung. It almost looks like you're praying. It's nicely drawn, too. Your lines are confident, and your colors are beautiful. I love the way the purples and blues are set off by these touches of pink and green. Really, it's just lovely."

I was sitting with Su Jung and MeiKai, whom Su Jung adored. I'd asked MeiKai to be part of this conference, hoping that would make it easier for Su Jung to talk.

My year with Su Jung had had its ups and downs. One day we'd talk about a story, compare experiences in our Presbyterian Sunday schools, or giggle as she told me about her younger brother's farts. On other days, she couldn't or wouldn't talk, and once I told her she had to talk or write or else go back to class. I gave her three minutes. She sat there, stone-faced, and watched the clock for three minutes exactly, then without a word gathered her writing folder and returned to the classroom.

Most of Su Jung's stories were sad, if not tragic—even brutal. I wondered if her stories might be partly a reflection of her native Korean culture. Once I asked the kids to bring in tales from the countries of their heritage. Su Jung's, told to her by her grandmother, was about a tiger who tells a woman he'll eat her unless she gives him all her possessions. She does, but then he eats her anyway. I figured this was Korean humor, and sometimes it seemed Su Jung's stories drew on that. In another story, meant to be funny, Su Jung wrote of "two horrible, nasty, disgusting, and irritating women" who "would kill people, pretend they were meat, and then sell it to the stores," but then the police came and killed the women. Ha, ha!

After a while, reading Su Jung's dreary stories got depressing. I told myself that at least her imagination was an honest one and didn't sugar-coat the world. I kept hoping her stories would help her work things through, get to a better place, but she kept writing the same unhappy endings over and over again. I came to dread reading Su Jung's stories, and I think she dreaded writing them.

"Su Jung, why don't you take us on a tour of your island?"

She said, "At the head of the island blah blah blah blah."

Firmly, I said, "Su Jung, today you have to talk."

Su Jung looked at me, lips pursed, saying nothing.

MeiKai tried to be helpful. She said, "I used to be like Su Jung. In first grade, we were in the same class. Remember, Su Jung? I was like that: Never talk."

"How did you overcome that?" I asked.

"Well, the teacher was gonna tell my mom, and my mom is very strict about things like homework and grades, so I just started talking."

"You forced yourself."

"Yeah. Now I can talk."

"You can do it, Su Jung," I said.

"Su Jung, pleeeeze," said MeiKai.

Long silence.

MeiKai said, "We're gonna stay here foreverrrrr."

I wasn't angry, but I told Su Jung, as I had told her many times, that I had other children to see, that I was behind schedule. I asked her please to understand and help me out. I said, "You have no idea how much I want to help you. But we can't just sit here and be quiet. It's not fair to the other kids. This is your time. Use it."

For a few minutes we sat quietly, patiently. Every now and then we smiled at one another. When it became clear she wasn't going to talk, I tried another tactic. As if nothing had happened, I looked at her map and said, "This is an interesting feature. Why did you name these the Choke Mountains?"

"'Cause you get sick, choke, and some people die."

She'd spoken, but I was careful not to make a big deal of it.

"And what about this?" I asked. "What's Anger Rock?"

"Whenever somebody's angry, they go on the rock and something happens and they're not angry anymore."

"Wonderful. You know, I could use that rock sometimes."

"When I don't talk you could use that rock."

"Do I get angry with you or just frustrated?"

"Frustrated, but I think sometimes you do get angry."

"Maybe a little angry," I agreed.

Our three heads leaned over the map, studying her island. "You've also got a Sorrow River," I said. "What's that?"

"Sorrow River is so thick that it takes years and years and years to cross and by the time you do, you're dead."

"Rivers aren't 'thick,'" I corrected her. "You mean 'wide.'"

"Yeah, wide."

I said, "And what about the Spike Mountains up north?"

"You can't climb them," said Su Jung. "'Cause there are spikes sticking out of the side, like a cactus."

"Okay, that's good."

Then I asked about the most remarkable element on her map, a black shape with a sun in its center. It divided her island in half, crossing her waist, filling her stomach. To me, it looked as if her praying figure was pregnant with a nighttime sun.

Su Jung didn't know what this mysterious black shape was. She said, "It might be a wall."

"Why is the sun there?"

"It's a carving of a sun."

"I see."

"It might not be a wall," she decided, picking up the map to look at it more closely. "It might just be a very tall flat rock, then they won't know there's a carving of a sun unless they climb the rock."

"Yeah, maybe the rock has stairs that go up it," I suggested.

"It could have a ladder," said Su Jung. "But then the village people, they never dared to go up there."

"Why not?"

"They was afraid something might be up there."

"What might make them afraid?"

"Maybe this thing is bigger than a mountain," she said. "Maybe they think God's up there, and God will get mad if they go up."

"So in your story someone maybe warns them, some wise person tells them it's forbidden to go up there. There's lot of ways you could take this story."

MeiKai said, "Or if he go up there, he gets hit by fire or it's going to be really hot and you melt."

"That could work," I agreed. "You could have characters saying you'll be destroyed by fire and others who say no, that's not right, God is up there . . ."

"But they don't know which one is real," added Su Jung.

"Yes," I said. "So this could be a story about a brave girl who one day decides . . ."

"To go up there," said Su Jung.

My heart leapt into my throat. I sensed she was on the brink of a breakthrough. Could a story change her life? I said, "What will she find up there on this great flat expanse?"

"Gold!" cried MeiKai.

I was repelled by this idea, so materialistic and crass, and was relieved when Su Jung didn't take to the suggestion either. She was thinking hard.

"I want to put Anger Rock in the story," she said.

"Yes," I agreed. "I think that's very important. It could be a really good way to start your story, to have your girl get very angry. What could make her angry?"

MeiKai said, "Her pet flew over the mountain."

"But I don't think she'd go to Anger Rock first," Su Jung said. "If my pet flew up there, I would go up the mountain first."

"But you're so angry!" said MeiKai, passionately. "You can't climb it! You're unh! Angry!"

Su Jung nodded, seeing MeiKai's point.

I said, "This doesn't need to be decided now. The point is something makes her angry and she goes to Anger Rock. What does Anger Rock feel like to the touch?"

"Cold," said Su Jung. "When you touch it, it will cool you down probably. And that's the way how it works."

I began jotting down notes for her. I said, "Okay, so she has a pet bird or something, and it flies off over the mountain."

Su Jung fell silent. She appeared to be studying her island objectively, as if someone else had drawn it. Struck by the way the black shape divided it in two, she said, "Up here, on this side of the mountain, a whole village lives, and down here only the girl lives."

"She's by herself," I said.

"Yeah, she's by herself," said Su Jung. "And the mountain is huge, like heaven."

"It could be a beautiful scene, when she climbs up the mountain and sees the other half of the island she'd never seen before."

"The carving of the sun, it could shine," said Su Jung. "She gets to the top and there's this big shiny light."

"Beautiful!" I said.

Suddenly Su Jung looked at the clock. "We have to go to band now!" she gasped. "We're late!"

They left in such a hurry that Su Jung forgot to take her island with her. I sat there alone, looking at her lovely island and feeling amazed and elated and hopeful.

Some days later, when the kids were writing their stories, Su Jung concentrated intently. She'd pause and stare into space, thinking, then return to the page. It took her several days to finish her first draft, and when she did, she looked exhausted. In the end, this was her haunting, ambiguous story:

THE BLACK PLAIN

Once upon a time on a deserted island with no name, there lived a girl named Lisa who was 15. She had a brother who had disappeared. Lisa also had a pet bird named Teeko. Lisa's father had died climbing Choke Mountain when Lisa was 12.

On the island, everything was eerie and strange. . . . There was a big wall with sun carvings and lots and lots of stairs. Her father had told her not to go up the stairs of the wall because if she does, the Earth would break apart. Lisa was angry that her father didn't let her go up the wall, but now she was furious that her pet Teeko had flown up the wall. Now, she was completely lonely.

She went to Anger Rock and when she touched Anger Rock, it was as cold as the Antarctic's icebergs. Soon, she felt better. Lisa started going up the stairs to find her bird, Teeko. She kept on going up the stairs.

She finally reached the top and saw a large plain. It was so black and there was nothing on the plain. Then she saw a boy painting the sky. He looked a lot like her brother. Lisa shouted, "Mike! Mike!" but all of a sudden, no one was there. She was just daydreaming. Lisa went to the middle of the plain. Lisa named it the Black Plain.

Lisa went to the other end and saw the other half of the island. She had always thought that behind the wall would be all dark, but it was beautiful. She named everything on the other half.

She went down the wall, got all her belongings, and brought them to the top of the wall, and that was her new home.

Party Island

Telling me their stories was the easy part. Writing them down was work. Most kids, I discovered, wrote a lot better in class than they did at home. Because I had the time, the children were able to do their first, second, and third drafts in school. Here are excerpts from my editorial letters:

Dear Aaron,

I like "Rex Island" a lot. But don't let your characters see the dinosaurs right away. Let them discover their presence slowly. They could see the footprints, perhaps, or hear strange sounds. Perhaps they find some skeletons. And use more dialogue.

Dear Maya,

This is very inventive and very ambitious. But I'd cut the first and second paragraphs completely. Cut to the chase, have Louise find the gigantic evil tree sooner, and be sure to describe it more fully. (Any tree near your home you could study?) I have trouble picturing the tree speaking. Does it have a mouth?

Dear Ella,

You have some really great images in this story, especially the green head and those horrifying giant fingers that grow on your island. The biggest problem is that you don't have a story yet. This is all description and no plot.

Dear MeiKai,

There is a lot of very good writing in this story. . . . You need to introduce the giant egg earlier, and you need to describe it. . . . And don't have the parents come to get the girl. That's too easy. Make her go to them. After all, getting what you want in life isn't easy. You have to struggle.

In their finished stories, six of the children's protagonists had always lived on their islands. The rest arrived following shipwrecks, except for Cesar's astronaut and Aliza's heroine, who'd been such a nuisance on an airplane that the stewardess had tossed her out the door. Eleven characters washed up on their islands' shores alone, the others with siblings or friends. All the protagonists were the same gender as their authors, except for the heroines in Cesar's and Matthew's tales.

Some islands had other inhabitants, not all of them friendly, and a few had talking animals, not all of them trustworthy. Seventeen islands were magical or fantastical, and six of those harbored monsters, like Carolina's Giant Cockroach, Ashley's Lion Queen, and Rosie's Princess of All Evil. Whether human or not, evil characters were either killed or banished, although Maya's malicious, gigantic talking tree survived triumphant.

Eleven stories were humorous, six had morals, four were horror stories, and thirteen were tales of adventure. Death made an appearance in a majority of the stories, and four included the tragic death of a loved one. I counted twelve heroes who saved the day, and most did so on their own. A few, however, got outside help, and MeiKai had a "deus ex machina" in the form of a "lady"—reminiscent of the Queen Mother of the West—who appeared to the story's heroine in a dream, telling her she needed to go home because her mother missed her.

Only a handful of characters returned to home and family at the story's conclusion. The vast majority stayed put, the young heroes independent, like the heroine in Matthew's story, which ended: "Ever afterwards and never again did I expect someone to do something for me. And I lived on the island for a very, very long time."

During the last days of the school year, we acted out the island stories in a two-day marathon. (Fatma was the only one who didn't have a story to perform.) The performance I remember best, though, and the one that makes me happy still, was of Ashley's "Party Island." Ashley, who was part Thai and part Chinese, had a radiant beauty. I have a poignant memory of her father. He walked Ashley to school each morning, and one day

I saw him standing outside the courtyard gate, watching Ashley play before the starting bell. He was oblivious to everything but her, his face expressing total, helpless love.

Ashley, who had recently had a birthday (but no party), made a map that was brightly, joyously colorful. Her island was called Party Island, and it featured the Disco Mountains, the Tap Dancing River, the Popcorn Beach, and the Balloon Tree Forest. At the end of her island story, all the characters dance, and when we finished acting it out in class, Simon had an inspiration. He put a tape in the boom box, and as the music played, the children, in a spontaneous show of collective joy, got up and danced. Everybody danced! Ashley danced, Cesar danced, Fatma danced! Even Miguel, whose religion forbade it, danced! School was nearly over, it was summer, and they danced! The children danced!

All of them, that is, but one. Su Jung stayed seated, smiling awkwardly, embarrassed, perhaps ashamed, and I knew how she felt. I wasn't dancing, either.

The Tree Project

� ✳ ❀

A Tree Is

As I walked through Central Park to the subway on my first day back that September, already leaves were beginning to turn. I was looking forward to the year with equal parts pleasure and dread, excited by the project I had planned but conscious that this would be my last year with these children, which meant the coming months would be a long good-bye and I'd be sad.

It was hot in their new classroom, an attic space with windows by the ceiling. Any breeze blew uselessly above our heads, and the students had nothing to stare out at when bored. Adding to this oppressiveness, the room was smaller, the children were bigger, and the number of students in the class had grown by nearly a third. Immigrant communities aren't stable, but that year an unexpectedly large number of families had moved into the neighborhood, and an unexpectedly small number had moved out, taking the school by surprise. No child could be turned away, of course, room must be found, so instead of twenty-eight kids, I had thirty-six, which made my task harder and sadder; with so many students, too much fell between the cracks. It was weeks before everyone had a desk; and once the added furniture was squeezed in, there was no room for displays or worktables. But at least we weren't as cramped as the bilingual class down the hall; there were forty-five kids in that room and their teacher was in tears.

My students' new teacher was Mrs. Hinton, an African American raised in New York and educated in its public schools. She'd been teaching fifth grade for a good many years and was gentle, steady, unflappable, and inscrutable. Although always polite and cooperative, she was distant and guarded with me. But she made the kids feel safe and loved, and they adored her.

I introduced the topic we'd be writing about throughout the year by asking, "What's a tree?"

"It's like a big tall plant," said Ella.

"A big plant, yes, but with a woody stem. Good."

I wrote "big plant with woody stem" on the blackboard, the start of a list. "What are the parts of a tree?"

Hands went up: Trunk. Leaves. Roots.

"Yes, good," I said, and added these words to the list. "What else?"

More hands: Wood. Bark. Branches. Twigs.

"Good," I said, and wrote those down. "Anything else?"

Silence.

"You studied trees a bit last year, didn't you? What's the green stuff in the leaves?"

Miguel, who always surprised me with the things that he remembered, said, "Chloro something?"

"Chlorophyll."

"Oh, yeah . . ."

And "chlorophyll" was written down.

"Can you name some trees from your native countries?"

"Palm," said Lucinda, from Puerto Rico.

"Ginkgo," said MeiKai, from China.

"Banyan," said Rosie, from India.

"Good," I said, and wrote them down. "Name other trees."

Maple. Oak. Redwood.

"Christmas trees," said Amarjeet.

"Yes, good," I said, and added all of those. "What do trees give us?"

"Oxygen and stuff," said Miguel.

"They clean the air of pollution," said Rosie.

"Yes!"

"What else do trees give us? Cesar?"

"Wood to build."

"Be specific! Build what?"

"Houses?"

"Yes. What else? Look around the room."

Eyes darted everywhere and kids shouted out the words I'd write: Chairs! Desks! Floor! Door! Pencils! Bookcase! Rulers! Flagpole! Broom!

"Keep going! What else in the world is made from wood?"

Clarinets! Ladders! Violins! Swings! Fences! Bridges! Boats! Chopsticks!

"What about food? What kind of food do trees give us?"

Apples! Oranges! Coconuts! Cherries! Peaches! Plums!

"Blueberries!" said Jessica.

"Actually, no. Blueberries grow on bushes, I think, not trees. What about nuts?"

Oh, yeah! Walnuts! Chestnuts! Almonds! Pistachios! Pecans!

"What other foods?"

Silence.

"Think pancakes . . ."

"Maple syrup! Maple syrup! Maple syrup!"

"Syrup" was added to the list. So was "firewood"—fuel for cooking, fuel for warmth.

"What do trees need to survive? What do they eat?"

"Water."

"Yes, mixed with minerals from the ground," I said. "What do leaves make, using energy from the sun?"

"Starch," said Miguel.

"Good! Does anyone remember what that process is called?"

Silence. I can see them searching: *Uh, uh, uh* . . . I wrote it on the board: "photosynthesis."

"Oh, yeah!"

"What else? What do trees give on a hot summer day?"

"Shade!"

"What fun things can you do with trees?"

"A base for tag!"

"Hide-and-seek!"

"You tie your jump rope to them."

"Climb them!"

"Yes! Oh, yes, yes, yes! When I was young, that was my favorite thing to do. How many here have climbed a tree?"

Three hands went up, no more, which broke my heart: ten years old and never climbed a tree! Out of all the things in a poor city kid's life, this made me saddest: how little time they spent outside. The school didn't even have recess, which was both tragedy and outrage, a kind of child abuse, one practiced by more schools in America than most people think. Without exposure to the outdoors, I worried, what kind of grown-ups would these children become?

I asked the class, "What about birds? How do they use trees? Nicole?"

"For nests?"

"That's right." "Nests" went on the list.

"What other animals do you see in trees?"

"Cats climb them and jump on you," said Rafael.

"Good! And no one's mentioned dogs. How do dogs use trees?"

That got a laugh, but it was true, so "place to pee" was added, too.

"What happens to trees in fall? Su Jung?"

"They change color."

"What colors specifically?"

"Red, yellow, orange."

"Purple!"

"Pink!"

"Yes! Yes! Yes! Let's have other adjectives. Describe a tree."

"Majestic," said Rosie.

"Beautiful," said Su Jung.

"When the leaves are gone, the tree is ugly," said Ella.

"They scare me!" said MeiKai.

"Always?" I said.

"Yeah, always at night."

I wrote down "beautiful" and "ugly" and "scary at night." I said, "What sounds do trees make?"

"Trees don't make sounds," said Jessica.

"Yes they do!" said Simon. "When comes the wind, they do like whoooosh!"

"Excellent! What other sounds?"

Okan made a creaking noise and Gary cried out, "Crash! Timberrrrr!"

"Yes! Yes!" I said and wrote it all down quickly, the list was growing fast and I was running out of room. I had to stick words sideways, cram them in the margins.

"Wait a second, let's back up! We forgot to mention bugs!"

"Ewwww," said MeiKai. "I hate bugs."

"How do bugs use trees?"

"Sometimes they eat leaves," said Okan.

Simon cried out, "Termites! Termites eat the wood!"

"Bugs" and "ewwww" and "eating leaves" and "termites"—all were added to our list.

"Who else are enemies of trees?"

That was obvious, and lots of happy kids cried, "Humans!" at which point Aaron raised his hand and slyly said, "But writers are the most worst enemies of trees 'cause they write books that murder trees!"

"Yeah!" they shouted. "Mr. Swope is a murderer! Call the cops!"

I wrote down "humans" and I wrote down "writers," too, then added "drought" and "flood" and "fire." By now our list was wonderfully long and could be longer still, but we'd done well, and it was time to write.

I love the first class of the year, all of us so eager, notebooks fresh and new, still tidy, everyone determined to do well.

"We made this list so we could write a special kind of poem," I told the class. "A list poem."

Poets have always been in love with lists. Homer has his sailors; Virgil, his kings; the Bible, its begats; Milton enumerates the angels; Rabelais, foods; Whitman catalogs New York; and Browning counts the ways. Not to mention Old MacDonald and his farm, the silly old woman who swallowed a fly, and the song that teaches us the ABC's. I pointed out how lists are kind of like a chant. I said they often employ repetition. I told the kids that poets sometimes break the pattern, though, to add variety and some surprise. I showed them, as examples, list poems written by young children Kenneth Koch had taught, then read them this from Charles Boer's wonderful translation of Ovid's *Metamorphoses* (no matter if they didn't get all of the words, they'd hear its music, catch the spell):

> . . . on hill a vast flat area, green
> with grass but no shade; when god-born
> poet sits here & strums resonant chords
> shade comes: the Chaonian tree & Helida forest
> of poplars, the high-leaved oak, soft lindens,
> beech, Daphnesque laurel, fragile hazels,
> ash (god spear trees), knotless firs,
> berry-bent acorns, friendly sycamores,
> colorful maples, river-dweller willows,
> water lotus, evergreen boxwood,
> thin tamarisks, double-colored myrtles,
> blueberried viburnums.
>
> you came too, flex-footed ivy,
> tendrilled vines & elms in vine-dress, mountain

> ash & pine, wild strawberries & palm,
> the reward of conquerors; & pine, hair up in leafy
> tops, favored by Cybele, gods' mother, since
> Attis shed human form for its hard trunk;
> cone-shaped (like race-course markers) cypress
> is there: tree now, but once a boy loved
> by god of bow-string & lyre string, Apollo.

I lifted back the cover from a giant tablet, and with light green marker wrote "A tree is" on the first line of the page. I said, "Each line of our poems will begin with those three words. Let's do some as a class. Who has a first line? Rosie?"

"A tree is brave."

"Good," I said, and wrote that down. "Another?"

Jessica said, "A tree is still and quiet."

Miguel said, "A tree is as full of life as the ocean."

"Okay, good," I said—but truthfully, I wasn't that impressed. I said, "Remember metaphor? Take a second now and close your eyes. Picture a tree. What do you see? What does a tree remind you of?"

Noelia got excited, shouted, "A tree is a lollipop of God!"

MeiKai said, "A tree is a big stiff statue."

Jorge said, "A tree is a pigeon hotel."

I said, "Now you're talking!" and after writing out those lines, I decided they were ready. "Okay, guys. Try writing on your own."

Everyone wrote, but when their exercises were handed in, just a few felt anything like poems or approached the rhythmic fever that can be a list. Most were monotones, a shopping list, but even some of those had a line or two that seemed inspired, or anyway fun, which was all that I could reasonably expect. Here's a selection:

> *A tree is like air, as quiet as can be.*
> *A tree is the shadow of God.*
> *A tree is patience, everyone's patience.*
> *A tree is brave, it doesn't run.*
> *A tree is a greedy old water sucker.*
> *A tree is a waterfall upside down.*
> *A tree is like a kid playing with the wind.*

A tree is a long bony jungle gym.
A tree is a place to be in when you are sad.

There was a single poem, though, that dazzled and startled me the way magnolia trees in blossom do. It was written by Maya, a Guyanese girl of Indian descent. With thick black hair, butternut skin, and huge red glasses (like a clown's), she'd always been so eager to please that it was hard to get to know her.

Maya, the oldest of three children, was lucky in her parents, who'd grown up in Guyana. Both were passionately devoted to their children's educations. No sacrifice was too great. So that his wife could stay at home to care for the kids and supervise their homework, Maya's father, a hospital technician, worked two jobs. He did this gratefully and told me, "We complain about this country, and it's not perfect, but nowhere else in the world do you have so much opportunity, can you choose what you want to be. I get tears in my eyes when I hear the 'Stars and Stripes.' Sometimes I cry right out loud. I love this country. I love New York City. When I went back to Guyana, and at eight o'clock the lights went out and everyone was going to bed, I said, 'Go to bed? At eight o'clock?! That's not what we do at home!' Mother said, 'This is your home.' I said, 'No, Mother, it isn't. Not anymore.'"

Maya was an excellent student and an enthusiastic writer who always did her homework, without complaint. But I'm sure she sensed that her writing never really captured my attention—not the way it did that day, the day she blossomed, found her voice, and made magic out of words:

A tree is a wedding gown in the spring
A tree is a giant Chinese fan
A tree is a great messenger of God
A tree is Mother Nature's child
    Strawberry trees!!
    Maple trees!!
A tree is a daycare center for baby birds
A tree is the giver of air
A tree is the reader of clouds.
    Apple trees!!
    Cherry trees!!

A tree is God's wig.
A tree conceals a beautiful story.
 Coconut trees!
 Palm trees!
A tree is a dog's toilet.
Scrapes the sky!
In the middle of nowhere,
Surrounded by vicious animals
A tree is an angel's choir.
 Red trees!
 Green trees!
A tree tells God about the sights on earth.
A tree is suffering in the desert.
A tree is a wise ancient teller of sense.
A tree is a tree.

When Maya finished writing, she was breathless, flushed, and looked as if she just might swoon. She'd always rushed when writing, though, which meant her stories were sloppy and incomplete. I'd forever be telling her, "Slow down! Don't hurry so!" but it did no good. She had no choice; writing was a passionate business for her, and if she didn't race, she'd never get it out. Her favorite genre was horror, and her stories were haunted by ghosts and evil spirits and children who came to bloody, grisly, "cursed" ends. I flamed her passion all I could, and when I asked her once why she loved horror so, she said, "It's just fun to have a chill go down your spine," and that made sense to me. Horror *is* sensual, making the heart pound and the skin crawl, but Maya also understood that it was a game. The quality I most admired in her horror was its humor, for Maya loved a laugh as well as a shiver, and her bubbly giggle was a delight to hear, burbling up from her tummy.

You can't predict what topic will inspire a child, but for Maya, in fifth grade, that topic was the tree, and it became her steadfast muse the whole year long.

"This is a beautiful poem," I told her.

"Really? You liked it?" she said, wanting to hear me say it again.

"I liked it a lot."

"Oh, thank you, Mr. Swope," she said, sweetly grateful.

I made a fuss about Maya's poem, typed it up and gave each kid a copy. I also showed it to her teachers, who were all impressed and told her so: "Wow, Maya!" Of course her parents were proud; her father said the poem made him think of Wordsworth. So Maya, told she'd written something special, sent her poem off to contests, won a prize or two, and got it published, saw her name in print.

If Maya does become a writer, most likely she will say this poem was a cornerstone of her career, and it will make her feel nostalgia for the days when words came easy in a joyous rush. If she doesn't, maybe years from now she'll come across her poem in a dusty box and say, "Oh, I remember this!" then think, "Not bad!" and wonder if she missed her calling.

Dear Tree

I grew up in Gettysburg, Pennsylvania, an old-fashioned American town with lots of trees. Early photographs of my childhood home, which was built in 1911, show a small, hopeful pine just off the front porch. By the time I was born, that pine was taller than the house. It was a perfect tree, with limbs like a ladder that made it easy to climb, and lots of branches to shield me from view. Nobody else used it; it was my secret hiding place. I would sit in it and watch the world and no one ever saw me.

I remember other trees. The pin oaks along the curb. The hedge of bristly hemlocks. The tamarack. Out back was a delicate tree, whose name no one knew. It held one end of Mother's clothesline; the other end was tied to the walnut tree, which Mother never liked because it was so "messy," dropping leaves throughout the summer. Behind the garage, there was the maple in which my brother built his tree house. But I got my love of trees from Dad. As a boy, I helped him plant a holly, a ginkgo, a locust, and a pink dogwood, which was his favorite tree of all. Yet Father never thought of any tree as "his" or even "ours." It was always "the" dogwood, "the" pine, "the" walnut. He knew he was just taking care of them, and that they'd be around long after he was gone.

There's another childhood tree burned into my memory, a white pine down the alley. The neighbors' cat got stuck in it one day, and their son climbed up to save it. But the tree's branches grew near a high-voltage line, which the boy touched. He died instantly. It was a while before anyone found him, and when they did the firemen weren't able to carry his body down for an hour, not until the power was shut off. I still see his body, limp in the tree. He was missing a shoe; his sneaker had somehow come off and fallen to the ground.

Throughout my childhood I was intimate with trees, but I never thought about them much. No one ever asked me to. They were just there, part of my world.

Dear Tree,

I know this sounds odd but I want to adopt you. This was a project from Mr. Swope and he told us to adopt a tree and to keep it all year long. I'm happy that we got this assignment 'cause I never really paid any attention to you.

My name is Sarah and you can see me from my apartment window. It's the one with the bright light. I will take very good care of you. I am responsible and have lots of time for you.

Sometimes I feel like you're just looking at me and what I do. Do you feel lonely when no one's paying attention to you, or when people are working and kids are in school?

Your leaves are changing colors and that's because you have to lose them and it's getting colder. You are a very big tree and I hope you live long.

Well, I have to go now. Bye!

Sincerely,
Sarah

Dear Tree,

I've sometimes looked at you when I'm sad or happy. I even spoke to you when my uncle died. I felt very lonely. I sometimes call myself dumb for talking to the tree right in front of me.

When I was a three-year-old boy I used to whistle at some pretty girls out my window, but hey, I was just three! I didn't know anything. So it would mean a lot to me if you would let me adopt you so you could be my best tree to talk to.

Your good friend,
Cesar

Dear Maple Tree,

When I look at you I see tallness. I see your bark but I can't see your canopy since you are so tall and I am just a midget. Plus I live on the first floor. I hate seeing plastic bags hanging from your branches. I see leaves that have fallen from your branches. I also see you standing nice and tall. I just love hearing you blowing in the wind.

Sincerely,
Nicole

Dear Tree,
I think we are the same age! Isn't that cool! Maybe we like the same things like I love water and the hot sun! You must like it because you need that to live! And you know what? When I was two I ate dirt! And I liked it!

Your pal,
Aaron

I've always enjoyed getting mail, and when the kids were in third grade, for homework I asked them to write me letters: "Tell me something about you that you think I'd like to know." Because they'd never written a letter, I had to start from scratch. I handed out envelopes and taught the kids how to fill them out. I said, "Most people don't know this, but you're allowed to draw pictures on an envelope, and that's a nice thing to do." I showed them sheets of colorful, interesting special-edition stamps. I said, "The post office sells two kinds of stamps, interesting ones and boring ones. When you grow up, please don't be the sort of person who chooses the boring stamps."

I told them, "After you've written your letters and sealed the envelopes, put the letter in a mailbox. I don't want you to put them in a slot at the post office—it has to be a proper mailbox on the street." I emphasized that they must mail the letters themselves; no parent was to do it for them. I wanted the children to have the experience of standing on tiptoe, pulling back the hinged lid, trying to see in, then placing the letter in the box's mouth and pulling their hands back before it snapped shut.

Over the next several days, I got a lot of mail from my beginning writers:

Dear Mr. Swope,
I hope you like my stories. Ashley told me she liked my story Watch out for Michael Johnston. I think you're funny. Can you get me a birthday present? Write back.

Your little writer,
Noelia

Dear Mr. Swope,

I have nothing to say but the only thing I could say is I played baseball. I love it and wanted to play agen. But no one wanted to play. The letter is short but. Can you come to my house neckts?

Senciry,

Aaron

Dear Sam Swope,

My life isn't very good you know, like your mom telling you what to do and getting a headige and doing homework and hearing Okan's bad jokes and starving while your mom, sister, and little sister play. I can't take it anymore.

Your buddy,

Rafael

I have a pleasant memory of sitting at my desk, writing replies, addressing envelopes, and licking stamps. After that assignment, every now and then I'd get a letter from out of the blue, but none came with better news than the one Su Jung sent the summer before fifth grade.

Dear Mr. Swope,

It is ten o' two at night. I'm lying on the bed that used to be my father's but now it's all mine. It's very big. It's a queen sized bed. My father moved. Before I tell you where and why he moved, I have something to confess. I told you my mom was in Korea, right? Well, my parents are divorced and I don't have a clue where my mom is. I didn't tell anyone this fact because I was ashamed but now I'm not. My father is getting remarried. But some times I still wish I was living with my birth mother. My father moved in with my stepmother and I'll move after fifth grade. My stepmother is nice. I like her a lot. She's not a total stranger because we went and still are going to the same church. Let's talk about something else. . . .

Letters are so quiet and intimate, and I was hoping that by writing to their trees, the kids would develop a relationship with them. Something like that happened for much of the class, but in life and in the classroom, you can't please everyone, and letters, as Fatma would remind me, are sometimes written with a poison pen.

Dear Tree,

Hey, man, hey babe, what's up? Like whatever! (Ha ha) You probably don't know me, but I want to adopt you. I know it sounds stupid, but I have to do this. For homework. We have to understand you guys and adopt and uh, you know, uh, study about you and other trees. So you're a great tree. And my teacher Mr. Swope says we have to write all about ourselves, even though I don't want to, because, I mean, come on, whatever I do is private, right? I can write all about you in my private notebook. But no way whatsoever am I going to tell you more extra things, like my secrets, especially the two BIGGEST secrets of all. And I know you're reading this, Mr. Swope, because sooner or later you had to edit this. I'm sure that my letter is different from everyone else because everyone else is gullible enough to write everything about themselves, but I'm not. You really do practice alot, don't you, Mr. Swope? And I really don't want to have a big conversation on this because it's no big deal. So let's just move on, people.

Your (legal) guardian,
Fatma

The Park

The day was perfect for a field trip—not too hot, not too cold, and lots of sunshine.

Gary, Simon, and Mateo had the task of reading the subway map and figuring out our route. They'd done well and brought us right to Central Park, where the leaves were colorful and bright. As we left the city gray for autumn color, the change was as dramatic as when Dorothy enters Oz.

Our final year was shaping up to be the best yet. For the first time, we had a patron. A paper manufacturer wanted to publish a book the class would write and illustrate, a book documenting our year with trees. It would be called *The Tree Book,* and the paper company planned to give copies to customers as a sample of its best paper. In return for our work, the company provided the class with boxes of different kinds of fine paper, art supplies, cameras, and film (processing included). Each kid would also get copies of the book, a book that would seal trees and what the children wrote about them into memory in ways I never could.

The thought of being published in a book was thrilling to the kids—a real book!—but I'd warned them it would be a lot of work. I said, "If we take on this project, it's a big responsibility. We have to work hard and see it through. Are you willing to work hard?"

"Yes, we'll work hard!"

All this was wonderful enough, but the best thing about *The Tree Book,* as far as I was concerned, was that it gave me a reason to get the kids outside in every season.

My plan was to take the class on numerous field trips to Central Park, at least two full days each month. The first hurdle was getting the support of Mrs. Hinton, who had responsibility for the class and would have to come along on our trips. Although Mrs. Hinton didn't seem much interested in language arts (the class didn't read a full book together that year), she loved the idea of the kids spending so much time in the park. But she doubted I'd ever get permission from the principal.

When I made my case to Mrs. Scalise, however, she immediately said yes. "How else will you get material for *The Tree Book*?" she said.

And so I began to plan our days in Central Park, days we'd spend studying trees as well as drawing, photographing, and writing about them in poetry and prose. "Check the weather forecast on the morning of a field trip," I'd tell the class. "If it's going to be cold, wear layers. And don't wear anything you can't get dirty!" On field trip days, each child had to pack a lunch as well as their nature journal, two writing pencils, a set of colored pencils, a pencil sharpener, and a magnifying glass.

If you want to study trees, Central Park is hard to beat. The park is vast, so big you can get lost in it, so big they say that you can see it from a spaceship. Because it has so many trees (some twenty-six thousand), migrating birds passing over the greater metropolitan area stop in, making it an excellent site for bird-watching, especially in spring. With 58 miles of meandering pathways and 843 acres, it's a park a king would be proud of. It has hills, meadows, forests, groves, lakes, ponds, streams, and waterfalls. It even has a castle.

On our first trip to the park, I brought along a gallon of water, but not so we'd have something to drink. I had the kids take turns lugging it from Queens, their bodies tilting from the weight. Our first stop in Central Park was a handsome purple beech, a tree so tall we had to lean back on our heels to take it in. I held the plastic jug above my head and said, "This is a gallon of water. In summer, every day a tree like this can send up to three hundred gallons of water from its roots to its leaves way up there. If I gave you that task, how would you do it?"

"Elevators," said Aaron.

"Very funny."

"I'd use a pump," said Okan.

"No pumps allowed."

"Then a pulley," said Okan.

"Uh-uh. No pulleys, either."

Noelia said, "I'd carry the water up. I'd climb up and down and up and down and up and down and up and down and—"

"But trees don't have arms and legs, so you can't use them, either."

"Trees have a heart to pump water," Ella said.

"No, they don't."

"They don't have a heart?" said Rosie, confused.

"Trees have *feelings*," said Ella.

"You could imagine that, but today we're scientists, and let me be clear: trees don't have feelings."

"My mom says that everything that lives has feelings!" said Rosie.

"I think she means they have a spirit, and maybe they do, but they definitely do not have a heart that pumps water the way our hearts pump blood. That only makes them more impressive. Listen to this—it's from a beautiful book called *Pilgrim at Tinker Creek* by a writer named Annie Dillard":

> It's amazing that trees can turn gravel and bitter salts into these soft-lipped lobes, as if I were to bite down on a granite slab and start to swell, bud, and flower. Trees seem to do their feats effortlessly. Every year a given tree creates from scratch 99 percent of its living parts. Water lifting in tree trunks can climb 150 feet per hour in full summer and a tree can heave a ton of water every day. A big elm in a single season might make as many as six million leaves, each wholly intricate; without budging one inch, a tree stands there, accumulating dead wood, mutely rigid as an obelisk, but secretly it seethes, splits, sucks, and stretches.

When I began researching trees so I could teach them, I was embarrassed to discover how little I knew. I didn't even understand the basics, like this business about water. For some reason, I assumed that scientists knew all about trees, that trees were something human beings had mastered inside and out, but that isn't really the case. Books about trees are surprisingly full of words like "probably" and "perhaps" and phrases like "it is thought that" or "most likely this is because" or "remains a mystery." And here's a fact I found humbling: laboratories can't replicate photosynthesis on the scale that a single tree can.

I did my best to explain to the kids what I didn't fully understand. I told them that water enters through the roots, travels up the trunk in tiny tubes, then evaporates from the leaves. I said, "So it's kind of like the sun sucks the water out of the ground through the tree like a straw." To illustrate the process, Aaron and Noelia helpfully made disgusting slurping noises. I said, "Seriously, guys, think about it! The tree has figured out how to beat gravity. Isn't that incredible?"

"Yeah," they said, nodding with more politeness than awe. None of them were flabbergasted and amazed, but this wasn't because they didn't get it—they did. They just couldn't understand what I was making such a fuss about: *Come on, Mr. Swope, it's just a tree!* Childhood is a time of wonder, but I suppose this was a kind of wonder only grown-ups feel; we better understand life's limitations, and thus can be astonished by a tree.

I changed the subject by putting one finger over my lips and saying, "Shhhhh." As if leading them someplace secret, I brought them under the beech's branches, which drooped down low enough to make a quiet space beneath, a shelter, different from the world beyond.

"Ooooh, cool!"

This was more like it! Here was the kind of wonder a child feels up and down their body. They sensed at once that this was an enchanted place. If I'd told them fairies lived there, they'd have easily believed me. But at the moment, we were being scientific, so I asked the kids to touch the bark, which was smooth, without the grooves of many trees. I pointed out how much the beech's bark looked like elephant skin.

Then Simon noticed that a lover long ago had carved a heart into the trunk, and MeiKai said that that was bad. I said, "Trees are long-suffering. They can take a lot of abuse. But here's a math problem: this heart is about five feet up the trunk, right? Now suppose the tree grows a foot a year. Twelve years from now, how much higher will the heart be?"

"Twelve feet higher," said Ella, a math whiz.

"That's what you'd think, but it's not so. The *tree* will be twelve feet higher, but the heart will stay right here, five feet up."

"That's not true!" said Ella.

"You're joking us!" said Rosie.

"It *is* true!" I said. "What happens is—"

"Hey, look! A worm!" cried Gary.

Oh the shrieks! Oh the squeals! The delight! The disgust! The sudden confusion of children crowding around to see! I stood there ignored. No one listened as I said, "Actually, worms are important for trees. They eat dead leaves, helping make more soil, they inch through the ground, breaking it up . . ."

I felt a tug on my jacket. It was Samantha, one of the new kids, a quiet, attentive Chinese girl eager to do well. She looked like a doll and was always by my side, as if the closer she was the more she'd learn. It was adorable, really.

"Yes, Samantha?"

"I have to go to the bathroom."

"Can't it wait half an hour?"

Samantha gave me an anxious look, so there was nothing to be done but make our way to the toilets. I'd spent the weekend before in the park, carefully mapping out our route, looking for cool trees and beautiful spots, then clocking how long it took to walk from A to B to C. But I'd drastically underestimated the time it would take to herd a group of kids. Some dawdled, some raced ahead, and some were just so out of shape and overweight they couldn't walk at a decent clip. To make things worse, I'd asked them to collect a variety of leaves that we would press and use in an art project. I'd imagined we'd pick leaves up as we went along, and hadn't factored in how distractingly beautiful leaves are when you stop to look at them, each one a masterpiece, some as big as the children's heads, some as small as their noses—*Wow! Look at this one!*—or how an indecisive kid like Jessica just couldn't choose which one was best . . .

"Pick one already! We haven't got all day!"

When at last we reached the bathrooms, the boys' was out of order, so we had to go in shifts. After everyone was finally done, the time had come for lunch. We were way behind schedule, and I knew I'd never get to half the things I'd planned.

We ate on some big sunny rocks (how the kids loved rocks!) and afterward, some of us rested, some played, a few read, and everyone was happy. I was sad Miguel wasn't along, but he'd forgotten his permission slip. When I'd suggested calling his home to see if his mom could bring it over, Mrs. Hinton had said no, Miguel was a fifth grader and had to learn responsibility. He'd been left behind, barely holding back his tears.

As we walked to our next destination, Fatma fell in step beside me, wanting to chat. I held my breath, wondering if today she'd be Fatma Jekyll or Fatma Hyde, but I needn't have worried. She was in a friendly mood. "So, Mr. Swope," she said. "How's life?"

"Life is good, thanks, Fatma. How about you?"

"Good. Mr. Swope, can I ask you a question? I don't think you read my last story."

"No, I thought you needed a break from me. It seemed like you'd had enough of my comments, so I gave it to Mrs. Hinton to edit. You're a good writer. I don't want to get in your way."

"She wrote on the top, 'Interesting story.'"

"I'm not surprised. Did she make any edits? Suggestions?"

"No, that's all she wrote. But I think the story's pretty good."

"If you want me to read it, I'd be happy to."

"Well, I really think it's pretty good."

"Then I have something to look forward to. How was your weekend?"

"Boring. Everything about it was boring. Except here's the exciting part. I saw a UFO."

"No! You saw a UFO? Really?"

"I think. I'm not *sure*. . . . It didn't look like an airplane. It looked like this vertical thing."

"A vertical thing? Can you describe it more specifically?"

"It looked like a vertical football with a ring around it and these, I don't know, these diamonds."

"Were you scared?"

"Not really. I was excited."

"Did you point it out to anybody else?"

"I tried. But my sister rolled her eyes. She said, 'You're so stupid. There's no such thing.'"

"Sounds like the beginning of a story: kid sees aliens, no one believes her—"

"Mr. Swope!" said Noelia. "I have a new technique for finding the age of a tree!" She had one palm against the trunk of an oak and the other on her forehead, like a psychic. "This tree is five hundred and a half years old."

Gary said, "Hey, Mr. Swope! Look how slanted down that tree is!"

The tree was growing at a forty-five-degree angle. "Interesting," I said. "How do you think it got like that?"

"Maybe the seed was put slanted in the soil, so it grew slanted."

"I don't think it works that way," I said, but there wasn't time to explain. I gathered them around and said, "Today we're going to do a new kind of writing. It's called nature writing. All you have to do is find a comfortable spot, look around, and write what you see and hear. Put your imaginations away. Let me repeat that: put your imaginations away."

I'd never tried this before, and I wasn't sure how it would go. At the very least, the exercise would force them to look at the world. Hopefully it would also introduce them to the pleasures of descriptive writing, which they hadn't yet discovered because at their young age, the main concern is plot, plot, plot.

"How many pages?" asked Samantha.

"Don't worry about that. Just write for half an hour."

Mrs. Hinton interrupted to say we didn't have half an hour. She said we had to leave for the subway in fifteen minutes. I was crushed, this was the most important moment of the day. But I could see from Mrs. Hinton's expression that this was not negotiable, so I said, "Okay, guys: write about nature for fifteen minutes."

Some got working straightaway. Maya plopped stomach down in the leaves, her knees bent and her feet in the air. MeiKai and Ella sat primly on a bench. Cesar found a rock. Lucinda and Paula, I was thrilled to see, climbed onto a tree, which gave others the same idea, and soon there were eight kids writing in trees, making me smile and smile. Then I saw Simon and Gary, whirling in circles in a little cyclone of leaves.

"Simon! Gary! Stop horsing around and write!"

Finally, everyone was settled, pencils in hand. Most looked around, then wrote; others got lost in their words. Here are a few uncorrected entries:

Today the sun wind come. I thought it might rain, but it didn't rain. The weather is very cold. Before we ate lunch Mr. Swope show us how tree suck up water. Then we went to the bathroom. After that we went to eat lunch. After we ate lunch we have to write. It's called nature writing. I see birds are flying. Trees are moving. Wind is blowing. Leaves are falling. Kids are in trees. Mr. Swope is stepping on leaves. The boys are playing with leaves. Mr. Swope is yelling. It is quiet.

SAMANTHA

The clouds move fast beyond the sun by the raging wind casting its spell on the leaves. I'm surrounded by millions of leaves, broken bits of bark and dirt. Birds tweet their beautiful chant through the wind. The fresh air of nature seizes beyond my calmest dreams. Ants walk the dirt and soil in their walk of amazement.

MATTHEW

Starting to change yellow. They have spots. They have veins. They're drying. They smell. They also have holes, some have white colors on it. There compound leaves. Have branches. The difference is that some are smooth and other bumpy. Some are sticky. Leaves jagged and smooth. Some have sticking up veins, some veins are inside of the leave. Some smooth and some rough leaves are breaking. They're curved. Some have wood. Bigger and smaller veins. Different color. Different shapes. More yellow. Have thorns. One wooden stem.

MATEO

The air is fresh, cool, and gentle.
The grass smells sweet and is so green.
Trees are waving in the wind.
They look ancient and beautiful.
Suddenly the wind blows, strong and fresh, just as
I'm taking off my jacket, the wind surrounds me, and feels so comfortable.
The trees all blow in one direction, pointing north.
Dry leaves fly out of the trees, towards my face, and
just before they hit me, they go in another direction.
This is a magical place, I can feel it.
The sun is bright, and warm against my face.
The clouds are as white as milk.
The sky is bluer than the sky in my dreams.
The air is so fresh and I inhale as much as I can.
The trees are so green, brown and orange.
They look so mystical and beautiful, I can't describe it.
I'm sitting in the middle of a grassy valley, lying
down on a bed of newspaper and my jacket.
The wind blows again, and moves every blade of grass.

MAYA

They were writing, and I begged Mrs. Hinton for a bit more time, but that was out of the question. She couldn't risk getting back to school after dismissal. Parents would panic, the principal would be furious, and the police might even be called. She said teachers who came back late weren't allowed to take any other field trips all year.

I sighed with frustration. Then a park ranger came along and politely told us that climbing trees was not allowed in Central Park. She was awfully sorry, but the kids would have to get down.

The Middle School Problem

I had an alarming conference with several students. They said the cop who'd come to educate them on the dangers of drugs had told them there were drugs and gangs at the middle school they were headed for, Intermediate School 138.

Rosie said she'd heard the police were called to I.S. 138 every day.

Su Jung said, "My cousin, she's at 138 and *oh my God!* She said older kids hit the sixth graders and if you tell on them, then they hit you harder."

Cesar said his sister went there. "She said that it's not good. She said it's overcrowded."

But Elena said, "My brother goes there. He likes it."

"My sister goes there, too," said Aaron. "They get to leave school at lunch and eat at McDonald's. That's why I want to go there. Plus you get your own locker."

"I'm scared!" cried MeiKai. "I don't want to leave this school!"

It's hard to separate rumor from fact, and so easy for fear to fuel a rumor until it assumes bogeyman proportions, especially when children are concerned. Worried, I asked the principal about 138. She was outraged to hear what the policeman had said and told me, "I.S. 138 is a good school that's done very well by our students." She added that its principal, another woman in her seventies, ran a "very tight ship," an assessment echoed by a guidance counselor, who told me, "Basically, 138 is a factory, a well-oiled machine. But it's badly overcrowded, with something like twenty-two hundred kids."

Drugs and gangs aside, the Dickensian image of kids marching up stairs each morning into a giant machine was horrifying. I asked the guidance counselor what other schools were available to these kids, but he knew of only one, a special middle school called Louis Armstrong. Admission was reserved for residents of Queens and was by application only. I went to Armstrong to check it out and liked what I saw. The teachers were passionate and devoted, and it had a good library, a fair number of computers, a band, an orchestra, a chorus, and a sports program. I was especially moved by its mandate, which was to mirror the diversity of Queens. This meant the school mixed races, nationalities, genders and academic abilities. *This is what a public school should be!* I thought. *This is where my kids must go!* Except that thousands of other children in Queens would also be applying for five hundred spots.

But it was worth a try.

I was sure there must be other options. I told myself, *This is New York. There are always ins and outs, ways around things.* Getting information wouldn't be easy, though, especially for parents who couldn't speak English. It was obvious that if I didn't make this my mission, no one would. So I started placing phone calls, talked to anyone I knew in education or could find. I badgered bureaucrats and principals and savvy parents who'd researched middle schools and knew the ropes. I asked a hundred questions. What are the best schools? What's good about them? What's bad? Which accept applications from kids in Queens? Which offer art and music? Sports? Which have a band? What do kids say about the school? How many get accepted into the best high schools? Are there tours for parents? When? Can you apply to more than one at a time? When are applications due? How can a kid increase her chances of acceptance?

I found no other options in Queens. Any good schools there were so overcrowded they couldn't take anyone from out of the catchment area. There were, however, schools in Manhattan that were undercrowded and accepting applications. Two had excellent reputations.

One of those, the Clinton Middle School for Writers and Artists, occupied the top two floors of an elementary school downtown. Being tiny, with 240 kids in all, it had little in the way of extras, and its "library" was heartbreaking, not really a library at all, just milk crates filled with random paperbacks. But the school was cozy and warm and safe, and its devoted principal greeted each kid by name every morning. Moreover, it did well by its students in math and science, got a good number of kids into selective high schools, and each day the place stopped cold for half an hour while everybody read. Even the secretary and the janitor read! Wow! Because of its size, Clinton couldn't accept many kids from out of catchment, but when the principal saw the work my students had done, he encouraged me to have them apply; he'd certainly have room for a few. "Especially boys," he said. "I'm low on boys."

The other Manhattan school, called the Wagner Middle School, was on the wealthy Upper East Side. It felt more prosperous than the others. With eleven hundred students, it had an impressive library, two bands, two art rooms, a drama program, interesting electives, after-school activities, and lots of sports. When Wagner's principal heard which school my students attended, he got misty-eyed: it was the same school his parents had gone to. For sentimental reasons, he was eager to help out, and he told me he anticipated having enough space for any kid from Queens who wanted to come.

I almost threw myself at his feet.

I also learned about Prep for Prep, a nonprofit organization that seeks out smart minority kids, prepares them for entry into New York's private schools, and provides them with scholarships. Prep for Prep helps elite schools attain diversity without risk, and the lucky few who get in are on an inside track to the college of their choice. You apply for Prep for Prep in fifth grade. Successful candidates pass three grueling tests but don't actually enroll in a private school until seventh grade. In the meantime, Prep for Prep goes to great lengths to get these kids ready for the rigors of private school. I was startled to learn what it took for public school kids to catch up with their contemporaries in private schools. After fifth grade, Prep for Prep kids go to summer school. Then they spend sixth grade in public school, but during the year have special classes after school each Wednesday and all day each Saturday. After sixth grade, Prep for Prep kids give up yet another summer vacation for school. Despite the sacrifice, there was a lot of demand for Prep for Prep, which meant the chances of getting accepted were slim: three thousand kids would apply for 150 spots.

With all this information in hand, I described what I'd found to the class, then asked the kids what they thought.

Of Prep for Prep, and losing summers, Noelia said, "That is the most horrifying thing I've ever heard in my life! Absolutely not!"

"I don't really blame you," I said.

MeiKai, however, liked the idea. "Summer is so boring, just stay inside all day."

"Yeah!" said Gary. "Me, too!"

Rafael said, "I don't know where I want to go to school. I only want to be a cartoonist. That's the only thing I'm good at."

"Maybe Clinton would be a good choice for you, Rafael. They're big on art there, and they don't have enough boys. You have to get your parents to take you to the open houses, guys. You have to check these schools out, see which ones you like best."

Mateo said, "I want to go to 138. Everyone's going there. All my friends."

"I'm not," said Gary. "I want a good education."

Mateo, Gary's best friend, shrugged, and Gary looked away, his feelings hurt.

"I'm not saying you'll get a bad education at 138, Gary. I don't know. I'm just telling you your options. You and your parents have to decide what's best for you."

Su Jung said, "My summers are boring but I don't want to do Prep for Prep. I'm just too lazy for all that work."

I knew there wasn't any point in pushing her; she'd only resist more. And she was right—she did suffer from laziness, the profound sort that descends on children who feel unloved and abandoned.

I sent them home with applications and a letter describing each school and listing the dates of open houses and the application deadlines. Several days later, when I asked what their parents' reactions had been, David, Noelia, and Rafael had lost the packets I'd given, and others said their parents weren't interested.

"But why not?"

Mateo said, "My mom said Armstrong is a racist school. I heard they don't take Spanish."

"But that's not true!" I said. "There are lots of Spanish-speaking kids there. Tell your mother that."

Rosie said, "My father doesn't want me to go to the Clinton School 'cause it's for writers and artists."

"But that's just the name. They actually have a strong science and math program. Tell your father that."

Lucinda said, "My mom said she might send me to Armstrong for high school."

"But Armstrong isn't a high school, it's a middle school," I said. "Tell your mother that."

Ella said her parents said Armstrong was in a bad neighborhood.

"Maybe so, but the school is completely safe, and a school bus will take you there and bring you back here. Tell your mother that."

MeiKai said the Queen Mother of the West didn't want her to apply for Prep for Prep because her mother hoped to send her to Taiwan next summer to learn Chinese.

"That would be wonderful!" I said. "But if there's even a tiny chance you won't go to Taiwan, you should apply. If you get accepted, you don't have to go. Tell your mother to tell the Queen Mother of the West that."

"My mom said she didn't like Armstrong," said Aaron.

"Why not?"

"I don't know, she just didn't like it."

It was clear the kids weren't able to explain the situation to their parents, so on parent-teacher night, I spoke to skeptical and worried mothers and fathers one after the other. Most didn't understand that applying to a school carried with it no obligation to attend. Once they learned there was nothing to lose, they were open to the possibilities, and especially to Louis Armstrong, which was nearby. Resistance was intense, however, to the Manhattan schools because the kids would have to take the subway, up to an hour there and back.

"Noelia is too young for the subway. She's still a little girl," said her father.

"Rafael is so absentminded," said his mother. "He's in his world, he'll get lost and miss his stop."

"I understand," I told them all. "But apply anyway. If we get lucky, they'll get into Armstrong. If they don't, maybe groups of kids can travel together, or parents can take turns riding with them. The principal of Wagner told me chances are *very* good they'll get in there. Go to the open house, you'll see the school is very safe. It's in one of New York's richest neighborhoods."

"Oh, really?" they said, their interest piqued.

"Don't close off any options. We'll figure out the transportation later."

No one from Su Jung's family showed up, and there wasn't any point in calling her home because, with the exception of her much younger brother, Su Jung was the only one there who spoke English, and she refused to consider Prep for Prep, no matter how I begged.

When all was said and done, most applied to Armstrong, twenty applied to Wagner and Clinton, and eight decided to try for Prep for Prep, setting in motion a process that would cloud the rest of the year in anxiety.

Max in Control

Every year an oak produces between ten thousand and fifty thousand acorns. It is estimated that on average only one becomes a tree, but none have a prayer unless they get out from under the shadow of their parent. To that end, trees have evolved solutions so clever and whimsical a child might have imagined them. Some seeds get gobbled up, then pooped; some are squirreled away, then forgotten; some hitch a ride on fur, then work loose; some whirligig in the wind, then drop; some drift out to sea, then wash up on a distant shore.

To teach this lesson in adaptation, one day we hunted seeds in Central Park. Because the park has a good variety of trees, I planned our route, ensuring we'd find lots of different seeds: dried-up maple seeds, prickly sycamores, stinky ginkgo berries, cute little acorns, fat fuzzy acorns, clam-like walnuts, earringlike locust pods, cranberry-sized apples, and plump dogwood berries.

Our hunt led us into the Ramble, one of Central Park's two forests.

"Mr. Swope!" said Rosie. "This place is like that book you gave me, *The Lion, the Witch and the Whatever . . .*"

"Why do you say that?"

"'Cause the lamppost in the forest!"

I told the kids, "As you hunt, don't go beyond that sidewalk over there, or that bench over there, or those huge rocks over there. And don't talk. Or goof around. I want you to be alone in nature."

The effect I was reaching for was a long, lazy day in which kids slowly get acquainted with nature the way kids in the country do, the way I had, by just hanging out in it. A bit wishful, wanting them to be alone in nature with thirty-six other kids as well as the dog walkers, the nannies with strollers, and the occasional cop car that snaked its way along the forest pathway. Nevertheless, something good was happening that day. The kids were quietly walking around, taking notes in their journals, and collecting seeds.

Miguel, however, was agitated. He stomped about and thwacked trees with his stick—wham! wham!

"You gotta calm down, Miguel. Take a deep breath. Listen to the quiet."

"I want to find a forest with like foxes and wolves."

"Yeah, that would be exciting. Bears would be good, too."

"Central Park wouldn't have, like, bears."

"No. But it does have hawks."

He shot me a look of disbelief.

"No, it's true. They roost on the side of a fancy building on Fifth Avenue. You sometimes see them soaring."

We looked at the sky, but it was empty, and Miguel thumped off. Every so often, I'd see him stop and rake the heavens with his eyes.

Miguel's adopted tree was in the school yard, where there were several large trees; yet he'd chosen the smallest, a laurel maybe eight feet tall with a slingshot shape. It had lost a major branch some time ago, but although damaged, it was a tough little thing, and Miguel, who wasn't small, shinnied up it as far as he could go, just a few feet. It sagged under his weight but didn't break. He told me, "I adopted this tree because I remember my dad used to put me up there, and then I'll fall down: ahhhhhhh!"

I couldn't decide whether that was a happy memory or not.

Miguel insisted everything was fine at home that fall. His mother, however, summoned to school because Miguel was getting into fights, said she and her husband were having serious trouble. She said, "The other night my husband told me, 'I'm moving out,' and so Miguel started packing his clothes too and said he was going with his father. That he didn't need a mother, he needed a man. So I told him, 'All right, go. But don't come crying to me when he makes you stay inside and doesn't let you play.' Because that's what my husband makes them do if I am not there. He makes them stay in the bedroom. They can't come out with him in the living room and play."

Miguel had named his adopted tree Max in Control. "I call him Max because all the stuffed animals that I have, I named them Max. I don't know why. And I named him 'in Control' because like there's so much stuff happening inside of him every season and every day. It's like a curse split the trunk in half and it means the control you have to take to absorb all the water and protect himself from damage."

When I asked him if he wanted to write a story about his tree, he shook his head, saying, "I'd rather write a poem. Because sometimes I think like a story and I make it way too long. I have to think. I can't control myself really."

"That's true about your stories," I agreed. "I think a poem is a good idea."

> I'm hiking climbing Mt. Everest
> falling rocks boom!
> one more step . . .
> I reached it
> I reached the top
> now get back into the world
> it was just my tree

On the day we hunted seeds, he came running up to me and said in a loud whisper, "I saw it, Mr. Swope! I saw the hawk!" I looked up, but he told me it was gone. "I'm so glad you saw it," I said, but I wondered if he really had.

Suddenly Maya shrieked in joyful horror, having come across the body of a dead and mutilated squirrel. Everyone gathered around and joined in the hysteria, screaming and jumping up and down. I had to force myself to look. The poor squirrel was a bloody mess, missing half an eye and its jaw torn off, but Maya was in seventh heaven. As she leaned over to study the carcass more closely, she was so fascinated that I thought she really would become a surgeon she'd once told me she wanted to be, so she could "look at people's disgusting insides."

The squirrel made Miguel happy, too. He was sure his hawk had killed it. "This is just the place where I saw him come down!" he told me. "I heard the squirrel cry out!"

"When you think about how nature works," I told the class, "the squirrel's death is good news for the tree. Now the nuts it buried won't get eaten, and maybe they'll grow into trees."

Absolutely no one was listening, but that was just as well because it wasn't true. Those nuts didn't have a chance, not in Central Park, which is full of nature but is in fact a work of art, an artificial construct that was blasted, dug, engineered, and landscaped. It's nature with sidewalks, lamps, and benches. It's nature controlled, its trees as pampered as a Park Avenue prince, and most upstart seedlings get yanked up by the roots.

When the time came for nature writing, again Miguel wanted to write a poem. He told me, "I used to think poems were like girlie things, like lullabies or something, but then I started putting a lot of effort in it. It's like you put twenty-five cents in those machines and you don't know what you're going to get. That's what happens to me. I put a coin in my brain and get a poem out."

> *Flash!*
> *Got a picture.*
> *I got the hawk flying with its prey!*
> *Run, run to develop.*
> *"Come back in an hour."*
> *Run, run to get my picture,*
> *pay my money without care,*
> *thinking that I'll get my share.*
> *When I open the little sack,*
> *I find the hawk with the hare.*
> *Hey, no fair!*
> *The hawk stopped!*
> *The photo is no movie,*
> *the photo is the past, with no more life.*
> *So run, run, run*
> *back to Central Park*
> *to find the hawk.*
> *No hawk now!*
> *This time I'll be ready,*
> *not with the camera,*
> *but with my eyes.*
> *Nature is the only true movie.*

On the subway ride home, many kids were in high spirits, but some, including Miguel and Rafael, sat by themselves. At Forty-second Street, a ragged, dirty man with a prophet's beard entered the train. He shook his paper cup with coins, then saw the kids and launched into a kind of sermon, silencing the car. "All you children, look at me and listen what I say! You stay in school! You do your homework! You stay away from drugs!

Or else here, look at me, I am your future. *Listen to me!* Stay in school! Work hard! Don't do drugs!" He paused as if he was about to say something more, then thought better of it. Scowling, he pushed his way into the next car, leaving all of us stunned and worried for the future. After a tense moment, a passenger down the car began to clap, then another joined in; everyone was clapping, even the kids, even Miguel was clapping.

Afros, Chinos, and Skittles

Rafael was a skinny, good-looking kid with black, watchful eyes, high cheekbones, and a single freckle on the end of his nose. When he ran away from home that fall, all he took with him was comic books.

Rafael's parents were divorced. He lived with his mother, her parents, and his two younger sisters, but he saw his dad several times a week, either in Queens or at his father's place in Coney Island, near the amusement park, where his dad had a job sweeping sidewalks. Rafael's mother told me that her son didn't speak till he was four years old. "He'd point instead," she said. Now ten years old, Rafael still didn't find speech easy. He stammered, sounding like a record needle momentarily stuck. Maybe that's why he loved comics, where words are few.

I asked him, "When you ran away, how long were you gone?"

"About two hours about two hours."

"Why did you run away?"

"Because because the kids were teasing me teasing me so I decided to run to run away."

"Who was teasing you?"

"Lucinda Lucinda Noorjahan um Simon Gary Jorge and Mateo and Okan."

"Where were you going to go?"

"I didn't I didn't know."

"Who found you?"

"My grand my grandfather. I was in I was in a Chinese store. They sell virtual pet toys and video games."

"You know I ran away once when I was a kid."

"How old how old were you?"

"Your age, I guess. I don't even remember why I did it, but I packed my toys in a little suitcase, screamed, 'I'm never coming back!' and stormed out the door. And do you know where I ran away to? It's funny, now that I think of it. I climbed this big pine tree beside our house, suitcase and all. From its branches I could see into the first- and second-story windows. I kept climbing up and down to look inside, waiting to see my parents freak out that I was gone and call the police or something."

"What happened?"

"Nothing. They just went about their business. They knew I wasn't serious, and after a while I knew it, too. When I got hungry I went back inside, and that was that."

I asked Rafael how the other students had teased him.

"Called me freakazoid and stupid."

"Well, freakazoid I can understand, but stupid? Never. You're not stupid."

"They also they also called me um . . . Afro."

I couldn't tell if Rafael was telling the truth or whether he just said that because he knew that word would get the other kids in trouble. Either way, it didn't make sense. Rafael wasn't African American and didn't look it; he looked Hispanic. It's also possible that Rafael didn't really know the definition of *Afro*. The kids were often confused about who was who and what was what. When I first met them, most were color-blind. I watched them gradually figure out that people can be categorized and then insulted. But the children didn't always know what they were saying. For example, they spat the word *gay* at each other, along with *mutant* and *retard,* without understanding what any of them meant. And once Amarjeet, an Indian Sikh, told me, "Kids on the street call me HBO"—Hindu Body Odor—"but I'm not Hindu, so I call them Spics."

"Were they Hispanic?"

"I don't care!"

Then there was Ella, who was Chinese. She said her parents didn't want her to go to Louis Armstrong because there were "black people there, and black people do all the graffiti and bad things." When I pointed out that Mrs. Hinton, whom Ella adored, was black, Ella got confused and did a double take—she hadn't put that particular two and two together yet.

The *Afro* incident caused a brouhaha. The offending kids were sent to guidance for sensitivity training, and Rafael went there, separately, to be comforted. After his session, he told me, "The counselor gave me Skittles Skittles, he gave me Skittles."

The year before, Rafael himself had needed sensitivity training, and Mrs. Melvern had been happy to provide it. One day she had the kids write instructions for brushing teeth, which is a difficult but useful writing exercise. When Carolina's instructions, hopelessly incomplete, were read aloud in class, Rafael laughed, hurting Carolina's feelings. To teach Rafael a lesson, Mrs. Melvern read *his* instructions out loud, mocking their incompleteness until Rafael was in tears. Then she drove her point home, saying, "See? You can dish it out, Rafael, but you can't take it. Now you know how it feels."

Rafael cried easily. I thought he might become an artist. He was certainly an artist type, with his sensitivity, his ready temper, the stubborn way he followed his own drummer, and his passion for comics and cartoons. This concerned his mother, a sad, gentle woman who'd left Cuba at age twenty to live in Queens. "When I first came to New York City, I was crying every day," she told me. "I had lost part of my life. My friends, my family. After I was here three or four months, I couldn't remember any faces. I kept trying to remember my sister's face. It was very strange." She met her husband, a Uruguayan, in New York, but shortly after Rafael was born, things went sour and the fights began. "When Rafael wasn't talking yet," she told me, "he'd look at me. His eyes were always worried, asking, 'Are you going to fight again?' Even now he still doesn't like to talk, not with me, not with his father, not with his sisters. He's very private. Sometimes I think he's a sad boy, that he doesn't love me. I'm his pain. I make him do things. All he loves is comics, comics and cartoons. Especially Garfield. He laughs and laughs."

Rafael almost never did his homework, and I'd get angry at him, but I also did everything I could to encourage his obsession. His preference for Garfield showed good taste. Rafael didn't care for superheroes or heavy-duty violence; what interested him were the ways in which people get on each other's nerves. So I gave him collections of *Calvin and Hobbes, The Far Side, Peanuts,* Winsor McKay's *Dreams of a Rarebit Fiend* and *Little Nemo,* and Jules Feiffer's novel *The Man in the Ceiling,* about a boy who wants to be a cartoonist. Because Rafael took comics seriously, I also let him hang out in my office while I worked with other kids. He'd sit quietly in a corner, making comics. Rafael had an intuitive understanding of the form's rhythm, which is difficult to master—it's not easy to tell a satisfying story in a few frames. When starting a new strip, he'd think for a long time. Not until he "saw" his idea whole would he begin to draw, which he did with methodical care, his lines confident and precise.

In fourth grade, Rafael invented a hapless character called Beef Jerky, who was skinny like Rafael but had spiky hair. In one cartoon, Beef Jerky broke a mirror. Although Beef Jerky thought that was why he always had such rotten luck, Rafael assured me that Beef Jerky was just kidding himself. "Really he just he just gets himself into trouble," he explained.

The hero of Rafael's island story comic was Beef Jerky.

In the first panel, Beef Jerky was on a boat looking through a telescope: Land ho!

In the second panel, the boat had landed, and a hopeful Beef Jerky made his way down the gangplank.

In the third, Beef Jerky was surrounded by crowds of nondescript people. His dialogue balloon said, "I can't believe I'm in an island full of Chinos. What are all these Chinos doing here?"

"Gosh, Rafael," I said. "That makes Beef Jerky sound like a racist creep. Is that what you intended?"

Silence.

"Do you not like Chinese people?"

"I like the food they make."

"MeiKai and Ella and David and Samantha are all Chinese. Do you think they're bad?"

"No."

"Don't you think the word *Chino* would hurt their feelings?"

"I don't I don't I don't really know."

"I'd be angry at anyone if they called you a Spic. It's not good to make fun of people that way."

He said nothing, so I moved on and continued reading his comic.

In the next two panels, Beef Jerky was beleaguered by loud radios and honking horns.

In the last panel, Beef Jerky found respite of the sort anyone can appreciate. His dialogue balloon said, "I can't survive the noise, I'm hungry. I'll just have a shrimp."

I laughed and said, "I love this picture of Beef Jerky eating a shrimp. Very nice ending. But you shouldn't have put a comma here, after 'noise.' That should be a what?"

He studied his mistake for a moment, then said, "Period."

"Right. And you know what else, Rafael? This comic would work just fine without the word *Chino*. You could use the word *people* instead and it would still be funny. And you wouldn't hurt anyone's feelings."

I handed him the comic and asked him to rewrite it, but he wasn't interested. On his way out the door, he crumpled it up and threw it in the trash.

The Willow Tree

Each day the park grew more colorful, as if nature were a symphony building to a crescendo. On one November trip, we had my favorite kind of weather, a classic autumn day—blue sky, upper fifties, wind in the hair. I was thrilled to be outside with the kids, and Central Park was in full glory. Some trees were still green, most had color, but enough were bare so the ground was full of leaves and fun to walk on, *crunch, crunch, crunch*. We'd come to a tucked-away pond with ducks, and as the children oohed at the reflection of trees in the rippling water, Su Jung said it all reminded her of the Impressionist paintings we'd seen on a visit to the Metropolitan Museum.

We moseyed along the weaving path that circled the pond, and I looked forward to the moment when a kid would spot the fruit an Osage orange tree had dropped. They'd rolled down the sloping lawn and were scattered around but pretty hard to miss, yellow-green and bumpy and strangely shaped, like some gangrenous digestive organ. Gary found one first.

"What's this, Mr. Swope? It looks like an alien brain."

I shrugged as if I didn't know what it was and let the children break the fruit open, puzzle out what it might be. I was trying not to say too much because I'd read an essay called "Children in the Woods" and wanted to be like its author, Barry Lopez:

The quickest door to open in the woods for a child is the one that leads to the smallest room, by knowing the name each thing is called. The door that leads to the cathedral is marked by a hesitancy to speak at all, rather to encourage by example a sharpness of the senses. If one speaks it should only be to say, how wonderfully all this fits together, to indicate what a long, fierce peace can derive from this knowledge.

I don't think I completely understood what Lopez was talking about, but I loved the sound of those words. I did know what he meant, though, about how teaching the names of things leads to "the smallest room." Ella, I'd noticed, was particularly good at identifying trees. It was an intellectual game for her, and the moment she'd pegged a maple, she'd dismiss it and look away. Next! It kept her from fully seeing the tree. But the mysterious peace that Lopez refers to, whatever it might be, would be awfully hard to find with a crowd of kids excited to be outside and wanting to laugh and shout and run around. Then there was this: much as I wanted to follow Lopez's advice and adopt a quiet, Zen-like presence, I didn't have it in me, and you have to be the teacher you are, not the one you'd like to be.

Besides, there was so little time, so much I wanted them to notice, like my favorite tree in Central Park. "See that willow on the far side of the pond?" I said. "Keep an eye on it. There's something very unusual about that tree."

From a distance, the willow wasn't unusual, but it was awfully pretty, with a mop-top head of yellowing leaves that drooped low, brushing the surface of the water. As we walked up to it, the kids were amazed to discover that its trunk was lying on the ground and had been so for years. Although it had fallen, the tree refused to die. Its branches had simply reoriented themselves and started growing up toward the sun.

The tree looked particularly human, and as we sat in front of it, I told the class the myth of Daphne and Apollo, and how the beautiful nymph vowed never to marry, but the god Apollo desired her, wooed her, pursued her. Poor Daphne fled and the god chased close behind until in desperation Daphne cried out to her father, a river god, to save her. As she reached the river's banks, just as Apollo was about to take her in his arms, Daphne's father transformed his frightened daughter into a tree, and Apollo found himself embracing a body becoming wood.

"This willow looks to me like it was human once," I told the class. "I've tried to write its story, but it refuses to tell it to me."

"It would have to be sad," said Noelia. "Now I know why they call them weeping."

"Did you ever notice how things aren't always what they seem?" I said. "Did you ever lift up a nice clean rock and find underneath a bunch of squirming bugs and worms?"

"Ew, gross!"

"Follow me."

When we stepped around to the other side of the willow's seemingly healthy, albeit fallen trunk, the kids got a shock. The trunk wasn't solid at all; it had a horrific gaping wound, a huge slimy hollow covered with moss, mold, and cobwebs. Viewed from this side, the tree was like a corpse, a hand reaching from the grave.

"Ew, gross!"

This interesting tree also provided an excellent demonstration of how a trunk functions. Nearly one hundred percent of a tree's trunk, I explained, the part we use to burn and build, is dead and serves only to support the tree and hold it upright. When the willow's trunk rotted through, the tree collapsed, but it didn't die because enough of the living tissue of the trunk, the cambium, that thin wet layer of cells beneath the bark, hadn't been severed. Since the cambium transports water and food between leaves and roots, the willow's trunk evidently still had enough on its healthy side to keep the willow alive.

It was time to write.

I said, "Spread out and take a walk around. Look for a tree that tells you a story."

"Does it have to be a sad story?" said Aaron, pointing out a sycamore whose branches pointed upward like arms raised high in an expression of joy.

"Happy stories would be good," I said. "But you don't have to write a story at all. You could also write a poem, or do some nature writing. Whatever the trees inspire you to write is fine with me, as long as you write."

The kids wandered around the grassy slopes overlooking the pond, inspecting trees and deciding where to sit.

Samantha, the tiny girl who never left my side, asked, "What tree should I write about?"

"Hmmmmm," I said, pretending to take her measure before looking around for a tree that would suit her. "I think that willow is the tree for you, Samantha. I think you're the one it'll tell its story to."

"Okay," she said, and quickly found a rock on which to sit and listen to the tree.

The ground was covered with multicolored leaves, like a carpet. I watched the children settle in, each kid alone, composition notebook open, pencil in hand. The sun glowed through the yellow maples, and gusts sent ginkgo leaves fluttering among us like butterflies. It was magical, and so intensely beautiful I felt a pang. It hurt to look at it; my eyes brimmed tears. Standing there, I had an image—the beginning of a story—that removed me from the moment. In my mind's eye the leaves on the ground knitted together, forming a Persian carpet, a carpet with a tree growing up out of its center, a magic carpet big enough to carry all the children and the tree into the sky. Up they went. The kids at first were startled, then thrilled, then scared and thrilled both. They ran to the edge of the carpet to look down. I saw them up there, peeking over the carpet's edge, waving, flying away, shouting, "Mr. Swope! Mr. Swope!"

That was all, nothing more; the image ended with no hint of what came next. But while I was imagining this magic carpet, Miguel, Aaron and Cesar had seen me standing transfixed, mouth slightly open, and they'd snuck up on me to see how close they could get before I'd notice. When I finally looked their way, they pointed at me and rolled over laughing.

"Very funny," I said. "Now get to work!"

Aaron and Cesar got ahold of themselves quickly, but Miguel's laughter escalated out of control. He was on his back, hugging his stomach, laughing so hard it hurt, and unable to stop. It was the sort of laughing fit I'd seen grieving people have, a laughter that has more to do with anguish than mirth. It was upsetting to see Miguel this way, but it seemed best to let him laugh it out.

I walked over to Samantha. She was hard at work on her willow tree story. Since she was new to the class this year, her writing wasn't as practiced, and her English prose had a heavy Chinese accent. She'd rewrite this story twice, making it easier to read, but I preferred the version she wrote that day in the park, unedited and uncorrected, there by the tree. As is often the case with children's writing, her first draft's roughness was more poignant and poetic than her polished later rounds. At times I heard in her sentences an almost Joycean music. I was pleased to find in Samantha's story the influence of Daphne and Apollo as well as the idea that pretty things (like the willow) aren't always what they seem.

Once upon a time a boy name Al like a girl name Amy. Evertime when Al past by Amy he said dumb thing like do de ya you ba. Amy alway go to the store and buy string to make boxes, butterfly, and zipper. Amy past Al they said hi together. Amy said what color is his favorite color they both said

"Green." Al said we are incoman. They become boyfriend and girlfriend. Amy said don't tell nobody that we are boyfriend and girlfriend. They dated together, but they never kiss because Al wanted to kiss her but Amy said "No." Amy never told Al or anybody that she was a ugly witch. Amy turn into a girl because she wanted a boyfriend. Evertime when Amy got kiss by anybody turn back to a witch but it never hapened. Al said come lets go. Amy said where are we going. Al said I taking you to Central Park. Al said let's walk anywhere you want. Amy went with Al to a pond and then they ate lunch. Amy order a chicken sandwitch. Al order a beef sand-witch. They finish there lunch. They walk and walk until Amy found a big space ground. Amy said stop let's stop here and rest. Al kiss her very fast. Amy turn into a ugly witch her mom came Al started to run away to tell people and his friends but Amy's mom put a spell on Amy and Al. Amy ask why mom why did you put a spell on me and Al, becase Amy you didn't listen to me. I told you not to turn into a girl but you didn't listen. Amy's mom only turn Amy back to a witch not a tree. Al stay as a willow tree for ever. Al got lonly and lonly. Al bend and bend. Al only feel happy when people touch him and look at him. Al forgot about Amy and Amy forgot about Al.

Gary, too, was writing up a storm. Like many of the kids, he hadn't chosen to write a story, which in his case was a relief, because his stories were so baffling they always gave me headaches. Nonfiction writing was much easier for him, and I was pleased by the clarity with which he described the day.

. . . I also stumbled onto something green that looked a lot like a brain. I wondered for a moment, then I observed it closely. It was a kind of fruit and was yellow green with continuous bumps all over it. It smelled like an orange. Okan found an open one. It looked like it had pieces of dirt inside. Those were probably seeds. When I first saw the fruit it looked like some-thing from science fiction. I called it a brain. What if it was from another tree? Maybe it was from the willow. I think Okan took one home.

When I checked on Miguel, he'd written only:

Trees are helpful. We should let Nature have its place. Animals are our friends.

"Miguel, look around you. Write what you see. Describe the scene, don't just write ideas."

"Mr. Swope?" he said. "I was just thinking, this place where we are right now? I want to come to here every time. I don't want to leave here. I was thinking, Yeah! Let's tell those police to throw a bomb in the city and then everyone dies and we can stay here. I like the ducks."

Oh, my. How do you answer that? I said, "Sit down and write something, Miguel."

"I'm thinking!"

"Think quietly."

My next stop was Esteban, another new kid in class. Esteban was Colombian, fine-featured. His hair was always neatly parted. He was very quiet and hadn't written a word that fall. Mrs. Hinton said she understood that things weren't good for him at home. I hadn't been able to get him to open up to me, though, and I had less time to try because the class was so much larger. Esteban smiled when I sat on the ground beside him, happy to have me nearby. I gave him a nod hello and started writing. I wanted to show him that this was easy, he could do it, too, and I invited him to read along as I wrote.

What a beautiful day! Right now I'm sitting next to Esteban on a gentle slope above a pond. He seems like a good kid. And guess what? A sparrow just talked to me! I was so surprised! It said that it had learned a secret about Esteban from a squirrel, maybe that squirrel over there, near MeiKai.

Startled to be addressed from the page, Esteban looked at the squirrel by MeiKai, then at me, wondering if this could be true. I kept on writing.

Anyway, the sparrow said the squirrel said that Esteban was going to write an amazing story today. She said the story is sitting in his head right now, even though Esteban doesn't know it yet. She said it was planted there, like a nut, waiting to grow. So how about it, Esteban? Stop reading what Mr. Swope is writing and get going. You have work to do!

Esteban looked at me in surprise. I ignored him, though, and changed position so he couldn't read my writing anymore. As I watched him from the corner of my eye, he looked around for a moment or two, and then I saw it—the moment of inspiration. It lasted only a second, but his body gave a little jolt, as if he'd had a small electric shock. A moment later, he was off and writing, pencil whizzing across the page.

THE TREE THAT LENT ME ITS BRAIN

I went to Central Park with my class and with my writing teacher, Mr. Swope. Mr. Swope told the class that we had to spread out and write. We all spread out and while I was running, I fell in a hole and wound up in a jungle.

I was walking through the trees. Man, were they scary! I decided to go back, but I couldn't because everything kept getting farther and farther away. Then I heard Mr. Swope saying, "Okay, let's go!" I was so nervous. I thought I was never going to get out of this scary jungle. My friends tried to find me, but they also fell in the hole. I told them, "Let's spread out!" And so we tried to find our way out, but we couldn't 'cause, as I said, everything got farther and farther away. Eventually Mr. Swope and Mrs. Hinton went to find us. They fell into the hole, too.

So there we all were, in the jungle. Mr. Swope said, "Esteban, why did you get us in this trouble?" I said, "It wasn't my fault!" But Mr. Swope said, "Who cares? Let's keep on looking at trees!" We said, "What are you, crazy?! We have to get out of here!" We started to look at different nasty, ugly trees with spiders and spider webs. Mr. Swope said, "Okay, now we could spread out since we're all together." So we did what the teacher said.

The trees I observed were all ugly. I couldn't see the trees very well because they were dirty and had so much green, gooey stuff. Man, was I scared! I went to this bright tree. Guess what happened? I was sucked into it! It felt like I was in a junk yard.

After like five minutes it threw me out and I became a tree, because while I was in his body, he sucked my brain, and he gave me his brain. I became a tree and couldn't tell anybody. I felt cold becoming a tree.

Then guess what? The tree started to talk like me, act like me, run like me, and walk like me. I was so nervous, but I had an idea if I sucked the tree's brain I could get my brain back. But I couldn't do it. The tree was too far away from me! I sucked as hard as I could. Then the tree who looked like me tripped and hit me and the tree gave me my brain and I gave him his brain. Man, was I happy!

The Muse is a fickle goddess. You never know when, or whom, she'll visit, bringing inspiration. I've noticed that assignments sometimes hit home runs in one classroom but strike out in others. I've also had low hopes for an assignment, then been pleasantly surprised. As it happened, the Muse would visit Esteban only once that year. I never got another story out of him. I decided Esteban was like the peach trees tended by the Queen Mother of the West, the ones that bear delicious fruit every three thousand years, then go dormant.

How to Draw a Tree

When the children drew trees, they looked like lollipops, so I asked an art teacher how to teach children how to draw trees. I gave her lesson to the kids in the park, and I was thrilled. It was uncanny, as if the children were channeling trees, as if the pictures were drawing themselves, and some of them were quite beautiful.

Aaron, Maya, Noelia, Simon, and Cesar were out sick for that field trip, so I took them into the schoolyard for a makeup class. I particularly wanted Aaron to learn to draw trees because he had a raw artistic talent that even after two years wasn't reflected in his leaden, halting prose—although in free verse, with its looser structure, Aaron could be wonderfully expressive:

THE BIRD GOD

In the bright air,
golden feather,
dark green eye,
sharp claw,
curved beak,
soaring, looking
like the sun.
It is: proud,
heading to the
crack in the
mountain,
a nest,

THE TREE PROJECT 229

bright eggs:
golden feathers
light the
cave
where pirates
come to worship!

The schoolyard had several good-sized trees, and I told the kids they'd be sketching three. When I asked for a volunteer, Aaron jumped up.

"Make like a tree," I said, and Aaron stuck out his arms.

"Where are Aaron's arms the thickest?"

"The top," said Simon.

"Yes, at the shoulder. And they get narrower and narrower the closer you get to his hands. What about his fingers, where are they the widest?"

The kids raced over to Aaron, studied his digits.

"The part by the hand."

"Right, just like the arms, wider to narrower. And it's the same thing with a tree. Look at the trunk, the roots, the branches, and the twigs. All of them start out wide, then get narrower."

The kids looked hard at the tree, taking this in.

I said, "Before you draw a tree, you have to look at its overall shape. They're not all the same. Some species have branches that grow straight out, others have branches that veer up, and still others have branches that droop down. Find me an example of each."

The schoolyard provided trees with branches growing out or up, but we had to look across the street to find a pine, whose branches drooped down. Next I handed out paper and pencil and said, "Using the side of your pencil, not the point, start at the bottom of the trunk and work your way up and out. Don't draw an outline, fill it all in. And don't draw every branch, just get the main ones—three or four or five will do. And don't worry about twigs yet. You can add those later. As you work, keep one eye on the tree and remember: don't stop drawing, don't hesitate, just keep going!"

As I gave this lesson, a deliveryman on his way into school stopped to watch. He told us, "I come from Jamaica, and every Friday we spent outside, learning the names of the flowers and the trees and the beautiful birds. American kids don't know the names of birds! They hardly even see them! You're doing a beautiful thing, man."

I said to the kids, "You hear that? At least someone appreciates me."

Simon gave a Bronx cheer, making everyone laugh.

Again, the lesson was a success. Aaron had drawn a particularly beautiful tree and when I praised it, he gave it to me as a present. (It's now framed and hanging in my home.)

It was such a pretty day out, I offered the children this choice: write a poem or return to class.

"Poems!"

Maya climbed to the top of the jungle gym to write. Cesar lay on his stomach. Simon lounged against the side of the school's brick wall. Noelia took longer to settle down. She strutted about like a chicken, saying, "Brock-brock-brock! I'm looking for a poem, Mr. Swope! A chicken tree poem!" Meanwhile, Aaron leaned against the tree he'd drawn, and wrote this:

> I went outside
> of the school
> with Mr. Swope
> so I could learn
> how to draw a tree.
> The first tree we sketched
> was HUGE.
> The second was split.
> The third was
> a strange tree.
> It was so small
> yet so cool because
> it had so many
> branches!
> Then a man came and said,
> "I love how you're teaching
> these kids about trees!
> Americans don't know about trees!"
> Mr. Swope said,
> "You see, someone
> appreciates me."
> "Yea, right," we said.
> We keep on drawing.
> It's like this:

You use the side of the pencil
and start with the trunk.
And then follow
it all
the way up.

AARON

Night Writing

That night there would be a full moon, and for homework I asked my students to go outside to do some night writing. "It's just like nature writing, except you'll be on the street. Write for fifteen minutes."

"No way my parents will let me go out at dark," said Noelia.

"You're a clever girl. Part of the assignment is convincing an adult to go outside with you. And be sure to describe your tree at night!"

"It would be dark," said Mateo. "I wouldn't be able to see my tree."

"You can see it in the streetlight!" said Rafael.

"Even if it's hard to see, describe what you *do* see," I said. "That's what night writing is all about."

Unfortunately it rained that night, obscuring the moon, but that didn't really matter. Here's Mateo's night writing, in which he gradually finds the beauty in an ordinary scene:

Well, I'm standing here next to my building. It's cloudy so I can't see the full moon. It's raining out here. People are rushing from work to their apartments and houses. Cars are swishing by in all the rain. The cars are wet. Pigeons are flying high in the air.

The little drops of water on the branches are going down second by second. The plants are taking showers happily. I had to stay right here in front of my building because of the rain. It's raining a little bit. It's not pouring. It's raining right at me. But I don't feel it because I have a hood.

Airplanes are flying high in the air. People are racing like ants. There's nothing really interesting. Everything just still, because it's night. People are going to stores for last minute lunch shopping for their kids. Some people are out just for fun.

It's a nice sight. It's raining and everything is still. The only things moving are the raindrops falling on the ground beneath me. There are also no stars because it's cloudy today.

"I love this, Mateo," I told him.

Mateo was a good kid, a jock, unfailingly respectful, and a hard worker. The year before, when the class had written poems describing their souls in terms of something else, in metaphor, Mateo compared his to an eagle "gazing through the sky" and ended with this stanza:

> *My soul is mad when*
> *I do something*
> *wrong.*
> *I feel my soul*
> *saying*
> *"OBEY THE RULES!"*

I'd smiled when I read that. Mateo had captured something true about himself. That superego breathing down his neck was maddening to him, no doubt, but it's what made him such a model student. I wondered if he'd ever loosen up.

I told Mateo, "You've described the wetness of the city well. I love the swishing cars. I love the details of the water beading off the branches and people buying last-minute things. All great stuff. I can see it. I get a sense of activity and movement, but also how it's quiet on a wet night. Excellent work. I'm very impressed. Were you outside by yourself when you wrote this?"

"My mom was with me."

What a woman! Mateo's mother was less than five feet tall, spoke no English, but was determined that her son do well at school. Mateo interviewed her once about her childhood in Ecuador and wrote it up. When she was a student, Mateo learned, his mom had studied hard and was at the top of her class:

Her wish that she wanted the most was to keep studying, but she did not get her wish even though her parents wanted it to happen. They did not let her because they did not have enough money and they wanted the older brothers and sisters to study, too.

This was a common phenomenon among these immigrants: the parent was determined that the child would have the education they'd missed. Mateo's mom did whatever she had to, even if she didn't understand why, even if it seemed odd and peculiar, like standing in the rain on a winter night so her son could do his homework.

Given the weather, Mateo was one of only a few kids who made it outside. Others just looked out their windows and wrote, but they still got something from the exercise, and the night inspired some lovely, quiet description, like this, from Okan:

> It is raining outside now. I am looking out my window. Not many cars are passing here and that usually doesn't happen on my street. About every two minutes one person passes by.
>
> My apartment building is very quiet and across from it I see a very tall tree. It breaks up a lot into thick branches that branch off into smaller branches, and so on. It still has leaves on it that are green and some of them are yellow. It looks very peaceful as the rain just swoops down on the unguarded tree.
>
> There is a full moon out tonight and the sky's color is a mixture of violet, blue, and black.
>
> There used to be a tree that was very close to my house but someone abandoned a dead car battery by the tree's roots, causing it to die. Later, the city cut that tree down. A very long time ago, when it was raining very hard, another tree on my street was knocked down by the wet winds.

Then there was Ella's, and its phony rapture annoyed me. If she was going to fake an experience, she could've done a more convincing job.

> The night is peaceful. The stars shining brightly. The tree really blends into the night's sky. The buds look so much like the branch bark. Only few cars pass by the street lights. The sky navy blue bring out the stars and lights. Oh, how beautiful the houses look in the dark blue sky. The sky so dark, I can hardly see my tree. At night there's not a single sound. Oh, how beautiful the sight looks!

I said to her, "This has some nice description, but you didn't write it outside, did you?"

"Yes, I did."

"But it was cloudy, so how could you see stars? And this neighborhood does have noise at night, yet you write there's not a single sound. You couldn't have been outside. You made this all up."

"It was raining! I'm just a kid! I couldn't go out!"

"Fine, okay! But you didn't have to *lie*. Other kids wrote about the city through the window. This isn't a description of your neighborhood after dark, this is some fantasy of night. I want you to look at the world, Ella, and write the truth. You're a smart girl. You're better than this."

She sucked in her cheeks, folded her arms, and rooted herself to the floor, waiting me out, but only because she had to, not because she thought I had something worthwhile to say.

The McDonald's Conferences

The kids took the first round of Prep for Prep tests on a Saturday morning in January at Trinity, a fancy private school in Manhattan. Trinity happened to be near my home, so I stopped by that morning with good luck cards and bags of candy to help the kids get through the day. It wasn't easy to find them among the hordes of hopeful, nervous kids packed into the hallways. I felt like I was in a war movie, trying to locate a loved one in a mob of refugees.

I saw Maya first. She was leaning against the wall, and her dark, pensive face lit up when she saw me.

"Mr. Swope!"

"I came to wish you good luck, Maya. Everything's going to be fine."

"Thank you, Mr. Swope."

Rosie, who wanted to go to Harvard and save the world, had already made a friend and was chatting away.

"Mr. Swope! What are you doing here?"

"I came to wish you good luck, and to tell you that whatever happens today, I think you're brilliant."

"Thanks, Mr. Swope."

Then I came upon MeiKai, who was a nervous wreck. Her slender body was quivering like a leaf, and I couldn't see how she'd hold a pencil, let alone concentrate. When she saw me, all she could only say was, "Enh?"

"I came to wish you good luck, MeiKai. Here's a little good luck gift."

"Enh?"

"Try to relax, MeiKai. Take some deep breaths. It's just a stupid test. Try to make it fun."

"How can a test be *fun?*"

"I know," I said. "But you have to relax."

"My mom says I won't pass."

What?! Why would her mother say such a thing?

MeiKai had told me several things that year that made me worry about Mrs. Li. Apparently, an envious woman was somehow draining her mother's healing powers. Her mother also thought there were evil spirits in their home. Then MeiKai told me that the Queen Mother of the West almost never let Mrs. Li leave the apartment, ordering her to adhere to a grueling schedule of study that gave her little sleep.

I told MeiKai that her mother didn't mean it. I said, "You're a very smart girl. Of course you'll do well on the test."

"Enh?"

The Prep for Prep monitors began herding the children toward the cafeteria, like cattle on their way to the slaughterhouse. I followed alongside MeiKai, saying, "This test isn't the end of the world."

"Enh? Enh?"

"Don't worry so much. Remember, you're a great kid, no matter what happens today. Prep for Prep isn't the only path. You can still have a good life, a wonderful life! Do you understand?"

"Enh?" she said, no longer hearing me, and I stepped aside as she was swept off in a river of children. "Good luck, MeiKai!" I shouted. She didn't turn around. I watched the back of her bobbing head until it disappeared, then turned and battled my way upstream through the kids.

I passed Fatma.

"Good luck, Fatma!"

I passed Gary.

"Good luck, Gary!"

I passed Najiyah, Aliza, Miguel, and Matthew.

"Good luck! Good luck! Good luck! Good luck!"

When the last kids entered the cafeteria, its doors were closed, and the hallway went silent. There was nothing more I could do.

Outside the school, parents were milling around, wondering what to do with themselves for the next three hours. I ran into Mr. Torres, Gary's dad, and he invited me for coffee at the McDonald's on the corner. Other parents had had the same idea, and the place was crowded. After we got our coffee and found a table, Mr. Torres told me he wanted very much for his son to get into Prep for Prep, but if that didn't happen, he'd decided not to send Gary to public school. He worried about the students there.

He said, "Gary is very innocent. He's my only son. I won't get another chance. I am not young. My son is my future." I told him kids in private school could corrupt Gary, too; there weren't any guarantees. This surprised Mr. Torres, and he shook his head, discouraged and confused. He asked me if I knew anything about parochial schools. I said I didn't. He said he'd heard the teachers were stricter there, and he also hoped the experience would bring Gary closer to God, something he couldn't give his son because he had to work Sundays.

I told him Gary was lucky to have such a devoted father, and he told me Gary was lucky to have such a devoted teacher. We smiled at each other in mutual appreciation, then I excused myself, having noticed that MeiKai's mother and brother were at a table across the room.

Mrs. Li gave me her huge smile, and I was relieved to see her looking so well. Although MeiKai's reports about her mother made me concerned about her mental stability, in her presence my worries evaporated. How could you not love this woman for her smile alone? Alan translated for us, and as we spoke, from time to time Mrs. Li affectionately stroked her son's arm. No one could deny she was a devoted parent who'd raised two decent, hardworking kids.

I asked if she'd really told MeiKai she'd fail the test. Mrs. Li smiled and nodded, explaining that this was a psychological device intended to make MeiKai angry and thus work harder to prove herself. "I don't think it's going to work," I said. "MeiKai was a nervous wreck in there." But Mrs. Li assured me everything would be all right: the Queen Mother of the West had said MeiKai would pass. Mrs. Li also said that the Queen Mother of the West had told her that MeiKai would grow up to write children's books. When she looked at me meaningfully, I shuddered. I hadn't detected a passionate love for writing on MeiKai's part, and if the Queen Mother was pushing MeiKai into a career she didn't want, I hoped she wouldn't blame me.

Gradually I became aware that I was being stared at by a pretty woman at another table, and when I glanced her way, she gave a shy wave. Was she flirting with me? It took me a moment to realize that this was Miguel's mother, Christina. I hardly recognized her. She'd lost a lot of weight, was wearing makeup, and no longer dressed like a Pentecostal. I was glad to see her because I needed to talk to her about Miguel. His recent stories were giving me the creeps. In one, a psychotic leaf saws off the paws of a kitty cat, the thought of which made Miguel cackle, "Now I'm *really* getting violent!"

I said good-bye to the Lis and went to Mrs. Santiago's table. "Nice to see you, Christina," I said. "Can I get you a coffee?"

"Thank you, Mr. Swope."

"Call me Sam, please. Don't be so formal."

She smiled, saying, "I'll try."

When I mentioned my worry about Miguel's stories, she started to cry. I handed her a McDonald's napkin for a handkerchief. She said, "The other day I said to Miguel, 'You can't lie to me 'cause I know you.' And his voice got very loud and he cried out, 'You don't know me! You don't know what I have inside of me!' And my mouth fell open, Mr. Swope, 'cause I was so hurt 'cause I had always been the one he talked to about everything. So I swallowed my pain and told him okay, that I was there for him whenever he wanted to talk, and he saw I was hurting so he said, 'You have to be patient, Mommy. I'll tell you when I'm ready.'"

As she spoke, Maya's family entered McDonald's. I nodded hello to them and gestured that I'd stop by later. Then I turned my attention back to Mrs. Santiago and asked, "How are things with your husband?"

"Very bad," she said.

It was clear she needed to talk, and if listening to her would help Miguel, I was glad to lend an ear. She said, "I am only happy these days when I am away from home on my own. Then I feel free. 'Cause when I get close to my house, I get migraines and I get very sick. I want to have a life, Mr. Swope!" she cried. "I want to go parties. I want to laugh. But I can't. I can't!"

I said nothing, just nodded sympathetically and handed her another napkin.

She lowered her voice and said, as if confessing, "I'm a bad mother, Mr. Swope."

"Don't say that, Christina. You've had a very hard life. You love your boys very much. Anyone can see that."

She looked in her coffee cup and shook her head. "You don't know. A very bad mother."

"Why do you say that?"

What followed was a terribly sad story, as painful for her to tell as it was for me to hear, but it explained Miguel's behavior last fall, his inability to focus, his anger, his banging through the forest, his bullying, his violent stories. Indeed, given the troubles at home, it was impressive Miguel had been able to function at all. Not only was he suffering, but he'd been warned not to talk to anyone at school about the family's problems at home, because his parents were afraid some government authority would call them unfit and send their boys into foster care. Terrified at this prospect, Miguel held his sadness in.

Troubling as Mrs. Santiago's story was, I didn't think it justified breaking up the family. There was suffering, there was pain, but there was also love and concern. Yet clearly help was needed. Not knowing what services were available to the Santiagos, or how good those services would be, I told her they should see a professional—a therapist, a social worker. I said, "There must some kind of mental health agency you can go to, isn't there?"

She said the school had given her a telephone number but her husband wouldn't allow her to use it. He wanted all their problems to be dealt with by the church. "But I am through with the church, Mr. Swope," she said. "I don't believe in a church where a man like my husband who is so involved there and he treats me like he does."

We'd run out of napkins, but Mrs. Santiago was still crying, so I left the table to get more, and was glad for an excuse to get away. My mind was reeling. I needed to catch my breath. I stopped by Maya's family to say hello; after the test they were taking Maya on an outing, as a reward. Lucky Maya! Such a warm, happy family! After chatting for a moment, I told them I needed to get back and, napkins in hand, returned to Miguel's mother. All I could think to say to her was "I'm so sorry you've had so much unhappiness, and it isn't fair. But you have to pull yourself together. There's no other choice. You have to find strength. You just have to. You have four boys who depend on you. You have to be strong for them."

Mrs. Santiago nodded silently. This wasn't anything she hadn't told herself many times. She forced herself to smile—Miguel's smile—and said, "I'm better now, Mr. Swope. Don't worry. I am getting better. The other day, you know, I passed the driver's test. First time."

"That's great!"

"Now I got my license, so I'm ready to take my boys to places we can play this summer. Outside. My husband doesn't like me getting wet and rolling on the ground with my boys. He says it's not ladylike. But I am not that way. I want my children to play. I want them to run around. And if I want to play with my children, Mr. Swope, I'll play. And nobody is gonna stop me."

"I'm so glad to hear you say that. Kids need to be outside."

I leapt on this scrap of hopeful news and smiled, trying to make it seem as if the danger had passed now, everything would be okay. I'd been at McDonald's for two hours and had to go, but before I did I asked Christina if she'd had breakfast. She said no, she'd had to scrounge for subway fare that morning. This kind of desperate poverty was incomprehensible to me, and I was glad I could buy her an Egg McMuffin with bacon and cheese and an orange juice. It made me feel less guilty about running off.

The Stalwart Boy

Miguel's mother gave him permission to confide in me. She told him he didn't have to worry, that I'd never do anything to put him in foster care. I met with Miguel the following Monday, and he cried and cried. I asked Miguel if he felt that the unhappiness at home was his fault.

He nodded, saying, "Because every time they fight my dad says *your* son and my mom says *our* son, and I usually hear both of them say my name, and they never say my brothers' names, so I think they're saying it's because of *him* this all has to start . . ."

"Oh, Miguel. It's *not* your fault. It's *not* your fault."

He cried so hard he couldn't speak. At last he said, "I sometimes think, like, I did something really bad. Sometimes I think that God doesn't love me no more. I know it's wrong to be angry with God, but that's how I feel because that's what the Bible says, to pray and give him prayer until your prayer is answered, but I pray and nothing's happened! It's hard for me, Mr. Swope! I can't deal with it!"

"It feels like you can't deal with it, Miguel. But you can and you must. Life hasn't been fair to you. Life isn't fair to lots of kids. But you have to believe that you can get through this. Because if you don't believe that, if you don't believe . . . It sounds ridiculous to say this, but the best way to help yourself is to do your homework and get your education. Then you'll have options. Otherwise, it'll be . . . harder. Do you understand?"

No words, just tears.

"Do you understand?"

Just tears.

"You remember that word I gave you for Christmas, in third grade?"

"Stalwart."

"Do you remember what it means?"

"Strong."

"Yes, strong in spirit. You have to be strong, Miguel. Can you be strong?"

Just tears.

"All right, my friend," I sighed. "It's time for lunch."

Before I asked the children to write, I often tried to change the mood in the classroom—I'd turn off the lights, play quiet music, or read them something. Several days after my conference with Miguel, I read the class the Brothers Grimm's *The Juniper Tree*, using Lore Segal's beautiful translation in an edition illustrated by Maurice Sendak. This strange, powerful story has familiar folktale elements. In it, a woman wishes for a child under a juniper tree, becomes pregnant, develops a greedy passion for juniper berries, and eats so many she becomes deathly ill. She then gives birth to a son, and "when she saw it she was so happy that she died." Her husband buries her under the juniper, and after a time he marries a woman who has a daughter of her own. Like many folktale stepmothers, she takes a hatred to her new son, and one day as the boy opens a chest and leans in to get an apple, she slams the chest's lid on his neck, decapitating him. After setting the boy's head back on his shoulders to make him seem alive, she tells her daughter, Ann Marie, to box the boy's ears. When Ann Marie does as she's told, she knocks her brother's head off, and her mother lets the poor girl think she's killed him. The father, returning home, worries that his son isn't anywhere to be found, but he sits down to dinner, not knowing that the stew, which he greedily devours, contains his son's hacked-up body. Guilt-ridden, Ann Marie lays her brother's bones under the juniper tree, and mysteriously feels better:

> The juniper began to stir and the branches kept opening out and coming back together again, just like someone who is really happy and goes like this with his hands. And then there was a sort of mist coming out of the tree and right in this mist it burned like fire and out of the fire flew this lovely bird that sang oh, so gloriously sweet and flew high into the air and when it was gone, the juniper tree was just the way it had always been and the cloth with the bones was gone.

The bird flies to the goldsmith, then to the cobbler, then to the miller's men, and to each it sings the same song not just once, but twice:

> "My mother she butchered me,
> My father he ate me,
> My sister, little Ann Marie,
> She gathered up the bones of me
> And tied them in a silken cloth
> To lay under the juniper.
> Tweet twee, what a pretty bird am I!"

In return for singing, the bird is given a golden chain by the goldsmith, red shoes by the cobbler, and a millstone by the miller's men. The bird flies back to the father's house with these gifts and sings the song three more times. The song, though tragic, is so beautifully sung it fills the father and Ann Marie with joy. The wicked stepmother, however, feels only terror. When Ann Marie runs outdoors to see the bird, it gives her the red shoes. When the father steps outside, the bird gives him the gold chain. Then the wife heads out, hoping for a gift, too.

And as she came out of the door, crunch! the bird threw the millstone on her head and she was squashed. The father and Ann Marie heard it and came out. There was steam and flames and fire rising from the spot, and when they were gone, there stood the little brother and he took his father and Ann Marie by the hand and the three of them were so happy and went into the house and sat down at the table and ate their supper.

This is the sort of Grimm tale people talk about when they remark how shockingly gruesome the original folktales can be, the sort of tale that reasonable people feel should not be read to children. I, however, lean toward the view of others, who feel these tales give cathartic shape to primal terrors children have—being abandoned by parents, as Hansel and Gretel were, or eaten by a wolf, as Little Red Riding Hood was. At any rate, my students were fifth graders and old enough to handle such a story, although as I read it aloud, those nine repetitions of the bird's strange song made me feel as if I were chanting some kind of spell, or conjuring deep magic I didn't fully understand, and indeed the story held the children rapt. Their mouths hung open when I'd finished; they were hardly breathing. Hoping they'd draw on the story's mystery and power, I didn't pause for discussion but asked the children to write a story about a mysterious tree. This was Miguel's:

DOESN'T MATTER

On a far away land named Joseph, people traded crops, meat, wine, clothing, seeds, etc. with Ecuador.

One day I went to Quito to buy some things for my family. When I got there, I bought a brown handsome male horse which cost me 907,421,180,906,452 sucres. Of course, I bought him with my money. Then I bought ten mangos, two fat pigs, fifty ears of corn, and a rifle. I don't know what my father wanted a rifle for, but I bought it. Orders are orders.

When I got home, my father took the pigs, killed them, washed the meat, cut the fat off, and cooked it. Meanwhile, my mother cooked twelve ears of corn, lentils, and mashed potatoes.

When it was time to eat, my brothers were the first ones seated. We ate. I was about to put the last spoonful in my mouth when I heard someone say, "You got to get to Quito, and fast!" I was heading for the door when my father said, "Junior, here. Take this. I told you to buy it because I thought it was time you got a rifle." He gave me the rifle.

I ran outside, got on my horse, and went full speed to Quito. When I got there, everyone was surrounding a man. But why? He just had in his hand one little seed. He noticed me and said, "Here, boy. Have this seed." I caught it. "On December 14, one minute before midnight, plant it. Don't plant it any earlier or later than that." That was one day before my birthday.

Quickly I went home and told my parents. So on the 14th of December, one minute before midnight, I planted it and then went to sleep. The next day I went to water it and saw a humongous tree with a vine as long as two adult pythons.

But very soon, came some bandits. When they were getting near me and the tree, the vine of the tree tangled all of them, choked them, and "swallowed" them.

I ran to my mom and told her the news, but of course she didn't believe me.

So that night she awoke because of a noise that startled her. She went down with my dad and saw fifteen bandits approaching them. They were twenty feet away from the tree. In the dim light my mom and dad could see the tree's vine tangle them, choke them, and "swallow" them.

The next morning, my parents couldn't talk. After breakfast, I went outside and got on my horse.

The man that gave me the seed came running to me and said, "That seed was watered with a venomous clear liquid instead of water. It's not supposed to swallow people. It's supposed to eat weeds and cabbage, butterflies and aphids."

"Doesn't matter," I said in a sweet, gentle voice.

"DOESN'T MATTER?" the man said in a leopard or lion-like voice.

"Yes, doesn't matter."

With that, my tree's vine tangled him, choked him, and "swallowed" him.

His eldest son came and challenged battle for his dad's death. I said, "I don't want to kill. Instead, since you have a horse and I do, too, whoever wins the race will keep both horses." I was serious. To let go of a horse that cost me 907,421,180,906,452 sucres was serious. He agreed.

The race started. I was a nose behind. My horse jumped over a log and was now two whole bodies ahead. We won, thanks to my horse. I kept both horses and gave the kid's horse to my dad.

And life continued easy and mysterious.

Emotion Recollected in Tranquillity

When I'd ask the kids what they'd learned about writing from me, they'd say, "More specific details" and "Never be boring." Those were my mantras. Nature writing, I'd hoped, would force them to write specifically about the world, but I discovered early on that nature writing without an organizing principal is unreadable, a scattershot list of random observations. Some kids intuited this right away and wrote their journal entries as if they were diaries. To help the others shape their observations, I suggested that they frame their nature writing as letters to their adopted trees. I told them, "Tell the tree where you're sitting and what you see and hear and let your mind take you to other places, to bigger thoughts. Let nature work its magic. I want you to be like the poet William Blake, who could 'see a world in a grain of sand and a heaven in a wild flower.'"

"That's pretty cool," said Rosie.

These "Dear Tree" letters, I explained, would be a recurring motif for *The Tree Book*. Letters mixed in among the poems, stories, and artwork would take us through the seasons. Although these letters were a literary device, a gimmick, it was something all the kids could do, and many did it well. Even Fatma came around:

Dear Tree,

Hello, once again. I'm now sitting on a rock. A dirty rock. But I don't mind. I think everything is beautiful. Even if this rock is dirty. I hear birds chirping and ducks making a whoosh, whoosh sound. Right now it got very cloudy. Just one minute ago it was sunny. Now it got sunny. Hmph.

You can never tell with weather, can ya? I love it when we walk around the park or write in our journals.

It is so peaceful and quiet. None of us students are talking and this way we can really listen to nature.

I saw some other trees which had moss or fungus growing on them. Right now a breeze just messed up my hair. But I don't mind. I want to go somewhere else where there is shade. I'm going right now. I also saw some moss growing on a rock. The wind shakes the leaves and it looks funny. Right now Mr. Swope said we have to go but I want to stay longer.

Your (legal) guardian,

Fatma

One day I asked some kids, "Tell me about what it's like for you to write in the park."

"I love it," Maya said. "Every time I go to Central Park, I feel like writing, I don't know why. Words come like a breeze!"

Su Jung agreed: "In the park, it feels so peaceful and nice there and when you, like, tell us to write, nothing comes to mind and then I keep on stare at the rock and everybody and all of a sudden stuff comes to my mind and I start writing."

But MeiKai said, "When I write in the park I get disturbed by the wind and the helicopters, and the squirrels can be very annoying. And sometimes when I write in the park other kids come over and talk to you and then that's what I hate."

Simon had a different take. "There's too much exciting to look at," he said. "I can't get everything down."

"What if you just took notes, then wrote your letters later, in school?" I suggested.

"Yeah!" said Simon.

"We'll give that a try, then. Maybe you're like William Wordsworth, Simon. He was a nature poet who said that poetry was 'emotion recollected in tranquillity.'"

"What the heck is that?" asked Su Jung.

"Well, *emotion,* you know what that means: strong feelings. And *tranquillity* means peaceful. So Wordsworth would be out in nature and he'd get these big, strong thoughts that got him excited, but he wouldn't write about them till he got home, later, when he'd calmed down and could think about them peacefully."

"But if you do it later," said Su Jung, "you don't really feel nature around you."

"You have your notes, so you remember," said Simon.

"It's best to see what you're writing about," said Rosie. "When you see it in reality, it's much better."

"At home, I'm not peaceful at all," said Su Jung. "At home, I don't feel anything, but I don't feel peaceful. I feel peaceful in the park."

In the end, some wrote in the park, and some took notes and wrote their letters later. Many of them produced their best writing under the influence of the trees, and I loved reading their impressions, loved this written evidence, clearly stated, simple and heartfelt, that they'd been touched by nature. Often I'd come across a sentence or two, or just a turn of phrase, that particularly delighted me. This may not seem like much until you consider that the legacy of many writers who appear in Bartlett's *Familiar Quotations* isn't more than a few words, either.

It is so calm and quiet in nature. Everywhere I go in the city it is so loud. I wonder why there can't be nature everywhere.

LUCINDA

I see stuff I never saw before. The water makes a squishy sound and the birds are singing twit, peep, twi, peeee. The wind is blowing. The trees shiver their leaves to the ground.

MAGGIE

Sometimes I feel like the wind, water, ducks, trees, well, I feel like nature everywhere is whispering in my ear but I don't understand what she is saying.

AMARJEET

I saw millions of trees. Some trees were slanted and bent. But many showed the twists and turns and oddnesses of nature.

ROSIE

Today at Central Park it was a wonderful feeling to take nature that's all around you and put it on paper.

MATTHEW

I saw a little bird today. It was brown with white spots on its back and wings. I wonder if he will come back. If he does, I wouldn't know if it was him or not.

CHARITY

I went toward the tree because among the rest of the trees, this one looked as if it was flying (not too high). The bottom part, the root, looked so light, as if it wasn't there.

NAJIYAH

I observed three pigeons. One was looking for a berry to eat. The second one was still and taking a nap. And the third one looked like it would like to go to the bathroom.

CESAR

Compared to two months ago, the world seems very empty. No green to light up the city. When I look out the window, I think of boredom.

GARY

I saw a little bird near me. I fed it bread, seeds, and some water. The little bird was happy but he was cold so I took my scarf off and covered him. Then he flew away.

SAMANTHA

Wow, it is all so beautiful!!!!

ELLA

Maya was the most sophisticated nature writer, and the most consistent. She'd found a voice, and she wrote about the world with a tender melancholy enlivened by vivid details that led her to a questioning sense of nature's mystery:

No sounds, no birds, no movement.

Complete silence, except for this pen against this piece of paper. The sky is completely white. Maybe it will rain, maybe it will not. Who knows? A bird flies overhead. Well, at least there still is some movement.

My tree looks sad. Well, it doesn't exactly look sad, I mean it feels sad, to me. I guess that's the feeling of sleep. (My tree is sleeping, you know.)

The wind blows by. It feels cold, but cold as in a "cold heart." I guess it's angry. I wonder why it's angry. I guess that the world isn't acting the way it should.

I have the feeling it will rain. The sky is white, everything is really cold, and so am I. A car passes by, destroying the silence. Silence is part of nature, in disguise, you know. Nature can be silent when a bird is laying its eggs. Sometimes nature needs quiet. How long does it take to keep nature completely silent? But, wait, there can never be complete silence, if you look at it in another angle.

Another bird (well, pigeon) flies overhead. It goes to the end of the block, then flies back and lands about a few feet away from me, looking (and pecking) for food. I get up and go near it. I am right behind it! Then, it flies away. Why do birds have that instinct? I've never been closer than a foot to any bird. It somehow knows that I'm there. First, it turns its head, then walks fast, then faster and even faster until it jumps up, flies away, and leaves me staring. Gone with the Wind, right?

Snow Poems

One Sunday morning I woke up to find my cat sitting in the precise middle of the windowsill and looking outside, mesmerized by falling snow—a quiet, wet snow with big, lazy flakes that covered the branches and twigs of the tree outside my window. Several inches had fallen, enough to play in. This was the winter's first snowfall, and I couldn't be sure we'd get another. I waited till nine o'clock, then got on the phone.

"Have you looked out the window, Miguel?"

"I was sleeping. Our shades are down."

"Pull them up!"

"It's snowing, Mr. Swope! It's snowing!!"

"Get your mom to take you and your brothers outside so you can play in it! That's your homework, do you understand? You have to play in the snow! Then when you come back in, write a poem about it. We don't have any writing about snow for our *Tree Book,* so be sure to look at your tree in the snow! And do me a favor, call the other kids on your team and tell them, would you?"

"Okay, Mr. Swope!"

I called other team leaders. I called Maya and Fatma, both still asleep. I called Gary, who wasn't home. I called Mateo, who was at church. Then I reached Cesar.

"Cesar, have you looked outside?"

"Yeah, it's snowing."

"Isn't it beautiful?"

"Yeah."

"Guess what I want you to do?"

"Um . . . I know! Write a poem?"

"Smart boy! But first I want you to play in the snow. That's your research. Then you write your poem."

"I was gonna go out later."

"No! Later will be too late! The snow will melt and get dirty! Go now! It won't last long! And call the other kids on your team and tell them, would you?"

"Okay, Mr. Swope."

Snow snow everywhere
I call Jorge to play
He comes right away.
We put our gloves on and count
to three—
A snowball in my face!
A snowball in his face!
Jorge slides down,
he falls.
Then I slide down,
but don't fall.
What a nice snowman we build!
We are happy three hours
playing,
and one hour in his house,
playing Monopoly
and resting,
because we are wet and cold.
Then I go home
and take a hot bath,
and then we talk
on the phone.

CESAR

The Bud Lesson

As we climbed a hill in Central Park, kids complained that it was cold. "Cold? You call this cold?" I said. "It's only forty-one degrees! This is nothing! Don't be such wimps!"

I was disappointed that it wasn't colder. For that day's lesson I'd hoped it would be twenty below. I couldn't think of a better way to get across the miracle of buds.

Su Jung, trudging beside me, asked, "What is winter like for the tree?"

"I don't think trees feel the cold."

"How do you know they don't?"

"They don't have a nervous system."

"Actually, if they did get cold, they'll probably freeze to death out here."

"No, not to death. These trees could freeze and still live."

"They can?"

"Amazing, isn't it?"

At the hill's top, we stopped in front of several trees of different species. I asked the class, "How would you describe a tree in winter?"

MeiKai said, "Bare."

Gary said, "Sad, ugly."

"Doesn't anyone think they're beautiful?"

Najiyah was surprised by my question. "Really? You think they're beautiful?"

"I do. See how their branches twist in interesting ways? See the different textures of the bark? Winter trees are like sculpture. If you open yourselves up to them, trees do something to you. They have an effect, emotionally. It's almost like they're communicating. I can't explain it. Don't say anything for a moment, just look and listen."

Simon, Gary, and Mateo were giggling, so I moved near them to stop their clowning, and we all stood silently.

I said, "Can't you see how beautiful they are?"

"If you concentrate on them, they don't look ugly," said Su Jung. "But they're not byoooooootiful."

For Su Jung, this was progress. Now that she had a stepmother and stepsiblings she liked (even if she saw them only on weekends), she was happier, more relaxed, less negative, and her silences were far less frequent. Moreover, that year she'd volunteered to help out with the kindergartners during lunch, and she did such a wonderful job she was made the head monitor. This made touching sense. In the third-grade production of *Peter Pan,* Su Jung had asked to play Wendy, the girl-mother, and I suppose that having lost her own mother, Su Jung had a greater need to be one. Su Jung was healing, I told myself. Even her writing sometimes showed a sense of humor:

> If I was a leaf I would be able to see
> everything that is going around me.
> I would give the tree color.
> If I was a leaf, I would have bugs
> all around me.
> I would have ladybugs and grasshoppers,
> ants and caterpillars on me.
> If I was a leaf, I would make food
> for flowers.
> If I was a leaf I would be friends
> with all the other leaves.
> If I was a leaf, I would get
> stepped on.
> But I wouldn't care because . . .
> I'm not a leaf.

I asked the class to look again at the winter trees, reminding them that in several months it would be summer. I said, "Right now these trees are bare, right? So tell me this: How do branches suddenly explode with leaves, flowers, seeds, apples, oranges? Where's all that stuff come from? Is it hiding inside the tree? Does someone push a button? Wave a wand?"

Their faces registered the improbability of that.

"Take your magnifying glasses. I'd like you to work in pairs. Study the twigs on these four trees."

Before long, Fatma said, "This twig has these, like, tiny green nuts."

"Those aren't nuts," I told her.

Before that year, if someone had asked me when trees grow their buds, I'd have said spring. But it turns out that buds grow in the summer, one at the base of each leaf stem and another at the end of each twig. Like the tiny green ones Fatma had spotted, most buds are small, so small it's easy to miss them. You have to look. What impressed and amazed me, though, was how buds sit on twigs all winter long, lonely and heroic, in rain and ice and snow. "You could write a story about buds," I told the class. "They're like treasure chests belonging to fairies, the place where they hide spring's leaves and flowers."

I asked the kids to pretend they were buds. I had them crouch on their haunches and hug their knees, tuck their heads in. I told them to imagine themselves on a twig, exposed to freezing winds and rain and sleet and long cold nights, covered with snow and icicles. Then I asked them to imagine at last a bit of warmth: the sun shines down, the sap begins to rise, it fills you up, you start to stretch, move a tiny bit, open up. You come to life gradually, reach for the sun! Stretch! Stretch!

"Mr. Swope?" said Noelia.

"Yes?"

"I think someone farted."

"Thank you for pointing that out."

I moved the class upwind, and we sat on an enormous sunny rock overlooking a lake. As they watched the ducks and swans, I read them the chapter from *The House at Pooh Corner* "IN WHICH It Is Shown That Tiggers Don't Climb Trees." Then I suggested that the kids write a story, saying, "Here's a beginning if you need one: It's your birthday. Your parents take you on a picnic to Central Park. You wander off by yourself and have an encounter with a strange tree."

Later, when I read over what they'd written, it was the usual mixed bag, but a wild story by Amarjeet took me by surprise and made me understand how much these kids were growing up. Amarjeet had never shown much fervor for writing, but to everything there is a season. All her pencil had needed was a jolt of hormones, and those just hadn't been available till now.

Amarjeet's preadolescent libido had been whipped into a passion by the movie star Leonardo DiCaprio. Poor Amarjeet: Leonardo was her god and she was helpless. She mooned, she sighed, she etched his name on notebooks and held his image in her heart. While waiting on the subway platform once, I saw her standing in front of a movie poster, eye to eye with Leonardo. She was spellbound—there's no other way to put it—and could hardly pull herself away. Oh, Leonardo! Amarjeet wrote this story just for you!

MY DREAM SEED

The whole family and my dog, Blue, were having a picnic in Central Park to celebrate my eleventh birthday . . .

While my parents packed up the basket with empty juice bottles and dirty napkins, . . . I ran into the Ramble, a forest in the middle of the Park. Blue came with me. As Blue and I crouched behind a maple tree, an acorn hit me on the head. I looked up and saw a squirrel. The squirrel leapt from the crown of the maple to a nearby evergreen, and then leapt to other trees further into the Ramble. All of a sudden, I had a strange feeling inside telling me to track down the squirrel. It jumped so fast I had to race to keep up with it. But finally, it stopped on a tiny ginkgo tree growing right in the middle of the path.

Right before my eyes, the ginkgo tree grew faster and faster until it was a full-grown tree. Blue barked at the tree. I was terrified and was about to run when I heard a voice cry, "Help!" I turned around and there in the rough bark of the tree's trunk I saw Leo DiCaprio's face! I was amazed and scared at the same time, but I didn't leave. I said, "Who are you?" He answered, "You probably don't know me, but I'm Leo DiCaprio. . . . Please help me! I'm trapped in this ginkgo!" Then, as the tree vanished before my eyes, Leo handed me half of a seed, saying, "This will help you!" And he was gone.

I stood there with my mouth wide open and the squirrel hit me on the head with a tiny piece of paper. As I opened it, it grew magically larger, just as the tree had. On the map, I saw Central Park's Belvedere Castle and a picture of Leo locked up in its dungeon. Blue and I raced through the forest, getting pricked by thorns, but I wouldn't stop until I reached the castle . . .

I ran down the castle's steps, opened the dungeon door, and . . . suddenly found myself sliding down a deep, dark hole. When I landed, I was in an underground cavern. Blue was nowhere in sight, but then I saw Leo tied up with ropes as the evil ginkgo poked his face with twigs, leaving bloody scars. . . .

I whistled for Blue and in seconds he came sliding down the hole and landed in my arms. Blue leapt to the ground, saw the tree and raced over to it and lifted his leg. "Ew!" screamed the tree and it waved its branches frantically, trying to dry its trunk.

I saw my chance. I raced over to Leo. He held out half of the seed and cried, "Quick! Get your seed and put it against mine!" I did as he said, took my half seed from my pocket and put it against his half.

Suddenly, he was free. The tree melted away as Blue ran over to me and scratched himself.

Leo had to leave so I asked for his autograph and he gave it to me. Then he handed me the ginkgo seed and said, "If you ever want to see me again, just shake the ginkgo seed!" After that he vanished, but I wanted to see if it was true, so I shook the seed, and he was there again!

What a birthday! Just what I always wanted—for Leo to come whenever I wanted him to! And to think it all started with one tiny seed!

Amarjeet had never written anything so long or so impassioned. Her script was fevered, frenzied. I tried to picture her that day in Central Park. Had she been sitting on a stump? Was she using a tree as a backrest? Or had she stood to write, as Simon had? No matter how I racked my brain, though, I had no memory of her, no picture of this young girl writing her heart out. She'd gone unnoticed.

As we left the park for school that day, Su Jung teased me, saying, "I hate you, Mr. Swope. Just when I start getting all these ideas for my story, you make us leave!"

"You could write it tonight."

"No!"

"What if I made it your homework assignment?"

She shook her head decisively and said, "Do you want me to do a bad job? Because I will. Do you want to read a waste?"

I sighed, defeated, giving up. She was such a stubborn and contrary girl. "No, you're right, Su Jung. I don't want to read a waste."

She saw she'd hurt me, so she said, "Maybe I could write a little bit."

"That would be wonderful."

Some days later she came to my office for a conference with her first draft of the story. I asked her, "How are your weekends at your dad's and stepmom's?"

"They want me to call her Mother but I can't call her Mother," she said. "It seems strange." She said no one ever talked to her in that home—not her parents, not her siblings.

My heart sank. I'd been so eager to think of her as happy at home. I said, "That must be lonely for you."

"Yeah," she answered with a shrug of steely resignation.

It was important to me to think that the kids I'd come to know and love were going to be okay, that life worked out. But some wounds don't heal easily, or ever, and we cannot always make things whole.

Because Su Jung didn't want to talk about her weekends, I turned our attention to her story. We'd lose ourselves in work. A quick glance showed me one thing wrong with it. "Why aren't there any paragraphs here? Not one! I know you know how to use paragraphs, Su Jung. You were being lazy again, weren't you?"

"I get my height from my father, my eyes from my father, and my laziness from my father. That's why I'm always lazy."

"You should fight that laziness, Su Jung. It's not a good quality." I read her story out loud. "'*The Strange Day*. My name is Nicole White and something strange happened to me on my 16th birthday. The weather was perfect. All of a sudden, my mom asked if I wanted to go on a picnic in Central Park.' It's interesting how you never use dialogue. What the mother says here could have been put in quotation marks, but instead you use indirect speech."

"I don't know why but I never use dialogue in my stories."

"You don't have to. Not all writers use dialogue. It's just another tool. Why don't you use dialogue in your next draft, though, for practice?" When she nodded, I continued reading. "'When my mom said that, I got scared.' Why is Nicole scared?"

"I didn't write that she was scared."

"Am I reading it wrong? Isn't this word *scared*?"

Su Jung looked at her story, then said, "She was scared because they never take her anywhere. She was scared they would leave her in the park and then come back home."

"Ah, that's interesting. Kind of like Hansel and Gretel. Okay, let's see. . . . 'When we reached Central Park, we went to Belveder Castle'—*Belvedere* has an *e* on the end—'we were eating our lunch when I found a seed in my pocket. I sneaked out of the castle while my parents were kissing and ran to the Ramble.' That's a vivid detail, I can picture that. Good."

It's impossible to know how close to fact her story was, but it didn't seem unlikely that Su Jung had seen her father kissing his new wife, or that this new relationship would cause Su Jung uneasy moments, moments when she wasn't sure if she belonged. I asked, "What was Nicole thinking about when her parents were kissing?"

"Nasty."

"And when she runs to the Ramble, is she running away? Or just getting away?"

"Getting away."

"Okay. So it would be good to have more—"

"—details—"

"—about what's going on in Nicole's mind. She's an interesting character psychologically: she has parents who never take her anywhere; she's scared they're going to leave her in the park; and they ignore her on her birthday picnic and kiss. Interesting. What is the seed doing in her pocket?"

"Maybe she found it on a class trip."

"Okay . . . you should make this seed seem somehow special, though, so she has a reason to plant it. 'She plants the seed and all of a sudden the seed opened up and then lots of gigantic enormous green buds grew shaped like a tree. It was amazing the buds started to open up and flowers grew, but it didn't collapse. It was still standing tall.' This is exciting, but can you describe that moment more? I'm a little unclear about what's happening."

"I don't know. The seed was there and then it's a tree. It's just that it doesn't have a trunk and a bark. It's just all buds."

"That's a wild idea. I like it."

Silence.

"Can you describe these buds beyond saying they were 'gigantic enormous.' Was it a beautiful sight, or a scary one?"

"Scary. It looked like this whole gigantic brain."

"That's good! I'm going to write that down here so you don't forget: 'gigantic brain, scary.' Okay, so you're scared—I mean, *Nicole* is scared. Can you describe the flowers?"

"Daisies, sort of. Like white and purple, I think."

"So at first it's this hideous huge bud brain, then it turns into a beautiful bouquet. Oooh, I love this! So how did you, I mean *Nicole,* feel, as she looked at those flowers?"

"A miracle."

"Ah! Then it ends: 'I heard my mom calling and I had to leave.'" I made a face and groaned dramatically. "Aw, mannnnnnnnn. Just when things start getting good you bail out!"

Su Jung giggled, then looked at the clock.

"Do you have to be somewhere?"

"I have to go. I have band."

"I'll just keep you another second. What could happen next in your story?"

"The tree turns her into a flower and people step on her."

I rolled my eyes. "Oh, please! Why must such horrible things always happen to your characters?"

"I don't know," she giggled. "It fits them."

"Couldn't you get picked, instead of stomped on? At least then you'd go home and be beautiful for someone to enjoy."

"The mother could pick it."

"Brilliant," I said. "That would be perfect."

"'Cause it's a surprise," said Su Jung.

"Excellent. Can you do a rewrite for tomorrow?"

"Maybe yes, maybe no," she said, half tease, half threat.

She did rewrite the story, adding a bit of dialogue, a detail here and there, and she also reworked the ending, but only enough so I couldn't complain. Her heart wasn't in it, and I didn't blame her.

Epithalamium

On a March field trip, Miguel asked, "What's that bird over there?"

"That's a robin."

"I knew it!" he cried, jumping up and down. *"That's my first robin, Mr. Swope! My first robin in my whole life!* It means spring is coming! A robin means good luck, right?"

I'd never heard that, but maybe there was something to it. Not long after Miguel saw his robin, he got three pieces of good news.

The first news came by mail. Miguel came home from school one day to find his mother smiling and waving a letter from Prep for Prep. She laughed and made Miguel chase her around the apartment before letting him read that he'd done well in the first round of tests and was invited to the second stage.

I said a silent prayer and fantasized a future for him: he'd get in and Prep for Prep would shape him up in ways I couldn't, make him toe the line so that he realized his potential, and one day—who knows?—maybe he'd get a job with the Wildlife Conservation Society, tracking jaguars in Central America.

Miguel's second bit of good news came during his interview at the Clinton Middle School for Writers and Artists. He'd sneaked a peek at what the principal had written on his application folder. "He put 'impressive,' Mr. Swope. He even underlined it!"

"You *are* impressive, Miguel," I said. "But don't get your hopes up yet. You never know till you know."

It was impossible not to hope, though. My hopes were sky-high. So much was at stake.

The third piece of news was the best of all. Miguel's parents had reconciled and were getting remarried in a commitment ceremony at the church. "I'm going to give my mom away to my dad," Miguel said proudly.

"That's wonderful," I said, knocking on wood. "Congratulations."

Without any prompting, Miguel came up with the idea to write a poem to his parents for their wedding gift. I said, "Poems written for weddings have a long tradition. They even have a name: *epithalamium*."

"Hunh?" he said.

"Say it: epithalamium."

"Epithamum."

"Ep-i-tha-LAY-mee-um."

"Ep-i-tha-LAY-mee-um."

It took Miguel several days to finish his poem. It was reassuring but also heartbreaking to see him work with such devotion, doing his poetic best to make his parents' marriage whole:

> *I give my mom away*
> *to my dad.*
> *The wind gives the seed away*
> *to the soil.*
>
> *A veil for my mom*
> *covers her face.*
> *What shall cover the seed?*
> *Its hard shell*
> *will be its veil*
> *which hides the*
> *beauty of a tree.*
>
> *Mom and Dad are one*
> *as a couple.*
> *The seed and the soil are one*
> *as a pair.*
> *My mom and the seed*
> *are brides.*
> *My dad and the damp soil*
> *are grooms.*
> *Mom, Dad, soil, and seed . . .*
> *new fruit*
> *which will bear*
> *more new fruit*
> *to continue life!*

The Story Trees

If Miguel was having a run of good fortune, I was not. April was the cruelest month, just one rotten thing after another. The weather, first of all, was a disaster. Four field trips in a row—rained out. I tried to convince Mrs. Hinton we should go to the park anyway, that rain was a part of nature, but this argument went nowhere. Another disappointment was how many kids forgot to observe their adopted trees each day and missed the magic moment when the buds opened. Mrs. Hinton told me it was hopeless. She said, "At this point in the year, you lose them. All they care about is finishing up. If they don't want to do something, they're not going to."

Then came a phone call with crushing news. The principal of the Wagner Middle School, who last fall had assured me he'd have room for lots of kids, had learned that his district's population had increased unexpectedly and he wouldn't be able to accept any kids from Queens. Not one. I had to tell the kids and try to give them hope: there was still Louis Armstrong.

But then the Armstrong letters came, and each one was the same. None of my students were accepted. Not one. When I spoke to my students' guidance counselor, he said, "That's why we stopped pushing kids to apply. I don't know if they've ever accepted a kid from this school." Angry, I called Armstrong to ask about their admission process and was told about a complicated formula, computer-based and somewhat random but preprogrammed by court order to favor certain neighborhoods over others. I said, "Then why didn't you explain that at your open house instead of getting all these families' hopes up?" There was no satisfactory response, so I asked if there was a waiting list and was told yes, but it was long; there were no guarantees. That night I wrote more letters to the students' parents, urging them to write to Armstrong and get their children on the list, but Maya's were the only ones to do so.

As for Prep for Prep, Miguel, MeiKai, Matthew, Maya, Gary, and Rosie were still in the running. Fatma and Aliza hadn't made it.

No news had yet arrived from the Clinton Middle School for Writers and Artists, but in any event that small school wouldn't have room for more than a handful of kids.

So there it was. After all the fuss I'd caused, most of the kids would be going to I.S. 138 anyway. When I saw the dismay on my students' faces, I wondered if I should have even tried. I felt awful. I felt I'd let the children down.

There was one bright moment in the month, however. Mr. Ziegler, the assistant principal, asked me if I had any thoughts on how the fifth graders and the kindergarteners might celebrate Arbor Day together.

Hmmmmm.

Because there wasn't anywhere to plant a tree, which is the traditional Arbor Day ritual, I suggested that we celebrate trees symbolically. Each fifth grader would write, illustrate, and create a handmade picture book and give it to a kindergartener. To show that these gifts were given as freely as trees give fruit, on Arbor Day the fifth graders would carry enormous green umbrellas (our symbolic "trees"), from which we'd suspend the books (our symbolic "fruit"), which the kindergartners would pluck and keep. The idea also had a nice circularity; the older students, who'd learned to read and write at the school, would write a book for younger ones, who were just beginning to.

Everyone thought it was a terrific idea.

Making a book is a complicated project; making an illustrated one is even more so. First you have to write, edit, and rewrite a story; then you have to make a "book dummy" or map, in which you figure out what text will go on each page, and what pictures. It's important to plan ahead or you'll end up having to cram half the text on the last page because you've suddenly discovered—oops!—that you've run out of room. Plus, the cover takes some forethought. Then, after you've planned the book, there's the execution. You have to cut and fold paper. Words have to be printed neatly, pictures clearly drawn, and the pages bound.

Given a limited amount of time, we bound these books simply. Blank pages were folded in half and nestled together; two holes were punched through the fold; a long rubber band was laid along the inside of the fold and its ends poked through the holes just far enough so a chopstick could slip under them, giving the book the spine that would hold the pages together.

My students had made several books over the years, in bindings of varying complexity. They knew what to do. This wasn't the case for other fifth-grade classes, though, whose teachers hadn't realized till too late that they were in over their heads. Not all their kids could write a decent sentence, much less a story, and they'd never made a book. With Arbor Day approaching fast, Mrs. Hinton smelled disaster. She had a powwow with her colleagues, made a tally, and figured out that we'd be one hundred books shy. Our class would have to take up the slack.

It was lucky we had Mrs. Hinton on our team. She knew what needed to be done. All other activities were suspended, a trip to the park was canceled, the bribe of a lunch at McDonald's was offered to any kid who made three books, and the class became a factory. "Get 'em out! Get 'em out!" cried Mrs. Hinton. "These books don't have to win a Pulitzer!"

You should have seen the kids go at it. I was thrilled, I was appalled, I was agog. What industry! What efficiency! What noise!

Bang, bang, done, next!

"Get 'em out! Get 'em out!"

The class was on a roll, and the kids were happy in their work. I couldn't keep up. Another book finished! And another! And another!

"Wait, MeiKai! I haven't read that yet! It hasn't been edited!"

"Wait, Simon! The colors are smearing. Do it again!"

"Wait, Okan! Why have you drawn a spaceship? Your story doesn't have a spaceship!"

"Get 'em out! Get 'em out!"

"Wait, Ella! You misspelled this word! You have to fix it!"

"Oh, Mr. Swope! It's only for kindergartners!"

"Only for kindergartners!" I cried. "Don't all children deserve our best?"

"Get 'em out! Get 'em out!"

Life is harder for perfectionists. I had to give up control, take a deep breath, step back, let go. I told myself, "Be like a tree."

In truth, most of the books were just fine, and many were more than fine. They were charming, heartbreaking, beautiful. I was proud, but also chastened to discover that I wasn't essential. The children made these books without me. I told myself this was a good thing, the whole point of teaching, after all.

But still.

The Mountain Climber

Rosie told me, "When I grow up, I want to be the leader, not just the assistant leader." She was the only kid with political aspirations, and I loved her for it. Here's what she wrote when I asked them to imagine themselves at the end of their lives, and writing a letter to their trees:

Dear Tree,

I'm 101 and I'm dead. I'm lying here in my grave. I'll tell you something. I did achieve world peace, so I died a happy woman. Now where you walk down the streets, there's no discrimination and no inequality or anything. My kids got accepted to Harvard. They're extremely happy. My daughter's going to be a pilot. My son is becoming a scientist. I'm very proud of them. Unfortunately, my husband died before me. He had leukemia. Now I'd dead. Someone assassinated me on my birthday. I still don't know who murdered me. But time will tell.

Extremely sincerely,
Rosie

Because Rosie seemed such a child of the 1960s, I was surprised to learn that her father was Republican. (This was unusual in a classroom where most students came from Democratic families.) Rosie explained that her father hated taxes and was a businessman. "So that's why he votes Republican," she explained. "'Cause I heard it's the party of business and no taxes, isn't it?"

Her father's candy store business was doing well. She told me proudly, "He just opened another store. In Manhattan!" What's more, the family had just purchased a house, and now Rosie had her own bedroom. Her father had come a long way since he'd emigrated as a teenager, but his success had a price. Rosie rarely saw her dad because he worked so much.

One day Rosie told me her parents wanted her to marry within her caste.

"Does that bother you?"

"Of course not!"

"Suppose you fall in love with someone else?"

"No, you can't. You just don't."

"Will your parents choose your husband?"

"No, I get to choose."

"Why do Indians marry within their caste?"

"I don't know. That's what they decided. That's, like, so long ago. Because this is what my dad says: he says if you marry in your caste, your religion and your culture will go on. If you marry someone else, it's going to be too confusing."

That made sense, but only to a point. It seemed to me Rosie's culture was already eroding and melding. She'd told me her father wasn't religious, the family wasn't strictly vegetarian, and each year they had a Christmas tree.

When I asked Rosie what she wanted to be when she grew up, she said, "Either a doctor or a lawyer. Sorry, Mr. Swope, no disrespect, but my parents don't want me to be a writer. My mom says writers are wackos."

"There's something to that."

"Like, take you. My family, we can't figure you out. Why do you do it? Why do you come all the way out here to teach us kids for no money and no appreciation?"

It was a reasonable question, one I often puzzled over myself. I said, "This is fun for me. I really like you guys. Your lives fascinate me. And I've told you that I want to write a book about you."

"You know what your big problem is?" Rosie said. "All you do is, you have fun with school."

"Is having fun a problem? Don't I seem happy to you?"

She laughed as if that was a silly question, "No!"

"Really? Gosh. I *feel* happy. Do you think I could be sad and not even know it? Of course I'm not *always* happy. Teaching can be awfully frustrating when kids don't do their work. I hate being the bad guy. I hate having to push, push, push."

"I want you to push me a lot, Mr. Swope. You should push all us kids into doing everything we can do, even though you might be the bad guy, because it's good for us!"

"You see, Rosie? That's why I do this, to hear you say wonderful things like that."

She smiled.

"And I do have another life, you know. I have a lot of friends."

"Oh, yeah!" she said. "I remember you told me about that book lady who liked my story."

"What book lady?"

"From that publisher that makes every great book, like, in America. With cancer."

She was talking about Gila Bercovitch, the editor in chief of the Library of America, which keeps in print definitive editions of the collected works of America's great writers. That year Gila had been diagnosed with cancer, and I'd spent a lot of time with her. In part because Gila had grown up in a poor immigrant family, she was as fascinated by my students and their stories as I was. Because Rosie was a regular at the public library, I'd told her how Gila had gone to her library as a child and systematically read through the children's shelves, one book after another until she'd polished them all off. Then she'd wandered through the nearest door, found the tail end of the adult fiction shelves, and methodically read her way backward through all those books, starting with the Z's. (Gila told me that somewhere along the way—at the H's, I think it was—she'd realized not all writers were equal. Some were great, some were just good, and some were hacks.) And one day, when I'd told Rosie that Gila Bercovitz, an important editor, was impressed with one of Rosie's stories, Rosie's eyes had popped. "No way!" she'd cried.

But now I had to tell Rosie sad news about Gila. "Her cancer got worse and she went to live with her son in Wisconsin. Not long after, she died."

"Oh," said Rosie, uncertain how to respond.

I smiled to show her I was okay. "The last time I talked to Gila, she said she had a view of trees from her bed, and that she loved looking at them. It was the same with my mother when she was dying, and with my best friend, too. As they said good-bye to this world, they were comforted by trees."

"I had an uncle who died," said Rosie. "And I cried but I'm not that sad anymore 'cause we all have to die sometime."

Earlier that year Rosie had written:

Dear Tree,

Now I am very fond of you because I know a lot about you. I know you have leaves that are colossal! Your leaves are of course compound and opposite which looks very good. From the living room, I see the middle of your trunk, and from the attic (my brother's room) I see your canopy which swerves wildly in the fall's great winds. It looks like you're having a quarrel with the wind. And sometimes if I look closely, I see the anger in you.

I feel very sorry for you. What happens to you on Halloween when people spray you with paint or hit you with eggs? Doesn't it hurt you? And in winter I heard that you die but then come back alive in spring. That's very amazing. If trees could come back to life, why can't people? . . .

My mom says always respect everything the same way you would want to be respected. I guess she meant you, too. You're lucky my mom is the one who wanted me to adopt you. She said there was something about you that was different from other trees. My family is the kind that really doesn't like to pollute or kill plants and animals. And there's something else you should know about my family. Our top priority is to have a lot of knowledge. You see, in my family the only thing that is passed down is knowledge. And if you don't have a lot, then you can't pass it down. My parents pass knowledge to me, and then I will pass it to my son or daughter.

What do you pass down?

Sincerely,
Rosie

At some point that spring, Rosie's writing fell off. Her recent "Dear Tree" letters had been a disappointment—cursory, clichéd, insincere. I was pretty sure what the problem was. Mrs. Hinton had arranged the students' desks in tables she called teams, and one, which included MeiKai, Ella, and Aliza, had formed a clique. What a nasty business this cliquish coven was, with its whispered secrets, coded notes, and wounding laughter. I hadn't seen anything like it since childhood, a clique as painful to the girls within as everyone without. How awful to see MeiKai, once the picture of happiness, transformed into something so unpleasant. Mrs. Hinton said it was hormonal, a developmental stage preadolescent girls go through. (Yet it wasn't universal; most of the girls, and all the boys, were still little kids—perhaps their time would come later.) Hoping Rosie would have a positive influence on the clique, Mrs. Hinton sat her at their table, but Rosie wasn't strong enough. She got sucked into that dark, unhappy place as well.

This didn't cause me to lose faith in her. I was certain she'd grow out of this, look back, and feel the shame that helps us to become better people. That's part of growing up. I knew Rosie respected me; all she needed was a little pep talk. I'd appeal to her better angel, tell her she had to be a leader, avoid peer pressure, be good to the other kids, get her writing back on track. And so, at the end of a friendly and productive conference with Fatma, I asked her to send Rosie down.

"Gladly," said Fatma, suddenly smirking.

"Why the smirk?"

"I'm not smirking!"

"There's smirk all over your face."

"Well . . . do you want the truth?"

Fool that I am, I said, "Of course."

Fatma savored her triumph. "It's just that Rosie hates coming down here," she said. "She finds it so *boring*."

"What a nasty thing to say. Why would you want to hurt me?"

"You always told us to be *honest*."

"You weren't being honest, you were being mean," I said, and gestured in irritation at the door. "Go back to class."

I didn't believe a word she'd said. I knew Rosie inside out, and if there was any kid who enjoyed my company, it was she. Nevertheless, when I heard her knock at the door, my heart quickened.

"Come in."

Rosie walked into my office, smiled wanly, and sat down, avoiding my searching eyes.

"You seem depressed," I said.

"I'm fine," she said. "I'm okay."

"How are things at home?"

"Fine."

"What's happening in your life? Any word from Prep from Prep yet?"

Her lip trembled, and I knew she'd been rejected. Poor Rosie! I understood better than anyone how much Prep for Prep meant to her, the first step she was taking for her father's sake so she'd get into Harvard.

"I'm so sorry. Has anyone else heard?"

"MeiKai didn't get in."

"No! What about Gary?"

"He didn't get in, either. Or Matthew."

"Poor guys. Miguel?"

"He and Maya are the only ones that didn't hear."

That was something, anyway. "I'm so sorry, Rosie. You must have been very disappointed."

"Yeah."

"What did your parents say?"

"I don't know. They didn't . . . They want me to go but . . . They were disappointed."

"What's wrong with those Prep for Prep idiots! Any school would be *thrilled* to you have as a student." I told her this was why I hated tests: they never tell you what is most important in a child, don't show you what is in her heart or put a value on her passion and creativity, her dreams and aspirations, the good she wants to do.

Instead of being comforted, Rosie was annoyed. "If you were in my shoes," she said, "you wouldn't be saying these things. What I go through and what you go through are different."

"I know. I'm just sorry you have all this pressure. You're too young."

She bridled, saying, "It's not because, you know, I have pressure from my parents. It's really hard for me. I can't just lay back and chill out. I can't just let it go smoothly. I have to try. In my family, the most important thing is knowledge. So if I don't pass this test, then I'm no good."

"Of course you have to try! You should always try your hardest! But don't think you're no good! Listen to me, Rosie: Don't let this test determine your opinion of yourself. You're a very special child."

She sneered, and I was hurt to see that my high opinion meant nothing to her. Nevertheless, I pressed on: "One day you'll look back on this rejection and see it was a blessing in disguise. You can still get into Harvard. Kids who get through public school are made of tougher stuff than kids from private school. It might even increase your chances."

She shrugged and said, "I didn't want to do Prep for Prep, anyway. Now I have my whole summer off."

"That's the spirit," I said, deciding that the best thing was not to make too big a deal of this but rather carry on, business as usual. Besides, I saw a way to bolster her confidence. I said, "I'd like to talk about *The Tree Book* with you. You're an excellent writer, one of my best, and your 'Dear Tree' letters are going to be a prominent part of *The Tree Book*. I love their combination of observation and philosophy. And the people at the paper company love them, too, by the way. But I don't have a good letter from you about spring. I want your voice at the end of this book."

"I did a letter about spring already," she said.

"Yeah, but that wasn't nearly your best work. You're capable of much more. I'd like you to try another when we go to the park next week."

She glanced away, somewhat guiltily, I thought, and muttered, "It's going to rain, anyway."

"We've had a run of bad luck, but it can't rain *every* field trip day."

"Oh, it'll rain," she said darkly. "I know it will 'cause I'm religious. It's already rained four times in a row. My mom says the Central Park trips are under a curse."

"Under a curse? What's that mean?"

She shook her head, bit her bottom lip, refused to explain, but I could see I had become the Enemy, that somehow in her fifth-grade mind she'd hatched a cockamamie fantasy in which the constant rain and trees and growing up and losing Prep for Prep were all tied up with me, my fault, I was a curse. This was a battle I was unprepared for. I didn't even know who my adversary was—her clique? her religion? her mother? her imagination? I was hurt and I was angry. I raised my voice. I told her this was superstitious nonsense, that I'd thought she was a leader. I said school wasn't over yet, she still had work to do, her writing wasn't perfect, needed help, and she had to do her best. I threw her metaphor in her face: "You always talk about climbing the mountain, Rosie, but when the going gets tough, what do you do? You give up! Well, *The Tree Book* is our mountain. Are you going to climb it or not?"

The intensity of her response was shocking, "I *will* climb the mountain, don't you worry about that! And no one's *ever* going to stop me! But it's gonna be *my* mountain, not yours!"

My hurt made my voice go icy cold: "Are you telling me you refuse to go the park?"

"I'm not going," she said tentatively. I could see what she was doing: she was testing her rebellion and discovering that yes, she could do this. "Yeah, that's it," she said, her strength growing. Then she looked me in the eye and said, "I'm not going." Her jaw was set. It was obvious she meant it.

It's not easy to stand up to authority, and even if Rosie's defiance was based on an absurd foundation, she'd showed courage, the sort of courage she'd need when she grew up, got some sense into her head, and set out to make the world a better place.

I said, "I'm extremely disappointed in you, Rosie. I expected more. Go back to class now, please, and send Jessica down."

Rosie gathered her things and left without a word. I sat there in a welter of confusion. How dare she do this to me after all I'd done for her! Traitor! Ungrateful brat! Yet after I had hated her awhile, I forced myself to look at things from her perspective and came to realize that she'd had no choice. For three years, Mr. Swope had been her muse and editor. For three years, he had given her assignments, praised her writing, criticized, suggested. For three years, he'd *observed* her, *taped* her, *made notes* about her. Of course she needed to be free. Any independent thinker would. And it wasn't as if Rosie hadn't tried that year. She had! For six months she'd written to her tree, and written well, but after all that time—enough already, Mr. Swope! Trees are boring!

What had I done? Despite my good intentions, I had failed—failed Rosie, failed writing, failed the trees, failed middle school, failed everything.

For half a second I wanted to abandon *The Tree Book,* but even if I could have, that wouldn't have brought Rosie back to me. Our time was finished. A teacher has only so much to teach, and she had learned all she could from me. Rosie needed to move on.

Then came a knock at the door.

"Come in."

It was Jessica. She gave me a big smile. "Hi there, Mr. Swope!"

"Hi, Jessica. How's it going?"

"Really good!" she said.

"Let's see what we have here," I said, and started looking through her writing folder.

"Can I ask you a question, Mr. Swope?"

"Sure."

"When Rosie came in the class, she was crying. Did you make her cry?"

"Really? She was crying?"

"She wouldn't tell anyone why."

Brava, brave heart! Such a strong child! Imagine what it had taken for her to hold her tears in during our fight and never show an ounce of weakness. Then upstairs, refuse to tell! Magnificent! What a fantastic woman Rosie was going to be!

A Spring Surprise

I wanted them to see the cherry trees in bloom. That year the grove was dazzling, with blossoms so intense that underneath the trees the light turned pink. There was magic in these trees, and this would be a special place to sit and write. But the blooms wouldn't last long. Petals already carpeted the ground. If we didn't go that day, we'd miss our chance.

The morning of the trip, I looked out the window and groaned. It was cloudy, and the forecast said there was a fifty percent chance of rain. I went to Queens, fingers crossed.

Mrs. Hinton agreed to risk the rain. As promised, Rosie and the girls' clique refused to go. This was disappointing enough, but then Mrs. Hinton told me that nine other kids (nine!) wouldn't be going either. She said they complained that I made them walk too much. I was horrified. Walk too much! At most on any given trip we'd walk a mile—two, tops. Lazy, out-of-shape couch potatoes! It was so depressing. I'd gotten them too late; only ten years old and already their bodies were lost causes.

No matter, no matter, no matter: the rest of the class was excited. So off we went, but on our way to the subway, it started to drizzle. It was only the tiniest nothing of a drizzle—really a mist—yet when Mrs. Hinton realized that only a handful of kids had brought umbrellas, she turned us around. No child would catch a chill on her watch.

The trip was canceled. Maybe Rosie was right. Maybe the trips to Central Park were cursed.

Maya was so disappointed she cried, which was a worry. Her mother had called me over the weekend, distressed because Maya was always in tears, upset for many reasons: grief at the death of an uncle, her feelings hurt by the girls' clique, terrible anxiety over middle school. When Maya learned she hadn't made it into Prep for Prep, her mother told me, she wept hysterically and cried, "I want to die! I want to die!"

Now that we weren't going to the park, I decided to make this Maya Day. She deserved it for all her good, hard work. I got permission to take her off school grounds, and we headed straight for Dunkin' Donuts, where we fortified ourselves with crullers. Then Maya took me to meet her tree. It was a grand old maple, more than a hundred years old, I guessed. I'd brought along a stethoscope, planning to have the kids listen to the cherry trees, but instead Maya and I held it up to her tree and heard the eerie slush-slush movement of its rising sap, a kind of heartbeat.

It drizzled on and off as we strolled through the neighborhood, but we didn't mind. Maya pointed out a house she said was haunted and a building where drug addicts lived, and we looked at trees and talked about friendship and books and growing up. She asked if I believed in God. I said I didn't know, that maybe I believed in something, some Presence that I couldn't name. I said, "Sometimes I wonder if the trees are God."

"What do you mean?"

I pulled my composition notebook with its marble cover from my backpack to read her a story I was working on, a kind of creation myth. I told Maya I'd gotten the idea when reading a book about trees and learned they'd been around for more than three hundred million years. I said, "Humans have only been on Earth for thousands of years, but trees have been here *hundreds of millions* of years, more years than we can possibly imagine. Trees saw the dinosaurs come and go. What we consider ancient history—the Pyramids, Stonehenge, the Great Wall—is nothing. It's a dot, a speck of Time compared to the history of trees."

I told Maya, "Scientists think the first tree grew in present-day China. Imagine that! The first tree! They have theories, but no one knows for sure how that first tree came to be. Anyway, this first tree grew, dropped seeds, and some of them grew into trees, which dropped more seeds, so gradually there was a little grove, then a forest, and bit by bit, over millions and millions of years there was this slow, silent, green migration until trees finally covered the planet, making animal life possible."

"I never thought of that," said Maya.

"I never had either. So anyway, that's what gave me the idea for this story." I found I was a bit embarrassed to read this rough draft to her, so I said, "It's not finished, you know. It's just a draft, not very good":

In the beginning, God made the seas and the land. But the land was barren, so God turned himself into a tree. When this first tree dropped its seeds, one of them grew into another tree, and this tree was God, too. Over time, more trees grew, and all the trees were God. When God saw there were trees enough, he made humans, and from that time forth he lived among his people, providing them with air and food and fuel and shelter.

I ended there, preferring not to tell Maya the rest. In fact, I'd abandoned the story because I couldn't find a way to finish it that wasn't completely depressing, with humans at first living in harmony with trees and understanding that trees are God, even communicating with him, but gradually becoming proud and arrogant until they forget the divinity of trees, and in their blind stupidity and urge for destruction, bring themselves and God to the brink of extinction.

Although I left it unspoken, melancholy Maya sensed this dreary theme, and when she asked, "Do you think the world is going to end soon?" there was such worry in her voice I rushed to say, "No, no, no, of course not, Maya. The world is going to be around for a long, long time."

We walked in silence, then stopped to admire a flowering tree. To our surprised delight, a tiny tropical songbird, yellow with lilac markings, landed on the branch in front us amid the blossoms and chirped hello. It was such an improbable sight, like something from a storybook, that I almost expected the bird to start talking. No doubt it was a pet that had escaped, but it was impossible not to see this delicate creature as a sign, or a blessing—*life does have miracles!*—and Maya and I headed back to school in lighter spirits.

> *Spring sweeps*
> *up winter,*
> *and puts it in a glass jar,*
> *and slowly,*
> *every day,*
> *opens the jar*
> *when September arrives.*
> *Spring brings calmness*
> *to a crazy person's mind,*
> *and blows a scentless*
> *soft wind upon you,*

flowering your hopes and dreams,
and sweeping nightmares away,
throwing them
into the garbage
cans.

MAYA

Who Is Su Jung?

In May the sun shone brightly once again and our trips to Central Park resumed. With nicer weather, everybody came along, even the girl's clique.

At school that month I met with children to go over all their nature writing and ask for last rewrites. It was time to make final selections about what would go in *The Tree Book*. As Su Jung, Maya, and I went through their writing folders, Maya mentioned that she kept a diary. "I write in it every day but I don't let anybody see it," she said. "It's where I keep all my secrets."

"I have a diary, too," said Su Jung. "It's very pretty, with a lock. It's just that I don't write in it. My place for my secrets is up in my head. That's why I get a lot of stress. I get a lot of stress 'cause I never tell everybody everything. I was ready to open up to MeiKai, but then I changed my mind."

Maya asked why.

"'Cause I had a good reason. But I'd rather talk to MeiKai than Ashley. That's how I feel."

"Ashley's nice," said Maya.

"To me, I feel that she cannot keep a secret. Or MeiKai or Rosie or Ella. They hang around with each other and they tell things to each other that other people told them. I don't know. I don't feel comfortable opening up to anybody in our classroom."

"Growing up is hard," I told her. "But one day you'll find someone you can trust."

"Maybe yes, maybe never."

"Don't say 'never.' If you say 'never,' it will be never. You have to have faith in life."

To tease me, Su Jung droned, "Maybe never maybe never maybe never maybe never."

There wasn't any winning with her; she always had to have the last word. But I did, too, so I sighed and said, "Then it will be never."

Su Jung's friendships never lasted long. Her need for love was too profound. She was drowning in a sea of loneliness and clutched the hand of any willing girl, dragging her down with her. First it was MeiKai, then Ashley, and both would smile uncomfortably as Su Jung told me they had everything in common, could read each other's thoughts, and were the perfect friends. This sort of friendship asks too much and cannot be sustained. Although I saw it coming, there was nothing I could do, and sure enough, both girls broke Su Jung's heart.

Her shell was hardening. Recently I'd asked how things were getting on at home and she'd said nothing, only sneered, an ugly goblin face that made me shudder: I imagined Su Jung years from now, a bitter, angry woman.

I said, "Here's something of yours from just the other day, Su Jung. I really like this part":

> I never noticed that a sparrow was this beautiful. I guess if you concentrate
> on something, you find its beauty. I wish I could keep the sparrow as a pet,
> but I think they're better off being free, flying across the sky.

"Mmmmmm," purred Maya.

Su Jung said, "Early this year I used to have a fondness of nature, but now I don't care about trees. It's like when somebody crumples up a paper and throws it away with nothing on it."

"Really?" said Maya, surprised.

I said, "I can't believe you don't have a fondness for nature, Su Jung. That would make these sentences a bunch of lies."

"Total lies," said Su Jung.

"You shouldn't write lies, Su Jung."

"I don't know. I just wrote them really emotionally to please you. I don't think I really meant them."

Maya saw that I was upset and said, "She's just teasing you, Mr. Swope. I think she really did mean them, but she doesn't want to say anything because she doesn't like to open up to people."

That was a wise insight, and it pleased Su Jung that Maya had noticed her. She shook her head playfully and giggled, "Nooooooo!"

"See?" said Maya, laughing too. "Proved!"

I said, "I won't believe you've only written lies, Su Jung. You've written some beautiful things about nature."

"That I didn't really care about!" she answered with a smile, determined to win the argument.

I'd hoped Su Jung would fall in love with words, that language would become her haven, but that didn't happen. Su Jung read, but not obsessively; she wrote, but not with joy. It was hard for me to learn that a teacher can only show his passion, not give it.

The year was winding down. On the day after the Multicultural Festival, I left school to get some lunch at a nearby burrito joint owned by a Tibetan refugee. On the way, I ran into Mr. Forti, the man who taught band. Short and slouched, with wild and wiry hair, Mr. Forti reminded me of Beethoven, but with a dazed, cartoon expression, like he'd just been clobbered by a frying pan. He was easy to make fun of, and the kids often did, but never nastily. They liked Mr. Forti. I'd heard he was a graduate of Juilliard and played in a professional chamber group, but he was a maddening colleague. Sometimes he'd wander into class without warning to say the band was having special practice, and like that—in the middle of my lesson!—his students, half of my kids, would get up and go away, the stories that they'd just begun now lost forever.

Because Mr. Forti was shy and hugged the walls and never met my eye, I'd never had a conversation with him, but I stopped him that day to congratulate him on the band's performance in yesterday's parade. I'd been impressed by how they'd improved over the years, and as the band had marched past the cheering crowds with Mr. Forti up in front waving his baton, the new America was meeting the old. All I had to do was squint to see them all in spiffy uniforms and playing "Seventy-six Trombones."

At first Mr. Forti was flustered at being addressed, but when I said we'd both taught the same kids for three years and asked what that was like for him, the words came pouring out; he needed to talk. "This was the first band I ever taught and I couldn't believe how good they got. What was so beautiful was all these languages and cultures, everyone different, how they came together in the band. It's really true what they say, you see it here in Queens: music is the universal language. I try to tell the kids, but they just look at me. They don't know what it means."

I asked him how he'd done it, how he'd taught so many instruments to so many kids.

"I didn't," he said. "That's what's so amazing. When I came to the school, the instruments were piled up in the basement, really in a pile, all beat up with missing parts. I took them home and fixed them up, but there was only so much I could do. They're still in lousy shape, and the kids have to blow themselves blue in the face, but somehow they get music from them. It's not because of me! I couldn't give them all lessons, just a minute here and there! But the smart ones figure it out and teach the others. It was . . . it was . . ."

Mr. Forti started crying. As he spoke he had to keep wiping tears away with the back of his hand. He said, "I'm just worried they won't keep it up, that the band we worked so hard to build, all this talent, will be wasted, and they won't be making music anymore. So many of them are so good. Gary on the trombone. MeiKai. But especially one, this girl Su Jung. You know her? She's the most amazing of them all. I couldn't even get a note out of her banged-up clarinet, but she stood up and hit all the high ones. I told her she's got talent and she won't believe me. I worry she'll stop playing, that she'll . . ."

Too overwhelmed to continue, Mr. Forti nodded and shuffled off, leaving me stunned. What a fine man he'd turned out to be, and what a further mystery Su Jung. Did I know anything at all about this girl I thought I knew so well? I never realized that she had a love for music, and I'd missed an obvious clue, the times in conference when she'd watched the clock, never wanting to be late for band.

Later that day I took Su Jung aside to tell her how highly Mr. Forti had praised her. I said, "He says you're *really* good. Maybe you could play professionally, Su Jung. Would you like that?" She said she wasn't sure she wanted to continue with the clarinet, that what she really wanted was a piano, but her family couldn't afford one. For a wild moment I considered buying her a piano and shipping it to her anonymously, but then I realized I couldn't afford it, either.

At the end of year, when the band members had to return their instruments, Su Jung said she couldn't find her clarinet. She said it wasn't at home and that she must have left it somewhere at school. A search was made, but her instrument didn't turn up, and gentle Mr. Forti didn't make her pay. I asked Su Jung what she thought had happened to it and she glanced away so fast I wondered if she'd stolen it, then hoped she had, because I hoped that music was so important to her that she'd steal.

Loose Ends

When Miguel finally got the news from Prep for Prep, he wasn't nearly as disappointed as I was. In fact, he seemed relieved, as if he knew he'd never have been able to keep up with all that work. Besides, the fact that he *had* gotten into the Clinton Middle School for Writers and Artists made Prep for Prep's rejection easier to take. He was thrilled at the thought of Clinton and had visions of this school for artists turning him into the next Picasso, his latest career choice.

MeiKai, Rosie, and Amarjeet had also been accepted to Clinton. I was happy for them.

Maya, too, had good news. She'd made it up the waiting list and would be going to Louis Armstrong Middle School after all. Another huge relief.

Gary, Rafael, Carla, and Maggie would be going to Catholic schools, and Aliza to a Muslim school. A handful of parents had discovered two small public schools nearby in Queens, schools I hadn't unearthed, and they planned to lie about their addresses so their kids could attend.

As for the rest, they were headed to I.S. 138. Some, especially those with older siblings at the school, were looking forward to it. I tried to be positive. I told myself 138 couldn't be as bad as the rumors; there must be some good teachers, and all you really need is one, that special one to see you through. Besides, my kids were smart, good kids,. They'd survive a lousy middle school—lots of people do. It doesn't mean they couldn't be happy and successful.

Mostly, though, I worried.

In the final week of school, Fortune's wheel took a surprising turn. Out of the blue, the Wagner Middle School principal called to say the projections had been wrong. It turned out he had lots of room. He said he'd take any kids who wanted to come. I said, "Thank you! Thank you! Thank you!" and flew up the three flights to the classroom, arriving breathless, and told the class the good news. I said, "Okay, guys. Who's game?"

No one raised a hand. They eyed each other warily, as if choosing Wagner over 138 would be a betrayal of their classmates, whom they'd been in school with since kindergarten. Or maybe by this point they'd made their peace with whatever school they were going to and didn't want to dredge that issue up again.

I said, "They say Wagner is one of the best middle schools in the city. Don't you want the best education you can get?"

Nothing. No response. I'd hit a wall.

Then Cesar's hand went up. "I'll go," he said.

Brave boy! One kid was all it took. Aaron's hand was next. I'll go! Then came Jorge's. Me, too! Then Nicole. Elena. Matthew. The tide had turned. Jalal. Lucinda. Simon. The hands went up, went up, until there were a hundred fingers dancing in the air: twenty kids!

That night I called their homes and spoke to any adult who understood a bit of English. School was nearly over, I didn't have much time, and in the end, the number twenty dwindled down to eight. For fear of the subway, several boys and all the girls would not be allowed to go to Wagner. But Aaron, Matthew, Jalal, Jorge, Joseph, Simon, Mateo, and Cesar would be going, and I was pleased.

So that was that. I'd done what I could, and all in all, things hadn't turned out so badly on the middle school front. At least everyone had made a choice.

As we headed into our final week together, I was ready for the end. My publisher had given me a contract for a new picture book and was interested in an idea I'd proposed for a novel. After so much time encouraging others to write, I was eager to get back to my own work. Of course I was also sad. I missed my students already, but then I'd been missing them for some time, missing the little kids they'd been and weren't, any longer. They were growing up, although not all of them wanted to. Aaron certainly didn't. Noelia didn't, either, and with her it was particularly poignant. All year she'd been trying to get me excited about her new imaginary friend, Naomi, but it was obvious Naomi wasn't real to her, not the way imaginary friends are vivid and real to younger children. Noelia was just pretending that Naomi existed, the way older kids pretend to still believe in Santa Claus after they've learned the disappointing truth. Without Noelia's belief, Naomi couldn't come to life.

One night that final week, I was in a nostalgic mood and, just as I'd done almost three years before, I made a ceremony of the moment. I put on some quiet music, poured myself a glass of wine, and sat in my favorite chair. With my cat in my lap, I reread my students' first stories, the ones they'd written when I'd said, "Write a story, any story."

I read Su Jung's "Living in the Jungle," Miguel's "Autobiography," Aaron's "The Summer Santa." I read them all. And as I did, I realized something new, something I never could have seen when I'd read this work the first time around: everything I'd come to know about these kids, their fundamental core, was already there. It was all there in those first stories.

Late in the afternoon of the next-to-the-last day of school, my phone rang. It was Miguel. He said, "Is it okay to call you even if I don't have nothing to say?"

I corrected his grammar: "Don't have *any*thing to say."

"Don't have *any*thing to say."

"Of course it's okay, Miguel. You can call me anytime. I want to be your friend. How are things?"

He said things were good. He said his parents were fighting "hardly at all." He said his dad had given his mom a watch, and she'd cried.

"That's wonderful," I said.

Now that I wasn't his teacher, I didn't really know what to talk to him about, so I fell back on old habits. "Tell me, Miguel. How many hundreds of stories have you written in the past week?"

"None, but I've been thinking about writing one."

"What's it about?"

His plot was about a boy who runs away to live in a forest and befriends a German shepherd, and as Miguel rambled on and on I only half-listened. I guess he'd never learn to cut to the chase, or maybe he would now that I wouldn't be there to force him. When his story introduced some older boys with knives who were going to fight the boy and his dog, I interrupted him, "Oh, Miguel. I hope you grow up to be a gentle, peace-loving person."

"Yeah, but my stories aren't peace."

"Why is that?"

"Maybe there's a little flame in me that wants revenge against something but I don't know what."

"What makes you angry?"

"Sometimes I get mad at my classmates for no reason. They bother me. Some girls say I'm a little tough sometimes—all right, fine. I can give you that. I admit it. But I really do want to be a good kid, but still, it's not only me who has to change. I would like a little help. Because it really makes me mad. Like when Okan calls me a farting chicken and stuff. I can't make them change, but if I could, I would because I don't even do nothing to them and they come picking on me."

"Kids used to make fun of me," I told him. "Once my friends whispered to each other, then counted to three and ran away from me, laughing. I cried and cried. I remember it like it was yesterday. I also remember the times I made other kids cry. Childhood is a rough place."

"Sometimes I have to cry and hide it. Sometimes I feel very hurt inside."

"Don't you think it's better to feel hurt than to get angry and fight?"

"I know, but sometimes my anger just blows up and I can't stop it. It's like my temper controls me and stuff. It's like King David, his emotions controlled him. He loved his son Absalom and when he died, he just couldn't stop thinking about him. He didn't want to go obey God."

"Christ wasn't violent. He was the Prince of Peace."

"Yeah, but he said to prepare the swords."

I wasn't going to argue theology with him, and changed the subject. "Miguel, you're going to have to work hard next year at school. You won't have me around to make excuses to your teachers for you. Will you work hard?"

Miguel didn't answer right away. At first I worried he was having an asthma attack; then I realized he was crying.

"What is it, Miguel? What's wrong?"

He voice was weak, a little-boy voice. "I don't really have confidence in myself that I can pass."

"Why do you feel that way?"

"I feel like God didn't put me here for no purpose and if this continues I'd rather die than keep up with this!"

I told Miguel, "It may be God won't tell you a reason. You might have to find the reason on your own. That's what I did. I was lost in my life three years ago. I felt my life was pointless. But then I decided to do something about it. I found your class and I made a commitment. No, it was more than that. I made a vow. I told myself that for the next three years I'd devote myself to you guys, do whatever I could to help. And it's been an amazing experience. You children changed my life. But *I* gave my life a purpose, Miguel. *I* did that. And you can, too. You have to imagine a different life, a good life for yourself, then work to make it come true. Do you understand?"

Miguel lowered his voice so his parents wouldn't hear. "It's really too hard right now. I just keep remembering everything that my father used to do to me. How he screams at me. I can even hear the volume in my ears how he screams at me."

"One day you won't have to live with your father anymore. One day you'll move out, be on your own. And one of your jobs in life, I'm sure, will be to find a way to forgive your father, Miguel. That won't be easy. Right now, though, the main thing is you have to do well in school. I don't know how to make you understand how important that is for you. Because if you don't . . . if you . . . well, it's just going to be a lot harder."

There was silence for a moment. Then a frightened voice said, "Can I run away from home for a while and live with you?"

Poor kid. I'd helped his imaginary heroes run away so many times. It was painful to have to tell the boy himself that no, he couldn't come live with me. I said, "Your place is with your family. Think how upset your mother would be if you ran away. Think how your brothers would miss you. The police would be called. Your father would be angry. Your parents might not trust you to take the subway to Clinton."

"But I wanna go to Clinton!"

"Then you can't run away."

My reasoning was airtight, no one could argue it, but all Miguel heard was my rejection. "Okay, Mr. Swope," he said, his voice so small it seemed a million miles away.

This child wanted more than anything to be good, to be a brave and stalwart savior, but with a deep down dread he feared his future, sensed he had to run away, escape, or he wouldn't be able to stop himself and he'd end up bad. Thank goodness he was going to Clinton. Clinton was a tiny school. The principal was a strong, decent man. He'd said he'd keep an eye on Miguel.

Miguel and I chatted some more. I got him to giggle a few times, and then I said, "Well, I have to go now. You be strong, Miguel. Keep your focus on your future. If you work hard, things will get better. Call me any-time."

"I will, Mr. Swope."

"See you tomorrow, okay? Last day of grade school!"

"Yeah!"

"Good-bye, Miguel."

"Bye, Mr. Swope."

I hung up the phone.

Good-bye and Good Luck

During the past few months, when I'd walk into the room, faces no longer lit up. Kids hardly even glanced my way: Oh, you. But when I appeared in the doorway on the last day of school, they whooped and hollered because they knew I carried copies of *The Tree Book,* hot off the press and in the nick of time. Everyone involved in its production had been so moved by the material they'd given it their all. As a result, *The Tree Book* was a handsome volume, beautifully designed and printed: a real book. Every kid was represented in its pages several times, and all the work was good. They could be proud.

As I walked through the classroom, passing out copies, hands reached wildly toward me. Then the children dove into their *Tree Book*s, squealing, laughing, searching for their names and shouting out one another's. Stories were autographed. It was thrilling to observe, the power of a book, the charge that comes from seeing yourself in print. Even the girls' clique, so determined to have nothing to do with me, couldn't resist its allure.

This was a gratifying moment, but a brief one. There was so much else for the children to think about that final day, so much intense emotion and so many games to play. The books were put aside, tucked into their backpacks, but I didn't mind. Like people who plant trees whose shade they'll never enjoy, I had confidence that *The Tree Book*'s most important moments lay in the future. No doubt most copies would survive the many moves these kids would make in their lives, although I could imagine some being mislaid, could even imagine Aaron managing to lose his that very day on his way home. When the kids were grown, from time to time they'd open their *Tree Book*s and browse, the pages like a message in a bottle from the past.

I imagined any number of them—Noelia, Gary, Nicole, Simon—reading their copies to their children. I imagined Su Jung, a teacher, reading hers each year to her students, until one student falls so much in love with her he steals her copy and she never gets it back. I imagined Fatma, now an arborist and a frustrated writer looking for a topic, coming across her *Tree Book,* which inspires her to write a successful memoir about how she'd come to love the trees. Or Rosie, now a senator known for her hard work on behalf of civil rights and the environment, turning to *The Tree Book* in a dark moment of her life to remind herself of the ideals she'd written of in childhood, and finding new resolve.

Or maybe one kid would be wildly famous—say Maya, in her eighties winning the Nobel Prize for Literature, causing the value of *The Tree Book* (with her first published writing) to skyrocket and providing a miraculous windfall to Cesar, whose grandson would need an operation the family could not afford. Even further down the road, I could imagine a *Tree Book* packed in an attic box, long forgotten, until a woman comes across it, thrilled to find her great-great-great grandfather Miguel's name inside, and reading the letters he'd written to a tree once way back when.

Meanwhile, on their last day of grade school, *The Tree Book*'s writers clowned around. Some hung out, some played cards, some checkers, some jacks. As I watched the children play, I felt out of place, a stranger at the party. Time to go, I told myself. Time to clean up my office and head home. I went from child to child, shaking hands and saying good-bye. Maya and Jessica cried. Gary and Mateo and Simon high-fived me. Fatma looked stricken, a little afraid, but tried not to show it.

"Good-bye, Fatma. Good luck."

"Good-bye, Mr. Swope. Have a good life."

Most of the kids were so out of their minds with excitement they didn't know what to say to me. Miguel was happy, though, as if our conversation of the night before had never happened. He gave me a gift from his mother (a gift the family could ill afford) and said, "Guess what? After school my dad is taking me to buy a bicycle for my graduation!"

"That's great, Miguel! I am so happy for you. Good-bye, my friend. Good luck."

"Good-bye, Mr. Swope."

Mustering all my dignity, I approached the girls in the clique and forced my way through their collective disdain. Performing for her friends, Aliza ducked under her desk and sat on her hands, giggling as she refused to shake mine. Ella made a lemon face as she extended her arm, princess style, offering me the back of her limp, cruel hand. MeiKai and Rosie weren't as rude, but there was no warmth in their farewells: "Bye."

"Good-bye, girls. Good luck."

I came to Noelia, who smiled her biggest smile and said, "Oooh golly wolly, Mr. Swope. I'm sure gonna miss you!"

"Golly wolly to you, too, Noelia. You have a heart as big as the sky, you know that?"

"I could make it as small as an eraser speck if I wanted."

"Impossible!"

"Nothing's impossible with me! I'm a cartoon! Nuts! Cuckoo! Absolutely no sanity!"

"Invite me to your first stand-up gig, will you?"

"Definitely!"

"Good-bye, Noelia. Good luck."

"Good-bye!"

Good-bye, Nicole. Okan. Samantha. Good-bye, Rafael. Najiyah. Amarjeet. Good-bye, Ashley. Carolina. Esteban. Good-bye, Matthew. Good-bye, good-bye, good luck to all.

I saved Su Jung for last. I said, "I'll never forget you."

In her eyes I saw her love for me as well as her hurt. *Mr. Swope is leaving, too, they always leave, no one will ever love me.*

"Good-bye, Mr. Swope."

"I'm not Mr. Swope anymore. You have to call me Sam."

She shook her head and smiled. "I could *never* call you anything but Mr. Swope."

"Write to me, if you get a chance. I'd love to hear from you."

"Maybe yes, maybe no."

"I hope it's yes. Good-bye, Su Jung. Good luck."

"Good-bye."

Aaron, Jorge, and Cesar wanted to come to my office and help me pack up, and I was happy they'd asked. It would be nice to end the story with such easygoing, uncomplicated kids. Once downstairs, we emptied my shelves of books, paper, children's writing and drawings, pencils, rulers, crayons, markers, and tree memorabilia.

Cesar asked how my cat was. He was always asking about Mike.

"You won't believe what she did the other day," I told them. "I overslept and was worried I'd be late to school, so I was rushing around and when I went in the bathroom, I saw Mike perched on the rim of the bath-tub looking in, her eyes fixed on a mouse cowering near the drain. I was amazed at how smart Mike was. She'd caught that mouse, then figured out if she put it in the tub it wouldn't be able to escape. You should've seen her. She was purring: her day was set. She could play with the mouse for a while, then take a nap, come back, play some more. But the poor mouse! I could see that Mike had already been playing with it. There were little dots of blood on its body where her claws and teeth had pierced its skin. I couldn't leave it there to be tortured all day, but I was late and I didn't know what to do, and I panicked."

"What did you do?" asked Cesar.

"I flushed it down the toilet."

"No!" said Cesar.

"Murderer!" squealed Aaron and Jorge. "Mouse killer!"

"I know! I thought I was being kind, but when I saw the mouse strug-gling in the water and swept in circles, I felt awful, and as it vanished down the drain, you're right: I *did* feel like a murderer."

Aaron and Jorge giggled, seeing me upset over a mouse, but Cesar asked, "Why didn't you just take the mouse to Central Park and let it live there?"

My mouth fell open. That would have been perfect! I said, "Oh, Cesar, I wish you'd been there to tell me what to do. Why didn't I think of that? That poor mouse! Now I feel worse than ever."

But Cesar told me, "You know you really shouldn't feel so bad about that, Mr. Swope. 'Cause at least you tried."

> *Whee! I am so happy!*
> *I am an airplane who likes to travel around the world.*
> *I have visited Canada, Vegas, Spain, and Brazil.*
> *A lot of people depend on me to get them*
> *safely to their destination.*
> *But I get to have fun going to those places!*
>
> CESAR

Epilogue

✱   ✪   ❀

Dear Class,

Wherever you are, I hope you are thriving and working hard at whatever it is you love most. I also hope you sometimes write and read for pleasure, and that you occasionally look closely at the world and notice things that make you wonder.

As you can see, I finally finished that book I set out to write all those years ago. By the time of its publication, you'll already be high school seniors, which means it's taken me longer to write this story than it did to live it. If you happen on these pages, I wonder what you'll make of them. How much do you remember?

I talked to Mateo once while he was still in middle school and asked him what he recalled from third grade. He looked puzzled at first and couldn't even remember who his teacher had been. Shocked, I cried, "How could you forget Mrs. Duncan? She was a genius! You all adored her!" Then Mateo said, "Oh, yeah . . ." and gave a little smile, as if recalling a pleasant dream. But when I asked him what he remembered specifically, he shrugged and said, "I just remember."

My memories of you are sharper, in part because I was paying close attention, knowing that I'd write about you. Condensing that experience into a readable narrative proved frustrating, however. There was so much I had to leave out! Events had to be telescoped, pruned, and grafted. Worst of all, I couldn't make each of you a character in this book. But even so all of you are in these pages, between the lines, a part of the rich and complex classroom world I've tried to describe.

I'm also sorry I couldn't use your real names, especially to credit your writing, but I wanted to protect your privacy. You were kids, after all, not completely responsible for your actions, still capable of change. Who you were then is not necessarily who you are now. I hope I've been fair in my representations, but of course I've told events only from my perspective. Each of you had your own experience of our years together, and perhaps one day you'll use your writing skills to tell your version of what happened.

Fatma, for one, may have already started. I'm glad to report that she's still writing, and recently she told me she was thinking about writing her memoirs. Others, too, have contacted me with news of their writing lives. Some of you worked on school papers; some won English awards. Rafael sent me some comics to show me he was still at it. Jessica noticed that writing was so much easier for her than for her new middle school classmates, and Cesar was disappointed that his teachers at Wagner rarely asked him to write creatively.

I visited your old school recently. Mrs. Scalise has retired, and the mandatory assembly programs as well as the Multicultural Festival parade are now things of the past. Of your teachers, only Mrs. Hinton is still in the classroom. When Mrs. Melvern had a second child, she left teaching to become a full-time parent. Mrs. Duncan, although young enough to have taught many more years, also retired. While she saw some value in the curriculum changes mandated by the city recently, in the end she couldn't live with them. The new curriculum requires teachers in underperforming schools to follow a regimen—exactly this many minutes for group reading, exactly this many minutes for responses, and so on. She said it took the joy and creativity out of teaching for her. (She also said a program like mine wouldn't be possible in the school today; there just wouldn't be time.) Although Mrs. Duncan felt that the new curriculum would help more children learn to read and write, she knew they'd end up hating school because the process was so boring.

What other news? Maya and Jorge reported their adopted trees had been cut down. Okan has made some public performances as a magician. MeiKai's family moved to a larger apartment, and Noelia's family bought a house. When Rosie sent news that she'd graduated as valedictorian from Clinton, she also thanked me for all the help I'd given her, and that was nice to hear. Several others sent reports that they'd gotten into some of the city's selective high schools. In my last telephone conversation with Miguel, he told me he was thinking about joining the Marines because he wanted discipline in his life. I also spoke to his mom, who said she'd finally separated from her husband. But she sounded strong and was going to computer school to learn a skill so she could be more independent.

That's all I know. I've lost track of most of you, and partly that's because I had to put some distance between us. It was too confusing to write about you when you were little and at the same time know you as teenagers. I needed you to be frozen in time.

Sometimes, though, I see you in my dreams. Recently I had a nice dream about Su Jung, whom I haven't heard from—at least not yet. In the dream, I was on a crowded sidewalk on a hot summer evening when I saw a teenage Su Jung driving an old Toyota, stuck in traffic. Elena was with her, and they were having the best time, both of them laughing. When the traffic cleared, I saw Su Jung shift into first, then second, then drive off.

As for me, I've published two more children's books, including a novel, portions of which I first tried out on you. And Mike the cat is still around, eighteen years old and blind as a bat, but amazingly spry.

I think fondly of all of you, and am grateful I had the chance to work with you so closely. I'll always wonder what's become of you. Teaching is like reading a fascinating novel that you lose before you've finished the story. Drop me a line if you get a chance.

Best always,
Mr. Swope

ACKNOWLEDGMENTS

Three people deserve thanks above all: Gail Hochman, George Hodgman, and Jim Tryforos.

I am also grateful to Michael Armstrong, Katya Arnold, Eytan Bercovitch, Felicia Blum, Christopher Bryson, Brenda Cullerton, Jill Ciment, Leslie Day, Richard DeLigter, Patricia Donahue, William Drenttel, Chris Edgar, John Elder, Michael Goldberg, Gail Goodman, Dixie Goswami, Robert Graham, Michael Josefowicz, Frances Kiernan, Howard Kiernan, Herbert Kohl, Gary LaTour, Wendy Lesser, Eden Ross Lipson, Alan MacVey, Carol MacVey, James Maddox, Lucy Maddox, Giovanna Marrazi, Arnold Mesches, Johnna Murray, Kirin Narayan, Jose Orraca, Ron Padgett, Ann Patty, Kathy Rich, Roland Rogers, David Sassoon, Catherine Shadd, Jacqueline Shannon, Nancy Shapiro, Rich Shea, Dennis Sullivan, Beatrice Swain, Cynthia Swope, Doug Swope, James Swope, Susan Swope, Jennie Vest, and the Child_Lit listserv.